REAL ESTATE
AFTER TAX REFORM

REAL ESTATE
AFTER TAX REFORM
A Guide for Investors

MARTIN SHENKMAN
Townsend, Rabinowitz, Pantaleoni & Valenti
New York, New York

JOHN WILEY & SONS
New York • Chichester • Brisbane • Toronto • Singapore

Library of Congress Cataloging-in-Publication Data:

Shenkman, Martin.
   Real estate after tax reform.

   Bibliography: p.
   Includes index.
   1. Real property and taxation—United States.
2. Real property tax—United States. I. Title.

HJ4181.S45   1987   343.7305'46   87-2196
ISBN 0-471-85984-2   347.303546

Printed in the United States of America

10 9 8 7 6 5 4 3 2

To my wife Shelly
and my son Yoni
("no more seven")

ACKNOWLEDGMENTS

Andrew E. Furer, Esq., a Vice President in the Mortgage Department at Salomon Brothers Inc, New York, reviewed the section on REMICs. Furer was integrally involved in the REMIC legislation working with Senator John H. Chafee (R–RI) and the other principal architects of the legislation. His comments and suggestions were greatly appreciated.

A number of people at John Wiley & Sons, Inc. deserve recognition for all their extra efforts in completing this book in a fraction of the time usually necessary for such a project: Michael Hamilton, Sheck Cho, Kirk Bomont, Marilyn Dibbs, and Kristine Karnezis. Michael Hamilton deserves special mention. His faith and confidence were a critical factor in this project beginning and succeeding in the face of ridiculous deadlines.

When a book of this length is written in a short 10-week period a long list of associates and word processing staff are usually thanked for their heroic efforts. This book, however, was written in a grueling solo marathon of my pounding on my Apple IIc every evening and weekend. As a result, those listed in the next paragraph deserve the greatest of thanks and gratitude, for their burden was far more than it should have been.

Thanks to the partners of Townsend Rabinowitz Pantaleoni & Valente, P.C. for their patience, tolerence, and support.

Finally, the most important of all, my thanks and apologies to my wife Shelly and my son Yoni, the cutest little boy anywhere, who were ignored for months while this book was planned, written, and edited.

M.S.

CONTENTS

PART ONE
THE REAL ESTATE INVESTMENT CYCLE 7

1 STRUCTURING REAL ESTATE OWNERSHIP 9
Introduction, 9
Partnerships, 11
Corporations, 15
S Corporations, 30
Mortgage-Backed Securities and Real Estate Mortgage
Investment Conduits, 34
Real Estate Investment Trusts, 41
Chapter Summary, 52

2 FINANCING REAL ESTATE INVESTMENTS 53
General Effects of Tax Reform, 53
At-Risk Rules, 56
Tax-Exempt Bond Financing, 60
Cancellation of Debt, 64
Original Issue Discount Rules and Imputed Interest, 65
Limitation on the Deductibility of Investment Interest, 67
Real Estate Syndications, 72
Chapter Summary, 80

3 DEVELOPING AND OPERATING REAL ESTATE 81
General Effects of Tax Reform, 81
Limits on Construction Expenses, 82
New Rules Requiring Capitalization of Interest Expense, 93
Accounting for Long-Term Construction Contracts, 97
Repair and Maintenance Expenditures, 99
Special Tax Credit for Rehabilitating Old and Historic
Buildings, 102
Chapter Summary, 106

4   LEASING REAL ESTATE   **107**
General Effects of Tax Reform, 107
Writing Off Leasehold Improvements, 112
Chapter Summary, 118

5   SELLING REAL ESTATE INVESTMENTS   **119**
Planning with the New Capital Gains Rules, 119
Effect of the New Law on the Real Estate Industry, 127
Tough New Installment Sales Rules, 135
Chapter Summary, 150

PART TWO
INVESTING IN RESIDENTIAL REAL ESTATE   151

6   RESIDENTIAL REAL ESTATE INVESTMENTS   **153**
General Effects of Tax Reform, 153
New Tax Credit for Low-Income Rental Housing, 154
Special Exemption for Certain Low-Income Housing from
   the New Passive Loss Rules, 160
Tax-Exempt Financing, 161
Vacation Home, 162
Chapter Summary, 167

7   YOUR HOME AS AN INVESTMENT   **168**
General Effects of Tax Reform, 168
Deducting Interest Paid on a Home Mortgage, 170
New Rules for Home Office Expenses, 173
Cooperative Housing, 175
Chapter Summary, 177

PART THREE
TAX PLANNING FOR REAL ESTATE
INVESTMENTS   179

8   GENERAL TAX PLANNING   **181**
New Tax Rate Structure, 181
Standard Deduction, 185
Itemized Deductions Generally, 187
Family Tax Planning Opportunities Curtailed, 190
Chapter Summary, 193

9 PASSIVE LOSS LIMITATION RULES MAY LIMIT YOUR
   WRITE-OFFS   194
   Introduction, 194
   Overview—Passive Loss Limitation Rules, 196
   When Can You Use Your Deferred Losses?, 201
   Who Is Subject to the Passive Loss Limitation Rules?, 205
   Loss Limitation Categories, 207
   Bridges Among the Three Income Categories, 213
   What Businesses Are Treated as Real Estate Rental
      Activities, 218
   Effective Dates of the New Passive Loss Rules, 226
   Chapter Summary, 227

10 DEPRECIATION WRITE-OFFS—SQUEEZING OUT TAX
    BENEFITS UNDER THE NEW RULES   228
    Introduction, 228
    What Is Depreciation?, 229
    Why Is Depreciation Important to Real Estate Investors?,
       230
    Calculating Depreciation—Old Rules, New Rules, 231
    New Alternative Depreciation System, 239
    Chapter Summary, 266

11 ALTERNATIVE MINIMUM TAX—TOUGHER TAX BITE
    TO WATCH   267
    What Is the AMT?, 267
    Tax Reform and the AMT, 270
    Tax Preference Items (TPI), 272
    Itemized Deductions, 277
    Calculating the Minimum Tax Due after Tax Credit and
       Loss Adjustments, 279
    Minimum Tax Credit Available to Offset Regular Tax
       Liability, 281
    Chapter Summary, 285

12 MISCELLANEOUS TAX AND ADMINISTRATIVE
    CHANGES   286
    Registration of Tax Shelters, 286
    Reporting Real Estate Transactions, 288
    Interest Charged and Paid on Tax Underpayments and
       Overpayments, 289
    Penalties Increased for Failure to File Required
       Information Returns, 289
    Penalties for Negligence and Fraud, 289
    Estimated Tax Payment Requirements, 290

Larger Penalty Imposed on Substantial Understatements of
    Tax Liability, 291
Use of the Cash Method of Accounting Restricted, 293
Certain Convention Expenses No Longer Deductible, 295
Solar Energy Tax Credit Extended, 295
Chapter Summary, 295

INDEX   **297**

INTRODUCTION

THE TAX REFORM ACT OF 1986 AND REAL ESTATE

On September 18, 1986, Congress approved, and the President signed, on October 22, 1986, what is perhaps the most sweeping tax reform bill in the last 30 years—The Tax Reform Act of 1986 (sometimes called "tax reform"). The changes are so extensive that for the first time since 1954 Congress has renamed the tax code—the Internal Revenue Code of 1986.

This dramatic new tax bill has affected the bottom lines of most American businesses and most Americans' investments. It has influenced the way many American businesses will organize and operate. It has changed where and how Americans invest. One of the segments of the economy most affected was the real estate industry.

Tax reform will affect property values, rents, cash flows, and rates of return on most real estate investments. This book will alert you to the factors causing these effects to help you to continue to invest profitably after tax reform. The significant decrease in tax rates from a maximum of 50% under prior law to 28% under the new law will affect how everyone involved with real estate views tax planning. Many tax planning strategies will simply be worth much less—a dollar in additional tax deductions will only be worth 28 cents instead of 50 cents as under prior law. Real estate investors and real estate professionals will have to ascertain carefully whether any specific tax planning program is worth the expense and effort under the new tax rules. The answer, as this book will illustrate, will still be yes in many if not most situations.

Tax reform simplified the tax system for many taxpayers. However, the new laws have complicated the task of the real estate professional, the real estate investor, and the homeowner.

1

A more all-encompassing minimum tax, extremely complicated new limitations on the deductibility of losses and itemized deductions, and a myriad of other tax changes make the task of tax planning far more complicated than ever before.

This book is designed as a convenient reference to guide the real estate investor and the real estate professional through this complicated maze of new tax provisions. The terms "real estate professional" or "real estate investor" are used in a very broad sense. Whether you are a major shopping center developer, an apartment mogul, or merely a homeowner, real estate is an investment for you. Whether you are a full-time broker, retailer, or developer, or merely a passive weekend investor in large syndications, you are a real estate professional.

The objective of this book is to guide you—the busy professional—to important tax planning ideas and to steer you around costly tax traps. The next section will show you how to use this book to get the information you need in order to start asking the right questions and how to work with your accountant, attorney, financial planner, or other tax advisor to make the right decisions after tax reform.

HOW TO USE THIS BOOK

Objective

The objective of this book is to direct you to the important tax planning ideas you need in order to consult with your tax advisors, make the right deals, and identify costly problems before it's too late.

Background explanations and detailed discussions of some of the more important new tax rules are provided. The book is organized and designed to enable you to find the type of information you want quickly.

Most chapters will give you a brief introduction, often raising the questions you should be considering. These questions will help you determine whether that particular chapter is important for the current deal you are involved in; if not, move on. Background material is provided for many of the tax planning ideas and new rules. Many professionals want to understand what the general rules are, to better understand the changes made and the planning opportunities which remain. If you don't need or don't want this background, the headings clearly identify it so that you can skip over it. If you're running for a meeting and just want a few quick ideas, you can easily scan the chapters relevant to a particular deal for the "Planning Tip" captions.

Divisions
The book is organized in three parts:

Part One: The Real Estate Investment Cycle. The five chapters in this part follow the chronological cycle of most real estate investments.

First, you decide how you're going to get involved. For example, you may invest alone, as a partner in a partnership, or as a shareholder in a corporation. The first chapter discusses some of the important changes the Tax Reform Act of 1986 made which will affect this decision.

Once you've decided how to invest, you may set up your financing in order to determine how much money you can raise. This in turn will set the parameters for the size of your investment. Chapter 2 addresses financing issues.

Next, if you aren't buying an existing property you will have to build a building. Chapter 3 will point out some tax points you should consider in the construction process. As a developer you will have to consider the new rules on construction period expenses. The special credit (as changed by tax reform) for rehabilitating certain old or historic buildings may be important. Finally, once the building is constructed, or once the purchase of an existing building is complete, you will have to manage the property. Chapter 3 will also point out a few tax considerations of operating a building. Since many of the planning ideas affecting developers also affect investors operating real estate, these two topics are covered in the same chapter.

Once your building is up and going you will want it to be leased (see Chapter 4). Although many investors would like to lease their properties before the building is complete or the financing arranged (the lender may insist on it), leasing follows next in the logical sequence of the investment cycle. A number of important changes were made by tax reform to the leasing area. (If you're leasing residential real estate see Part II.)

Finally, once you have owned a property for a while you may decide to sell it. The Tax Reform Act of 1986 made a number of changes to the taxation of the proceeds of real estate sales. The favorable capital gains rules were repealed. The rules for installment sales were also changed. Chapter 5 explains the new rules you will have to work with and gives a number of examples showing what the new rules mean to real estate investing.

Part Two: Investing in Residential Real Estate. The two chapters in this part discuss the many changes affecting the holding of residential real estate as an investment, whether it's your home or a large apartment complex. If you're developing or investing residential real estate on a commercial scale, the tax benefits of home ownership will be important to you: Knowing what your customers face will help you plan better. Chapter 7 will analyze many of the changes important to homeowners and to apartment dwellers considering owning. Some of the new rules affecting vacation (second) homes and the new special credit for investing in low-income housing are discussed in Chapter 6.

The following examples will illustrate how the book's organization will help you quickly find the information you need:

You're in the financing and structuring stage of a project. Chapter 2 will alert you to the major new ground rules affecting financing decisions. If you're making a real estate investment for cash (i.e., no debt) then you can save time by skipping this chapter. If you're using tax exempt or nonrecourse financing this chapter will highlight some important changes and planning ideas you should consider. If you plan to construct a building Chapter 3 will advise you of the tough new rules affecting interest paid during the construction period.

Are you evaluating an investment in a partnership that will build a low-income housing project? Chapter 6 will tell you about the new tax credit for qualifying low-income housing. Since the partnership will be building the apartments, Chapter 3 will be important—new rules will limit the tax benefits your partnership will get for construction costs. What can you do? This chapter will give you a number of ideas to limit the impact of these harsh new rules. Discuss them at the next meeting with your partners and tax advisor. Chapter 9 will discuss how the new passive loss limitations will limit your ability to use any losses generated.

Are you a retailer? Chapter 4 will alert you to new rules on writing of leasehold improvements. If you're financing the improvements take a look at Chapter 2 on financing. Since you're doing construction, Chapter 3 on development could have some valuable tax tips.

Are you buying a home, or acting as a broker for someone buying or selling a home? The new rules on home office deductions and the new way home mortgages will be structured could affect what the home will cost on an after-tax basis and could affect how mortgage financing will be arranged. The changes in itemized deductions may eliminate (or dramatically reduce) any benefits you get for your home mortgage interest and property tax payments. Chapter 7 will explore many of these considerations.

Part Three: Tax Planning for Real Estate Investments. Whatever type of deal you're involved in, whatever role you occupy in the real estate industry, you should consider these important changes.

The value of any tax benefit to you will depend on your personal tax situation. Chapter 8 reviews many of the changes tax reform made and how they will affect the after-tax results of your real estate investments. All real estate, except for land, is usually depreciable. The depreciation chapter (10) will tell you how the new depreciation rules will affect you; more importantly it will give you many ideas to minimize the harsh impact of the very long write-off periods now required. The new passive loss rules and the tougher alternative minimum tax rules will affect how every investor and developer is taxed. These rules may force you to reconsider the very structure and organization of your business.

Caution. Although every effort has been made to provide a complete and accurate review of the new laws, the area is too new and too rapidly changing to guarantee completeness or accuracy. Also, every deal is different thus no general book on tax planning can address every situation. Finally, since this book has been written for the real estate professional and not the tax advisor, discussions of complex exceptions, transition rules, and many other nuances have been omitted. Therefore, don't act without carefully consulting your tax advisor.

Part One

THE REAL ESTATE INVESTMENT CYCLE

1 STRUCTURING REAL ESTATE OWNERSHIP

INTRODUCTION

Many factors should be carefully considered in deciding, with your tax and legal advisors, which type of ownership vehicle to use for your real estate investments. Some of these factors include:

Potential liabilities you may face.

Impact of the new passive loss rules on each ownership structure and on your personal tax situation (See Chapter 9).

Whether the real estate investment will generate tax losses or income and the extent to which you will be able to benefit from those losses.

How you will be able to raise the necessary capital for the investment, and any preferences your investors or lenders may have for one structure over another.

The number of other investors in the deal (many ownership structures have minimum or maximum investor requirements).

The dollar value of the prospective investment. The cost of setting up the investment structure should not be prohibitive relative to the amount being invested.

Your relationship to the other investors. This will, in part, determine how the investment relationship should be structured.

Any state or local law requirements (e.g., in the past corporations were sometimes used to avoid local usury law limitations).

The accounting and reporting requirements and burdens associated with each type of entity.

Any additional flexibility which one investment vehicle may have over another for purposes of your estate planning.

The desire for privacy. Some investment forms will require much more disclosure than others.

Any other factors which you and your advisors consider relevant to your particular situation and the specific investment being considered.

The discussions in the following pages will highlight the changes made by tax reform and some of the factors you should be considering after tax reform in choosing one investment vehicle over another. The discussions are designed to provide general insights and planning ideas which should be considered as you review your real estate and related investments and activities in the aftermath of tax reform. A complete discussion of the tax consequences of each investment vehicle is obviously not provided. Thus many important considerations like the tax and legal consequences of transferring real estate to each of the various entities, payment of salaries and other benefits, tax elections, and so forth, have not been reviewed. Finally, no comments have been made about holding your real estate directly, as a joint tenant, or as a tenant in common. Many of the income tax consequences of these forms of ownership are discussed throughout this book (e.g., see Chapters 6 and 8). Thus the final decision, as well as the follow-up planning for the ownership entity chosen, must be made in consultation with your tax, legal, accounting, and estate planning advisors.

The discussion of each type of investment vehicle is followed by a comparison of that form of ownership with the others being discussed. This approach should help your decision-making process. The best approach would be to review the discussions of each investment form being considered. Each section's comparative discussions are fairly complete (at the cost of some redundancy) to enable you to contrast the form you have just read about with the other forms available.

PARTNERSHIPS

The most important facet of a partnership structure from a tax perspective is that a partnership is not taxed. All of the income and deductions flow through to the individual partners and are taxed to them. This has been advantageous from two perspectives. First, there is no tax at the entity level. This compares favorably with a corporation, for example, which is taxed at the corporate level. Distributions from a corporation are then taxed again to the recipient shareholders. Partners and partnerships avoid this second layer of taxation. This conduit characteristic of a partnership is the reason the partnership has been the most preferred vehicle for structuring real estate transactions. This conduit or flow-through feature enables individual partners to use the losses generated by the partnership on their own tax returns to offset other income.

Since the partnership is in many respects independent of its partners, many tax elections (such as depreciation) are made at the partnership level. Income or loss is determined at the partnership level. Thus the partnership must choose a tax year. Tax reform requires that the partnership's tax year be the same as the majority of its partners. This will generally mean that partnerships will have a December 31 fiscal year-end.

Once the partnership's income is determined it must be allocated to the individual partners. The simplest approach is to allocate income, deductions, credits, and so forth to each partner in the same proportion as that partner's interest in the partnership. For example, a 12% partner would be allocated 12% of all partnership items—12% of cash flow, 12% of net income or loss, 12% of any tax credits (e.g., the rehabilitation tax credit), and so on.

Allocations, however, do not have to be made in the same proportions as each partner's interest in the partnership if the partnership agreement calls for a different method. This has been, and may continue to be, one of the principal advantages of the partnership form. This flexibility sets the partnership apart from the other forms of organization discussed in this chapter.

For example, some partners may be given a priority distribution of cash flow (e.g., limited partners may receive all cash flow until they have been paid 8% preferred return on their investments). One partner may receive 80% of the gain ultimately realized on the sale of certain property (such as land and a building which that partner contributed to the partnership). The general partner may receive 25% of the remaining profits on the eventual sale and liquidation of the partnership, although he only had a 1% interest in the partnership's profits and capital (this could be offered as an incentive fee to the general partner to encourage his performance). This freedom to allocate provides an opportunity to devise a compensation system to best motivate all parties involved.

Can these special allocations be made with total freedom? Not quite. For these allocations to withstand IRS scrutiny they must have what is called "substantial economic effect." Defining this term has proven to be one of the most complicated tasks the Treasury Department, IRS, and courts have faced. In very simple terms it means that the special allocations should have more than mere tax consequences. They should have some meaningful economic and nontax impact on the partners making them.

These three factors—avoidance of double taxation, ability of partners to deduct losses of the partnership, and great flexibility in allocating tax results—have made the partnership the preferred real estate investment vehicle. Tax reform may not change this, but it clearly has affected the process of deciding whether to use the partnership form.

Choosing between a Partnership and Other Types of Investment Vehicle After Tax Reform

Partnerships will probably continue to be the preferred form of owning real estate. Tax reform, however, has minimized some of its advantages. The advantages a partnership provides by permitting investors to use the partnership's losses will be minimized. The many restrictions on deductions, most importantly the new passive loss rules (see Chapter 9), make this attribute less important. The flexibility to allocate income and other items will continue to be important, but the degree of importance will greatly depend on the extent to which the IRS will permit allocations of losses and tax credits to partners not subject to (or at least not as constrained by) the new passive loss rules. It is unlikely that allocations of losses to a partner solely because that partner has excess passive income to offset will withstand IRS scrutiny.

The passive loss rules will also be critical in choosing among the various types of partnerships. Although these rules are discussed in detail in Chapter 9, a few general comments are necessary here to facilitate the discussion. The passive loss rules divide all activities (and the income or loss they generate) into three categories: (1) passive (activities in which the taxpayer doesn't materially participate, such as a passive tax shelter investment); (2) active (activities in which the taxpayer does materially participate, such as full-time real estate leasing); (3) portfolio (interest, dividends, etc.). Passive losses can't generally offset income in the other two categories. Unused passive losses are carried to future years until they offset other passive income or until the taxpayer's entire interest in the activity is sold. With this brief overview, some of the advantages and disadvantages of different types of partnerships can be reviewed:

1. *General Partnership Interests.* A general partner is one who can be held personally liable on partnership debts (i.e., beyond his initial capital contribution). A general partner is also allowed to actively participate in the management of the partnership's affairs. Thus, if the activities of the partnership constitute an active business, and the partner materially participates in those activities, then the general partner will receive active income or loss. If this activity will generate losses and the general partner has other active income, it will be advantageous to invest as a general partner in order to offset other active income with these losses.

2. *Limited Partnership Interests.* A limited partner is one who can't participate in the active management of partnership activities according to state law. Further, a limited partner can generally only be held liable up to the amount invested. The new passive loss rules generally treat any income or loss received as a limited partner as passive income or loss. Thus, if an investor has unusable passive losses and is contemplating another investment which will produce income, a limited partnership interest which will produce passive income (which can thus be used to offset the investor's otherwise unusable passive losses) would be preferable over a general partnership interest which (if the investor materially participated) would produce active income. Obviously, the investor's involvement in each situation must conform with the active or passive result desired.

3. *Master Limited Partnerships.* These are large, publicly traded limited partnerships. They offer investors tremendous liquidity as compared with most other partnership or direct real estate investments. Their size usually indicates an opportunity

for much greater diversity than most real estate partnerships. A master limited partnership still retains the important partnership attributes of no entity-level tax and the flow-through of tax results to each partner. Master limited partnerships are often formed in one of two ways. Some sponsors (such as a large corporation) may "roll out" or spin off to outside investors a package of real estate holdings. Another common approach is for a sponsor of real estate limited partnerships to "roll up" a number of independent partnerships into one large entity.

Since passive-losses can only be used to offset passive income, the master limited partnership could become an ideal vehicle. It could plan its acquisitions and activities to zero out any income generally. This could alleviate the problems investors will have of monitoring their own investments to obtain the maximum tax benefits under the new passive loss rules. Another result may be to see master limited partnerships structured to either generate passive income or loss, in each case with a diversified portfolio. This would enable investors to pick an investment suited for their own passive income/loss mix. For example, an investor with passive losses from prior real estate holdings would choose a master limited partnership generating income. A first-time investor would probably prefer a balanced (no income or loss) master limited partnership.

Planning Tips. Apart from the tax considerations, investors contemplating an investment in any master limited partnership should carefully review each of the properties "rolled up" or "rolled out." The possibility of the sponsor burying a few lousy properties in the much larger master limited partnership should be carefully analyzed. Bigger is not always better. Carefully weigh the advantages of supposedly increased liquidity and diversity against the possibility of trading a good investment for a dog (or part dog).

In considering an investment in a master limited partnership, review two technical tax matters with your tax advisor. First, some partnerships, particularly large, publicly traded ones, often begin to take on the appearance of a corporation. If the IRS proves that these entities have predominantly corporate characteristics (see the discussion of corporations later in this chapter), the IRS could reclassify the master limited partnership as an association taxable as a corporation. This approach could have dire consequences for your investment. All the projected tax benefits could be lost, a second-level tax at the corporate level could be assessed, and so forth.

Second, consider the passive loss rules. It was noted earlier that unused passive losses may have to wait until the taxpayer's entire interest in the activity is disposed of. While it appears at the time of this writing that a master limited partnership's (or another partnership's) disposition of one real estate property may often be sufficient to trigger any unused passive losses with respect to that property, this may not always be the case. The result will depend on the activities the partnership is involved in, the relationship between each of the activities and properties, as well as eventual IRS interpretations of the new passive loss rules. The IRS has expressed disfavor with the concept of publicly traded limited partnerships in the past. Before investing, check with your tax advisor to find out the latest developments.

If you don't need to earn passive income to offset otherwise unusable passive losses, and you want a diversified, liquid real estate investment, consider real estate investment trusts (REITs) and real estate mortgage investment conduits (REMICs) (discussed later in this chapter).

Conclusion
The partnership form of investment will probably continue to dominate the real estate field. However, the decision to use this form has been made far more complicated by the types of partnerships available and the complications created by tax reform. In some situations one of the other investment vehicles described in the sections that follow will be preferable. Thus consider all options, and review the matter with your advisors before committing yourself.

CORPORATIONS

There are two types of corporations, C corporations and S corporations. C corporations, or regular corporations, are the common type of corporation most investors think of when the term corporation is used. C corporations are referred to as C corporations, regular corporations, or simply corporations. They are described in the discussion in the following section. S corporations are closely held corporations which elect to have special tax rules apply. They are described in the next section of this chapter.

The corporate structure has never been a popular one for real estate ownership. It has been common for real estate related activities such as maintenance or leasing operations, development, retailing, and so forth. Tax reform is likely to make the corporate form less desirable for all of these endeavors. Before reviewing the changes made by tax reform the nature of the corporate entity should first be reviewed.

What Is a Corporation?

The corporation is a legal entity independent of its owners. It is an entity formed under the laws of a specific state. Thus the rights and nature of any corporation are dependent on the specific state statutes governing its existence, and it must adhere to the requirements of the statute under which it was formed. These requirements can include the filing of a certificate of incorporation or charter which identifies the purpose for which the corporation was formed, the principal place of its business, the corporate name, its duration (usually perpetual), and so forth. The corporation will be governed by a board of directors chosen by the shareholders. The ownership interests in the corporation will be evidenced by shares of stock.

The corporate structure has a number of characteristics which are important to consider in evaluating the various alternative vehicles for investing in real estate. As these characteristics are reviewed, comparisons will be made with other ownership forms.

1. *Centralized Management.* A corporation is managed centrally by individuals delegated management authority by the board of directors. Although the shareholders may vote at shareholder meetings concerning certain fundamental corporate changes, and they may elect directors, they may not generally be involved in daily management affairs. Limited partners, shareholders in an S corporation (see the section on S corporations later in the chapter), and REIT face similar situations. A general partner in a partnership may, however, have input concerning the daily management affairs. And in a closely held corporation or S corporation a shareholder may negotiate certain rights to influence daily management affairs and have those rights included in a shareholder's agreement.

2. *Continuity of Life.* Corporations can exist perpetually if the state law and corporate charter so permit. This contrasts with a partnership which will be dissolved by state law in certain circumstances.

3. *Free Transferability of Interests.* The ownership shares in a corporation can often be transferred freely. This contrasts with shares in a partnership which often can only be transferred with consent of the general partner, or with the consent of a specified number of other partners. Some partnerships offer what appears to be almost unlimited ease of transferability, despite various legal limitations. In a closely held corporation shares may not be freely transferable. Often closely held corporations have shareholders' agreements which significantly restrict the rights and abilities of any shareholder to transfer shares as he chooses. Often the shares must first be offered to the other shareholders or the corporation itself subject to a right of first refusal. Other agreements may prohibit the sale of shares to anyone other than the corporation at net book value, or some other figure which may be significantly less than market value.

4. *Limited Liability.* Perhaps the most important attribute of the corporate structure is the availability of limited liability. This means that in the event of suit or other liability, the creditors can generally only proceed against the assets of the corporation. The personal assets of the shareholders will generally be insulated. Often, however, this attribute of limited liability is unavailable. For a new or undercapitalized entity, lenders, suppliers, and others may insist on personal guarantees of the shareholders. This would obviously drastically reduce the availability of limited liability. Also, limited liability can be achieved in S corporation or limited partnership format. These latter forms offer some important advantages over the corporate form, as will be discussed later in the chapter.

Overview of C Corporate Taxation

A corporation is taxed separately from the shareholders who own it. The corporation must pay a tax (or minimum tax) on its profits. These profits are computed based on the various tax elections (such as depreciation method, etc.) and tax year determined at the corporate level (i.e., independent of the tax elections and tax year of its owners). When these net of tax profits are ultimately distributed to the corporation's shareholders as dividends, the shareholders must generally pay a tax on the amounts received. This results in two layers of taxation or double taxation. This can be rather unfavorable when compared with the result obtained with a partnership or S corporation. These two entities generally don't pay a tax at the entity level; rather, their earnings are distributed to their owners, who pay any tax due.

Another result follows from this corporate tax scheme. If the corporation is subject to its own tax system, then if the corporation realizes losses, the shareholders can't benefit from these losses. Again, this contrasts unfavorably with the result available with a partnership or S corporation; these entities can pass any tax losses they realize through to their owners. Prior to tax reform the owners of a partnership or S corporation were generally able to use these losses to offset tax that would otherwise be payable on other income. This factor was the major reason real estate was owned in corporate form much less frequently than in these other forms.

There is an important exception to this double tax scenario for corporations. In many closely held corporations the owner is also an employee. As an employee, much of the corporation's income can often be distributed as salary. Since salary is deductible by the corporation as a business expense the corporate-level tax (and hence double taxation) is avoided.

Caution.   The ability to pay salaries is not absolute. The salaries paid to owner/employees must bear a reasonable relationship to the services provided. If they don't the IRS could challenge the compensation as excessive and recharacterize it as a dividend. When a salary approximating the income of the corporation can be justified, however, the many disadvantages of the corporate form may not be important.

With this brief overview, a number of additional observations can be made about the advantages and disadvantages of the corporate form for conducting real estate activities after tax reform.

Comparing the C Corporate Structure with Other Investment Vehicles After Tax Reform

As noted, a significant drawback to the corporate form of real estate ownership before tax reform was the inability of the owners to use the tax losses which were often generated (from depreciation and interest deductions, etc.) to offset income from other sources. As will be discussed throughout this book, real estate will no longer be able to generate the significant tax losses it did in the past (because of the investment interest limitation, at-risk rules, less favorable depreciation benefits, repeal of the investment tax credit, etc.). Even if a significant tax loss is somehow generated, it may not be of any benefit because of the stringent new passive loss rules (see Chapter 9). Thus, if real estate investments are made for economic, rather than tax reasons, so that income rather than tax losses are produced, the fact that a corporation can't pass tax losses through to its shareholders will often be unimportant. This scenario, however, makes other tax reform changes more important.

A number of other factors must also be considered. Tax reform has lowered corporate tax rates. However, the tax rates faced by corporations will be higher than the maximum tax rates faced by individual investors. Therefore, unless the income at the corporate level can be reduced to near zero (by depreciation and other real estate deductions, salary payments to owners, and other planning), it will be preferable in many post tax-reform planning scenarios to opt for a vehicle other than a corporation.

The double tax burden faced by corporations can be a significant cost when trying to remove real estate investments from the corporate structure. In the past a corporation was often able to take advantage of certain exceptions in the tax laws to liquidate and distribute its real estate (and other) holdings to its shareholders without incurring the corporate-level tax. Tax reform generally eliminated these exceptions. As a result the double tax will almost always result in attempting to distribute real estate, liquidate, or sell the corporation's assets.

The new passive loss rules (see Chapter 9) must also be carefully considered in choosing the type of entity for your real estate investments. As noted in the earlier discussion of partnerships, there are three basic types of income: (1) active (a business you materially participate in); (2) passive (rental real estate, and activities in which you don't materially participate); and (3) portfolio (dividends and interest). Generally, passive losses can't offset income in the other categories. Each individual investor's situation with respect to these three types of income, the passive loss rules, and the investment being considered, must be carefully evaluated. For example, certain closely held corporations can offset active business income by losses incurred on passive real estate investments. Individuals are generally unable to do this. Therefore, subject to all the caveats discussed in this section, there may be instances where it appears favorable to own real estate in corporate form. However, if the investor has unusable passive losses and the rental real estate investment will generate passive income, the limited partnership form will be preferable.

Caution. Before concluding that the lower individual tax rates, or other changes, make the partnership form of ownership preferable over the corporate form, carefully review the impact on all shareholders with your tax advisor. Certain tax exempt institutional shareholders may be hurt by the change to partnership form as a result of the unrelated business income (UBI) rules. Also, certain foreign shareholders could be hurt depending on the provisions of the tax treaty they are relying on. Tax treaties sometimes treat dividends on corporate stock differently than partnership distributions.

If your real estate is presently in a corporation and you and your tax and legal advisors agree that it would be preferable to hold it in another form, what can you do? It is possible to liquidate the corporation and hold the real estate personally or in a partnership. This, however, could result in a significant tax cost (including recapture of prior tax credits and depreciation deductions). The corporation could elect to be taxed as an S corporation. This approach will also have some drawbacks as explained in the latter sections dealing with S corporations.

Planning Tip. This comparison has focused solely on tax considerations. This is not to say that the business considerations (limited liability as one) are unimportant. Rather, this discussion presumes that you have already discussed and evaluated the nontax factors with your attorney and have then begun a tax analysis. Never let the tax factors eclipse essential business considerations.

With this background a brief review of the corporate tax changes made by the Tax Reform Act of 1986 can be presented.

A Summary of the C Corporate Tax Changes Made by Tax Reform

The changes tax reform made to corporate taxation are numerous, complex, and profound. Every investor considering the corporate form should carefully evaluate the effects of these changes.

The following discussion can at most only highlight some of these changes.

1. *Lower Tax Rates.* One of the most important changes was the drastic reduction in tax rates. The maximum corporate tax rate was reduced from 46 to 34%. Importantly, for the first time the maximum corporate tax rate is greater than the highest individual tax rate. The new corporate tax rates are:

Taxable Income	Tax Rate
0–$50,000	15%
$50,001–$75,000	25%
Over $75,000	34%

The benefit of the lower tax brackets will be phased out for corporations with taxable income over $100,000. The phaseout is accomplished by imposing an additional surtax of 5% on income over $100,000 (i.e., a rate of 39% until the benefit of income taxed at the lower brackets is recouped. The phaseout is completed by an income level of $335,000. Therefore income above this amount is taxed at a flat rate of 34%.

2. *Dividends-Received Deduction.* Corporations have been entitled to exclude a large portion of the dividends they receive from other corporations in calculating their income. The reasoning behind this exclusion is that corporations are subject to tax on their income. When a corporation distributes its income to shareholders there is another tax—this time paid by the shareholder. If that shareholder is an individual, the second tax is paid (so-called double taxation). If the shareholder is another corporation, it too would have to pay tax. When this second corporation eventually distributed the funds to its shareholders yet another level of tax would have to be paid. To prevent burdensome, multiple layers of tax on earnings paid by different corporations before they reach the ultimate individual shareholders, an exclusion was provided. Under prior law this exclusion had been 85% of the dividends received. Tax reform reduced this exclusion to 80%.

3. *Allocating Purchase Price on Buying a Corporation.* When buying a business, a prescribed method for allocating the purchase price among the assets acquired will now have to be used by both the buyer and the seller. This method is called the "re-

sidual method." This is the approach the IRS had advocated for certain corporate transactions before tax reform made it mandatory for many types of acquisitions. When a business is purchased, the purchase price must be allocated to cash, securities, equipment, real estate, and all other specifically identifiable assets. Any unallocated purchase price must then be allocated to goodwill and going-concern value. The drawback of this approach to purchasers is that goodwill and going-concern value are intangibles for which no tax deductions are permitted. For additional details see Chapter 10.

4. *"Greenmail" and Stock Redemption Payments.* The newspapers have been full of hostile takeover attempts, including many of firms with significant real estate holdings. A practice which had become too common for Congress' liking was the paying of a premium over the market value for stock to get it out of the hands of a hostile suitor. The target corporations making these payments often deducted them for tax purposes as a cost of doing business. Tax reform makes these payments, as well as related legal and other expenses, nondeductible.

5. *Property Distributions Taxed.* As discussed, one of the drawbacks to the corporate structure is the burden of double taxation—the corporation must pay tax on its earnings and the shareholder must also pay tax on his receipt of the earnings as a dividend. In a number of important situations this double tax could have been avoided, under the theory of what became known as the "general utilities doctrine." In very general terms, a corporation was allowed to distribute appreciated property (i.e., property with a fair value in excess of the corporation's investment or tax basis in it) to its shareholders, and terminate its corporate existence (i.e., completely liquidate) without any corporate-level tax. A corporation could also sell its assets and distribute the proceeds to its shareholders in a complete liquidation without having to recognize any corporate-level tax. Alternatively, the shareholders could sell all of their stock and the purchaser could make a special election to treat the selling corporation's assets as if they had been sold. All these transactions could have been effected without a corporate-level tax. There were a number of exceptions to this result of no corporate tax; however, the benefits of the general utilities doctrine were still significant in many situations (see Chapter 10).

Tax reform has dramatically changed these rules and with

them the way corporations will be bought, sold, and liquidated. Apart from some complicated transition rules, the benefits of the general utilities doctrine are gone. Now both the corporation and its shareholders will face a tax cost. When a corporation distributes appreciated property to its shareholders, it will now have to pay a tax on the appreciation.

One approach to minimize this problem is to convert to S corporation status. (See the discussion of S corporations later in the chapter.) If this conversion is made after 1986, however, the problem cannot be entirely avoided. Any appreciation which occurred before the conversion from a C (regular) corporation to an S corporation (called "built-in gain") will be taxed if the property is sold within 10 years of the conversion.

6. *New Limitations on Using Losses After Change in Corporate Ownership.* These provisions are complicated, but they are very important to many corporations. Corporations which may have incurred tax losses as a result of real estate and related operations will be significantly affected. Income of a corporation is measured on an annual basis. If a corporation incurs expenses in excess of its income in a given year, it will have a loss. Recognizing the potential unfairness of taxing corporations on income in the good years only, the tax laws provide that the losses from bad years (called "net operating losses") can, subject to various rules and limitations, be carried over to offset income in the good years.

This simple concept becomes difficult when there has been a significant change in the ownership of a corporation with losses. Have the new owners acquired their interests because they found a good business investment, or have they sought an interest in the company solely to take advantage of its net operating losses? Although Congress deemed it appropriate to permit corporations to use these losses to offset income in other years, it did not consider it proper to permit taxpayers to buy and sell operating losses. Strict new rules have been enacted to enforce this dual objective. These rules generally replace the rules existing before tax reform, although they incorporate some of their concepts.

These new rules are only triggered if there has been a significant change in the ownership of the loss corporation to create a concern that taxpayers may be dealing in net operating losses. Since such a test would be too subjective to administer, a mechanical test was provided. The new law has two mechanical tests to determine whether a sufficient change in ownership has occurred. Both tests are generally applied over a three-year period. Thus a number of individual changes occurring over a three-year period could be combined for these tests and together trigger the new limitations.

The first test is called an "ownership change" test. An ownership change occurs when the percentage of stock owned by shareholders who own more than 5% of the loss corporation's stock increases by more than 50 percentage points over the lowest it had been during the past three years. For example, a publicly held company has no shareholders who own 5% or greater interests. Three individuals each acquire 25% of the stock. An ownership change has occurred since the interests of these three (more than 5%) shareholders has increased by more than 50 percentage points (i.e., from 0 to 75%).

The second test is called an "equity structure shift." This test was designed primarily for publicly held companies. Congress was concerned that even though many publicly held companies would not have the 5% shareholder shifts described previously, structural changes could occur which should also result in limits on the use of the net operating losses of the "prechange" corporation. An equity structure shift occurs when the ownership interests of the loss corporation's shareholders have increased by more than 50 percentage points as a result of a reorganization, merger, or public offering.

Example. A corporation with a large net operating loss is merged into a profitable corporation. This is done by issuing stock in the profitable corporation to the shareholders of the loss corporation. The profitable corporation survives the merger. As a result of this transaction the shareholders of the former loss corporation end up owning 30% of the surviving entity. This means that the former shareholders of the profitable corporation own 70% of the interests in what had been the loss corporation. Since this is more than a 50 percentage point increase, an equity structure shift has occurred.

Once it is determined that either an ownership change or equity structure shift has occurred, you must determine whether a "business continuity test" is met. If it is not met then none of the net operating losses can be used. The reason for this is that .

if there has been a significant ownership change and neither the business nor assets of the former loss corporation are retained, then to permit the losses to be used would permit the dealing in tax losses which Congress sought to stop. This test requires that for the two-year period beginning on the date of a change, the historic business of the corporation with the net operating losses must be continued, or a significant portion of that corporation's assets must continue to be used.

If the business continuity test is met then the new limits are applied to the net operating losses. In its simplest terms this new limitation allows the use, in any year, of the net operating loss only up to the fair value of the loss corporation just before the change, multiplied by a long-term federal interest rate to be determined by the Treasury Department.

Example. The loss corporation which was merged in the previously discussed example had a value of $500,000 just before the transaction, and the prescribed federal interest rate was 10%, only $50,000 of net operating losses could be used in any year ($500,000 value × 10% federal rate).

7. *Corporate Alternative Minimum Tax System (AMT).* This is perhaps the most fundamental and dramatic change affecting corporate taxation that has occurred in many years. Every investor using or contemplating using a corporate structure should carefully review the impact of the new corporate minimum tax. Congress has replaced the prior corporate minimum tax provisions with a comprehensive alternative minimum tax system which is very similar to the individual alternative minimum tax system described in detail in Chapter 11. This new corporate minimum tax is best viewed and planned for as a separate tax system. Planning under the regular corporate tax system alone could be a costly oversight for many taxpayers.

The structure of this new corporate alternative minimum tax is illustrated in Figure 1.1. Since the concepts are similar to the individual minimum tax discussed in Chapter 11, only the more important differences will be discussed here.

Real estate investors must consider all the required adjustments, even nonreal estate ones, since any combination of adjustments may be sufficient to trigger the minimum tax. The tax

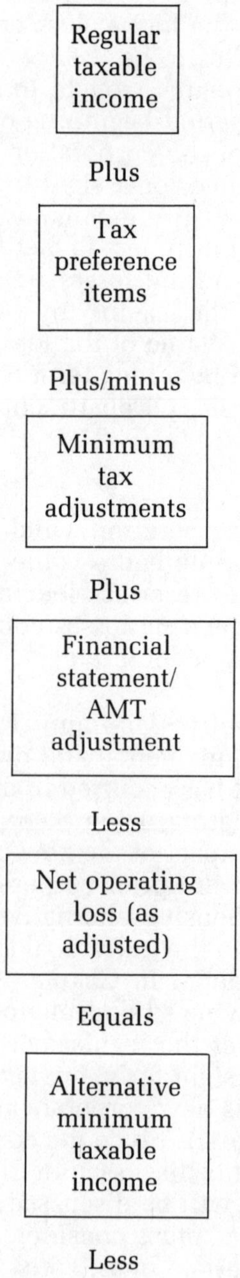

Regular
taxable
income

Plus

Tax
preference
items

Plus/minus

Minimum
tax
adjustments

Plus

Financial
statement/
AMT
adjustment

Less

Net operating
loss (as
adjusted)

Equals

Alternative
minimum
taxable
income

Less

Figure 1.1 Simplified overview of corporate alternative minimum tax

```
┌─────────────┐
│  $40,000    │
│  exemption  │
│ (subject to │
│  phaseout)  │
└─────────────┘

     Equals

┌─────────────┐
│  Minimum    │
│    tax      │
│    base     │
└─────────────┘

    × 20%
    equals

┌─────────────┐
│  Minimum    │
│    tax      │
└─────────────┘

      Less

┌─────────────┐
│  Allowable  │
│  foreign    │
│ and invest- │
│  ment tax   │
│   credits   │
└─────────────┘

     Equals

┌─────────────┐
│  Minimum    │
│    tax      │
│  (pay to    │
│ extent exceeds │
│ regular tax) │
└─────────────┘
```

Figure 1.1 (*Continued*)

27

preference items and adjustments which must be made to corporate income include the following items, which are similar to those for individuals (see Chapter 11):

Depreciation on real and personal property put into use after 1986 to the extent it exceeds depreciation calculated under the new alternative depreciation system (see Chapter 10).

The completed contract method of accounting for certain long-term contracts must be replaced with calculations made under the percentage completion method.

The tax preference for intangible drilling costs now applies to all corporations.

Use of the installment method of accounting for gains on certain sales is no longer allowed.

Certain tax-exempt interest is not excludable for minimum tax purposes.

Untaxed appreciation on contributions of property.

The tax preference for the excess of percentage depletion over the adjusted basis of the property.

The special amortization deductions for certain pollution control facilities must be adjusted.

Mining exploration and development costs must be adjusted.

The special amortization deductions for magazine and newspaper circulation expenditures must be adjusted. This only applies to certain corporations.

The excess of accelerated depreciation over straight-line depreciation on leased personal property and real estate. This only applies to certain corporations.

In addition to these preference items and adjustments, which are similar to those for individuals, corporations face five additional items:

A special deduction for certain tax-exempt insurance providers must be adjusted.

Moneys deposited in certain capital construction funds of shipping companies, and the earnings on these funds, must be adjusted for.

Passive activity losses of certain closely held and personal service corporations are allowed to offset certain other income for purposes of the regular tax (see Chapter 9). These are not allowed for purposes of the minimum tax. NOTE—before the passive activity loss can be subjected to this minimum tax limitation, it must first be adjusted to reflect all the other adjustments required for minimum tax purposes (such as depreciation).

The excess of bad debts calculated using the reserve method over the bad debts which would have been allowed using the experience method, for certain financial institutions.

One-half the amount by which income for financial statement ("book") purposes (as adjusted) exceeds alternative minimum taxable income. The purpose of this adjustment is to prevent corporations from reporting profits in their financial statements and reporting no income for tax purposes for the same year.

. This adjustment is the most complicated and difficult to deal with of any of the minimum tax adjustments and preferences. It is an entirely new concept added by tax reform. As a result, regulations and additional guidance will be necessary in order to implement it. In very general terms this adjustment will be calculated as follows. Start with income from the corporation's financial statements (rules are provided to determine which financial statements to use). Adjust this financial statement income to remove or add the effects of companies included or excluded in the financial statements which are or are not reported on the same tax return. The financial statement income must be adjusted so that it is on the same year-end as the tax returns. The effect of income taxes should be removed from book income. Compare this adjusted financial statement income to the minimum taxable income (before the adjustment for this item and before the net operating loss adjustment described in the following paragraph). One-half the excess of the adjusted book income amount over the minimum tax amount is an additional adjustment item for the corporate alternative minimum tax.

Once all the adjustments and preferences described have been considered, the minimum tax net operating loss is calculated and subtracted. This is the same concept as the regular tax net operating loss. It is, however, adjusted to reflect all the changes previously discussed for calculating minimum taxable income.

The resulting amount is the corporation's alternative minimum taxable income. This is reduced by a $40,000 exemption, to the extent available. This exemption amount is reduced at the rate of 25 cents for each dollar of alternative minimum taxable income in excess of $150,000. Thus when alternative minimum taxable income exceeds $310,000, no exemption will be allowed.

The amount remaining after reducing the alternative minimum taxable income for the exemption is multiplied by 20% to obtain the tentative minimum tax. This tentative minimum tax is reduced by certain foreign and investment tax credits to arrive at the final tax due. Technically, this final minimum tax is only paid to the extent that it exceeds the regular corporate tax.

One final step is necessary. A minimum tax credit must be computed. This credit is a portion of the minimum tax paid for the year. This amount will be available to offset the corporation's regular tax in later years. (The concept of the minimum tax credit is more fully developed in Chapter 11.)

Conclusion

The decision to use, or to continue to use, a corporate form of ownership after tax reform must be made very carefully. The cost of an incorrect decision could be much greater than before. In many instances investors will be better off with a different form of ownership. In some situations, such as where a significant salary can be paid, a corporate structure may still be reasonable. However, as the brief summary of the changes tax reform made to corporate taxation makes clear, the decision is very complex and should therefore only be made with the advice of your tax and legal advisors. Tax reform may have been sold as tax simplification, but it's hard to tell by looking at the corporate tax provisions.

S CORPORATIONS

Whether called a "tax option corporation" or a "Subchapter S corporation," S corporations have been commonly used for many real estate related activities, such as brokerage, leasing, and maintenance operations. They have not been commonly used for holding real estate investments. However, tax reform may change this. An overview of S corporations will help to understand why.

What Is an S Corporation?

S corporations are a hybrid between the partnership and corporate forms discussed in previous sections. An S corporation is a regular corporation which, by meeting additional requirements, elects to be taxed in a manner similar to that of a partnership. An S corporation also has the corporate benefits of limited liability (the shareholders can generally be held liable only for the amount of their investment). This benefit often proves illusory because many lenders and creditors will require personal guarantees from the shareholders.

Since an S corporation is taxed similarly to a partnership, there is generally no tax at the entity level. The S corporation's tax attributes flow through to the shareholders who then report any income or loss on their personal tax returns. Prior to tax reform, this was a considerable advantage over a regular corporation since these losses could be used to offset income the shareholder would otherwise have to pay tax on (such as salary).

Another tax attribute of the S corporation is not as favorable. An investor can generally only deduct losses from an investment up to the amount he has invested, that is, up to the amount of his tax basis. In the case of an S corporation shareholder, this generally includes the amount paid for the stock in the corporation and amounts loaned directly by the shareholder to the S corporation. Thus, if the S corporation takes out a mortgage on property it owns, no part of the mortgage can be included in the amount of the investor's tax basis. Under prior law, this could have significantly limited the amount of tax deductions which the S corporation shareholder could have used. This limitation was very unfavorable when compared with a partnership arrangement. If a partnership took out a mortgage on property it owned, each partner could include his pro rata share of the partnership debt in his tax basis. As a result, a partner would often have been able to deduct far more tax losses than a comparable S corporation shareholder.

S Corporation Compared with Other Investment Vehicles After Tax Reform

Tax reform will make the S corporation look much more advantageous than it had in comparison with a partnership or regular corporation. An S corporation structure enables a shareholder to avoid the double tax burden which a shareholder in a regular corporation will face. Tax reform, however, makes this savings potentially more valuable for two reasons: (1) corporate-level tax and (2) the relationship between corporate and individual tax rates.

A regular corporation often avoided the corporate-level tax on a sale, liquidation, and/or distribution of its assets to its shareholders. As discussed more fully in the preceding section on regular corporations, tax reform has generally repealed the special rules which permitted this. Now a regular corporation will generally face the burden of the corporate-level tax in most situations in which it attempts to distribute real estate and other assets. Since an S corporation generally pays no tax it will be far more cost effective from the perspective of liquidating and distributing its real estate and other assets. In addition, tax reform has changed the relationship between corporate and individual tax rates. Corporate tax rates now exceed the individual tax rates for the first time. This provides an even greater incentive to use an S corporation when the corporate structure is necessary. For a discussion of converting a regular corporation to an S corporation see the earlier discussion of regular corporations. Also, carefully review with your tax advisor the possible applicability of certain additional rules that could affect an S corporation that was formerly a regular corporation.

Before rushing to convert a C (regular) corporation to an S corporation review the effect of the change on your pension plan and on any outstanding loans due to the plan with your pension consultant. There could be some costly problems with an improperly planned conversion.

The disadvantage which an S corporation previously had relative to a partnership concerning the inclusion of entity-level debt in the owner's investment (amount at risk) still exists. However, now the trend in real estate investments will be toward investments which produce economic benefit and taxable income, rather than tax losses. To the extent that this generalization holds true, the relative advantage that the partnership form has over the S corporation form with respect to supporting tax deductions will be far less important. Also, the S corporation form avoids a risk which many real estate investment partnerships face, namely recharacterization as an association taxable as a corporation. If a partnership has more corporate characteristics than partnership characteristics, it could be taxed like a corporation. This could be very detrimental from a tax standpoint, in part because an S corporation election would not be in effect and the corporate-level tax cost could not be avoided by such an unfortunate partnership. An S corporation avoids this risk and obtains similar conduit or flow-through of tax benefits.

One characteristic of the partnership form may prove advantageous after tax reform. How advantageous, however, will depend on the results of regulations issued and IRS actions. Partnerships have a great deal more flexibility than do S corporations in allocating income and deductions among their owners. If certain conditions are met, a partnership can allocate deductions, tax credits, and other tax consequences in a manner different than each partner's interest in the partnership. For example, a partner who owns 50% of the partnership may be entitled to 60% of the rehabilitation tax credit. Depending on future developments, this could prove advantageous when the passive loss limitations are involved (see Chapter 9). If it is possible to allocate more deductions to partners who won't be limited by the passive loss rules, the partnership form could prove very advantageous. It is, however, questionable whether the IRS would permit such allocations (see the discussion on partnerships earlier in this chapter).

Requirements to Elect S Corporation Status
In analyzing whether an S corporation form is best, the detailed requirements which an S corporation must meet should be considered. These strict requirements have been, and will continue to be, a major disadvantage of the S corporation form. Many business situations will simply not lend themselves to being organized within the stringent S corporation guidelines. Therefore it is important to be aware of these requirements in order to make an informed decision as to the appropriate business structure for your real estate investments.

The following requirements must be met:

There can only be one class of stock. This means that each share of stock must confer the same rights as every other share as to corporate profits and corporate assets if the corporation is liquidated. The shares are allowed to differ with respect to voting transfer, repurchase, and redemption rights.

Planning Tip. An S corporation can issue a valued employee stock which, on the death or termination of the employment relationship must be resold to the corporation at fair market value. This won't violate the one share of stock requirement.

There can be no more than 35 shareholders. A husband and wife are treated as one shareholder for this limitation. This requirement has prevented the use of S corporations for many larger real estate transactions.

Only U.S. resident humans (i.e., not corporations, etc.) can be shareholders. Certain trusts and estates, however, are allowed to be shareholders.

A timely and proper S corporation election must be made.

An S corporation may not own 80% or more of another corporation.

The S corporation must be a domestic corporation (generally organized under the laws of one of the states).

Planning Tip.   Many state and local governments have special rules affecting S corporations. Some of these taxing jurisdictions recognize S corporations, others do not. Also, some have their own requirements for electing S corporation status. Don't make a decision to use an S corporation until your tax advisor has carefully reviewed the state and local tax ramifications.

Conclusion

An S corporation, combining many of the advantages of both the corporate and partnership forms of doing business, warrants careful consideration after tax reform. Be certain, however, that the disadvantages and caveats noted in the previous discussions do not eliminate the potential benefits in the particular situation you and your advisors are evaluating.

MORTGAGE-BACKED SECURITIES AND REAL ESTATE MORTGAGE INVESTMENT CONDUITS (REMICs)

What Is a REMIC and Why Did Congress Create Them?

The mortgage-backed securities industry—the pooling ("packaging") of real estate mortgages and selling of security interests in these pools—has grown tremendously in recent years. The

federal government has encouraged this private sector participation to foster liquidity and flexibility in the mortgage market.
The tax laws, unfortunately, had not kept pace with these trends
on Wall Street, and tax problems resulted. These tax problems
hindered the ability to structure, for maximum economic, reg-
ulatory, and accounting benefits, a mortgage-backed vehicle to
attract both issuers and investors. Consistent with the federal
policy of encouraging private sector participation in the mortgage-backed securities area, Congress recently amended the tax
rules affecting mortgage-backed securities to address these problems. The response was primarily the provision of a new real
estate investment vehicle created by the Tax Reform Act of 1986—
REMICs.

When a pool of mortgages is packaged for sale, these packaged
securities are not owned directly by the ultimate investors, but
by some type of intermediary. One reason for this approach is
to accommodate one of the techniques used to package and sell
these mortgage-backed securities to investors, namely the provision of different types of income and principal interests ("multiple-class arrangements"). Multiple-class arrangements typically
create securities that differ from the underlying mortgages with
respect to the coupon rate, credit risk, and so on. The advantage
for the use of multiple-class securities is increased flexibility to
provide a security with the investment characteristics which best
meets the needs of investors. Such multiple-class arrangements
could not be provided for if direct ownership of the underlying
mortgages was transferred. Importantly, the use of an intermediary's securities as the means of ownership made the interests
in the underlying mortgages more readily transferable than a
mere direct interest in underlying real estate mortgages. Thus a
partnership, REIT, corporation, or grantor trust would acquire a
pool of mortgages. The security interests in this intermediary
would be structured to meet perceived market needs and would
then be sold to investors. The securities of this intermediary
would be backed by the real estate mortgages.

The use of such an intermediary entity created a number of
potential tax problems. One of these problems, specifically addressed by the new REMIC legislation, is the taxation of the
intermediary—that is, the taxation of the mortgages at the pool
level. If the intermediary were a corporation, the corporate intermediary would be subject to tax. Thus the corporation and
the ultimate investors would both be taxed—double taxation.

This result was very burdensome when compared with the results an individual investor would obtain by directly investing in a pool of mortgages. One option around this tax at the pool level would have been to elect to be taxed as a REIT. This solution was insufficient because the many requirements a REIT must meet made it too cumbersome a vehicle to serve the needs of the mortgage-backed securities industry adequately. (See the discussion later in the chapter concerning REITs.)

The partnership form of organization also presented difficulties in the context of a pool of mortgage-backed securities. For example, the special elections which would have to be made on the transfer of partnership interests to assure proper tax benefits are too cumbersome for mortgage-backed securities.

Another type of vehicle used to hold the pool of mortgages was a trust. When properly structured, the trust would not be taxed, only the beneficiaries would be. However, a major problem faced by such trusts was the risk that they would be recharacterized by the IRS as an association taxable as a corporation because their characteristics would be predominantly corporate in nature. This risk became particularly acute when the trust had different classes of ownership interests—something that was often essential from a marketing standpoint to best meet investor needs. A trust is generally not permitted to have more than one class of ownership interest. If multiple ownership interests were demanded by the marketplace, the trust would risk being treated for tax purposes as an association taxable as a corporation. Finally, some trust arrangements exposed certain investors to personal liability.

A number of other tax, accounting, and marketing problems existed. These further hampered the growth of the mortgage-backed securities market.

In response to these problems, Congress created the REMIC. Congress also addressed a number of ancillary tax problems such investments could create. (Some of these are dealt with in the following discussion.) The result should be further growth in the mortgage-backed securities market. This should provide a valuable investment opportunity for many issuers and investors. In time, the commercial mortgage market should also benefit from the creation of the REMIC, and an improvement of the financial markets for real estate investors who finance acquisitions and development should become evident.

Key Benefits of a REMIC

The key benefit of an entity being taxed as a REMIC is that there will be no entity-level tax—that is, no tax will be assessed at the mortgage pool level. The only limited exceptions to this no-tax rule are that a REMIC will be taxed on certain prohibited transactions (see section below concerning taxation of a REMIC). So long as the REMIC requirements are met, there will be no risk of the IRS recharacterizing the entity as one which would be subject to tax. The sponsor of a REMIC will be able to choose the entity (trust, partnership, corporation) which is most advantageous from a business perspective, without affecting the tax benefits. From an accounting perspective a number of problems have also been eliminated. The tax law changes made by tax reform provide flexibility to select the appropriate investment vehicle which will provide the desired accounting results. Establishing certain structures will be treated as a sale under current accounting conventions. For example, a sponsor setting up a REMIC can now qualify to treat the transaction as a sale by using a pass-through form to issue REMIC securities. In the past, many issuers were required to treat similar arrangements as liabilities on their financial statements. This was a significant deterrent to many mortgage banks.

Requirements to be Taxed as a REMIC

A number of stringent requirements must be met to qualify for the favorable tax treatment afforded a REMIC and those investing in a REMIC. If the requirements are not met at any time, the entity will not be afforded the favorable REMIC benefits. The Secretary of the Treasury may permit a REMIC to continue to be treated as a REMIC if its failure to meet the REMIC requirements discussed below was inadvertent and quickly corrected. Since the Secretary of the Treasury only has the right to permit the continued treatment of the entity as a REMIC, and is not obligated to do so, great care should be exercised to assure continued compliance with the requirements discussed below.

The objectives of many of these requirements are to assure that the REMIC serves as a conduit for investors to invest in real estate mortgages. The entity must make an election to have the new REMIC rules applied to it, and it must report its earnings and payments on a calendar-year basis.

The asset requirements form the heart of the REMIC concept. With very limited exception, substantially all of the assets of a REMIC must be certain mortgages. Mortgages which are permissible (so-called qualified mortgages) include only mortgages secured by an interest in real estate. Qualified mortgages must be transferred to the REMIC before its inception (i.e., as part of the organization of the REMIC) or they must be purchased by the REMIC within three months of its inception. In addition to a direct interest in mortgages, obligations directly or indirectly secured by mortgages are also acceptable. A participation or certificate of beneficial ownership interest in such a mortgage is also a qualified asset. Therefore, debt instruments such as collateralized mortgage obligations (CMOs) can be transferred to a REMIC. Replacement mortgages are permitted when substituted for mortgages in the REMIC's pool which have defaulted.

Nominal amounts of cash and other liquid assets may be maintained for meeting cash-flow requirements (e.g., to make the required interest payments to its security holders). Thus a REMIC can temporarily invest cash flow in passive-type investments before such funds are distributed to its investors. The REMIC may hold a limited amount of assets as a reserve to meet certain expenses and to meet the required payments due to certain REMIC investors (a "qualified reserve fund"). A REMIC may also own regular interests in another REMIC (see below).

A REMIC may also own property acquired on the foreclosure of one of its qualified mortgages. However, to prevent the REMIC from becoming actively involved in the managing of this foreclosed property, a strict time limit is imposed. The REMIC must dispose of foreclosed property it acquires within one year.

Extensive reporting requirements must be met by REMICs. These requirements are designed to provide each member of the two classes of investors with the information which is necessary to determine their tax liability.

Types of Ownership Interests in a REMIC

There are only two classes of owners under a REMIC: regular interest holders and residual interest holders. A regular interest is an interest akin to a debt instrument. These investors obtain an unconditional right to receive interest at a fixed rate (a variable rate may be provided as allowed for in future regulations) and specified principal payments. The timing, not the amount, of these specified principal payments can be made contingent on the actual prepayments of the underlying mortgages. Thus, regular interests generally have most of the characteristics of pass-through mortgage obligations.

A residual interest is an interest akin to that of an equity holder (shareholder). Any interest which is not a regular interest will be a residual interest. There may only be one class of residual interest holders. For example, an interest in a mortgage that resembles excess servicing can qualify as a residual interest because it is contingent on prepayments on the underlying mortgage pool. Excess servicing can be illustrated as follows: The person originating the mortgages (e.g., a mortgage banker) originates a loan with an 11% rate. The market rate for similar loans is only 10% when he sells the loan. Since investors generally won't pay a premium because of the risk that the loan will be prepaid before the premium is amortized. The mortgage banker will therefore sell the loan at par, 10%, and will retain the extra 1% interest. This retained interest is known as excess servicing.

These investors receive a pro rata return based on the following factors:

The rate of return on the REMIC's permitted investments

Contingent payments received, such as equity kickers on mortgages held

The prepayments received on the REMIC's mortgage portfolio

Transferring Assets to a REMIC
To permit the ready transfer of assets to a REMIC, no gain or loss will have to be recognized for tax purposes on the transfer of assets to a REMIC in exchange for a regular or residual interest in that REMIC. The investment (tax basis) the investor has in the assets transferred to the REMIC will become his tax basis in the REMIC interests he receives on the transfer. However, any difference between the issue price of the regular or residual interest and the tax basis of the property contributed will generally be amortized as income or expense, as the case may be, over the term of the REMIC.

Taxation of a REMIC and Its Investors
To meet the objectives a REMIC was designed for, it cannot pay tax as an entity. This is in fact the result. If all the requirements are met, the REMIC will be treated as a conduit passing all of its taxable income, computed on an accrual basis, to its two classes of investors. Each investor will then report his allocable share

of the REMIC's income. In computing the taxable income for a REMIC, a deduction is allowed for amounts paid to regular interest holders as if such amounts were interest expense on debt instruments. The remaining income of the REMIC is generally allocated to the residual interest holders.

Regular interest holders report their income as interest income on an accrual basis regardless of the holder's own method of accounting. If the instrument is issued at a discount (original issue discount) special rules will apply. Since a regular interest holder is analogous to a creditor, the income to be reported is the income which an accrual method holder of a debt instrument, with terms similar to those of the regular interest holder, would report.

The residual interest holders report their allocable share of the daily taxable income (or loss) of the REMIC. This income will be taxed as either interest or dividends, the law is not clear. Actual distributions by a REMIC are treated as a return of the investor's capital to the extent that the distributions do not exceed the investor's tax basis plus income previously allocated to that investor which hasn't been distributed. Payments in excess of all of an investor's capital will be taxed as gain realized on the sale of his interest in the REMIC (i.e., if Congress reinstates the capital gains rules, these amounts would be treated as capital gains).

To enforce the stringent requirements the REMIC must meet, Congress has provided for some tough penalties. If the REMIC earns income on a prohibited transaction, a 100% penalty tax will be assessed. Prohibited transactions include earning income from nonqualified assets, compensation for services rendered, or from the disposition of a qualified mortgage unless the disposition was for the purpose of replacing a defective mortgage with a nondefective mortgage, or incident to replacing a mortgage in default.

Although the Tax Reform Act of 1986 has eliminated the ability of most corporations to liquidate and distribute assets to shareholders without incurring a tax, REMICs will be allowed to liquidate without an entity-level tax. To liquidate without recognizing any gain on the sale of its assets, the REMIC must adopt a plan of liquidation and liquidate within 90 days.

A special rule was also enacted for foreign investors in REMICs. Thus the same withholding tax rules which apply for mortgage pass-through securities issued after July 18, 1984 apply to all interest paid to foreign regular interest holders. Foreign regular interest holders should therefore receive their remittances free of withholding tax. Under prior law, mortgages issued prior to this date were subject to withholding tax. For foreign residual interest holders, withholding tax is charged at the statutory 3% rate, or a lower income tax treaty rate if applicable.

Miscellaneous REMIC Rules

A number of miscellaneous rules were enacted as part of the REMIC provisions. For example, a REIT can hold an investment in a REMIC without disqualifying itself as a REIT since the interest in a REMIC will be treated as a qualified asset for purposes of the REIT rules. Also, certain savings and loan institutions can treat their investments in a REMIC as qualifying real property loans for purposes of computing their bad debt deduction. Since the ownership of corporate debt instruments would not generally be treated as a qualified asset, this special rule was necessary.

Conclusion

The REMIC vehicle seems to answer many of the practical accounting, tax, business, and marketing problems faced by the mortgage-backed securities industry. If actual experience proves this true, REMICs could become a major factor in real estate finance. They could provide a valuable new investment opportunity for passive investors interested in the yields real estate mortgages can provide. For developers and other owners of real estate, REMICs could become a valuable source of financing.

REAL ESTATE INVESTMENT TRUSTS

A REIT is a special form of real estate ownership which permits a widely held entity to own real estate and pass through the income to its owners without the entity incurring a tax. A large number of investors pool their capital in an entity (a corporation or trust) and the entity invests in a diversified real estate portfolio. Thus a REIT is to real estate what a mutual fund is to stocks and what a REMIC is to real estate mortgages. The key advantages to investing in a REIT are the same as investing in a mutual fund or a REMIC: diversification and liquidity. Diversification comes from the sizable portfolio which a REIT can own.

Liquidity is available since the REIT shares are generally traded on a major stock exchange. It's obviously much easier to dispose of publicly traded stock than to dispose of actual real estate investments.

The key advantage to REIT status is that if all the complicated REIT requirements are adhered to, the REIT itself will not be subject to any tax. Thus the double taxation normally imposed on corporations and their shareholders can be avoided. Most income would be distributed to the shareholders and taxed to them.

For a number of reasons REITs are important to the real estate industry. They can provide an excellent investment vehicle for even the smallest investors. Also REITs can be an excellent source of capital, either for a lender (REITs can hold mortgages) or for a purchaser of your existing real estate.

Tax reform has liberalized a number of the requirements an entity must meet to be taxed as a REIT. These provisions will generally make it easier for an entity that wishes to be taxed as a REIT to be so treated. The changes, however, are not so fundamental that they would make a REIT the preferred choice for an investment vehicle if it wasn't the recommended choice before.

REITs Compared with Other Investment Vehicles After Tax Reform

Tax reform should make REITs a more desirable form of real estate investment for reasons other than the liberalization of some of the technical REIT requirements discussed below. Tax reform has eliminated, in many instances, the benefits of being able to deduct tax losses at the individual investor level. (See Chapters 2, 9, and 10.) A primary reason not to use a REIT in the past had been that real estate investments generally provided significant tax benefits. A REIT could pass through cash flow (taxable income and capital gains) to its shareholders. It could not pass through tax losses. This factor was often sufficient to end consideration of a REIT in favor of a partnership in many instances. Now, however, since investors should be looking more for economic deals, rather than tax benefits, there could be a resurgence of interest in REITS.

However, two factors may offset this potential for resurgence. This factor is a result of the new passive losses (described in Chapter 9). Investors who have tax losses from passive investments that cannot be currently used because of the passive loss limitations will be inclined to invest in real estate limited partnerships which will generate passive income that can be offset by their otherwise unusable passive losses. This is because REIT income will be treated as portfolio income rather than as passive income under the new laws. Since portfolio income cannot be used to offset passive losses, a REIT would not be the recommended investment for an investor with unused passive losses. This result is an anomaly since, as will be discussed below, a REIT's income may be predominantly from sources which, if invested in directly, would generate passive income. The apparent rationale for classifying REITs as portfolio investments in spite of their underlying nature is that REITs usually generate income to their shareholders and they can't pass through tax losses.

The second key factor, according to many, is that Wall Street has not always valued REITs in a manner reflective of the underlying real estate holdings. Often REITs have been lackluster performers. Given Wall Street's sophistication with real estate (witness mortgaged-backed securities) the reasons for this valuation problem are unclear, if it exists at all.

Other factors to consider in evaluating the type of entity to be used for real estate investments include the very complicated requirements which a REIT must meet in order to continue to qualify as a REIT. If, however, you are merely going to be a passive investor rather than an active principal, these complications will not particularly affect you. The REIT and its accountants will have to deal with these matters. What a REIT does offer a passive investor is liquidity. You merely sell shares of stock to reduce or dispose of your investment. Also, the uncertainties which a partnership can face as to its status as a partnership if challenged by the IRS are not faced by a REIT. Shareholders in a REIT can exercise greater control over their investment than can limited partners in a partnership. Limited partners cannot exercise any control over the management of partnership affairs. However, REIT shareholders can vote at annual shareholder meetings and elect directors or trustees.

Requirements to Maintain REIT Status

To maintain its qualification as a REIT, the entity must meet a number of strict technical requirements, which are best understood when divided into a number of categories:

1. *Organizational Requirements.* Numerous types of entities can elect to be treated as a REIT—a corporation, a trust, or an association. There are no differences in how each of these electing entities are treated under the tax laws. However, some differences may arise in how the different entities are treated under state law. Whichever type of entity is used, it must be managed by trustees or directors who have continuing and exclusive authority over the management of the REIT's assets. A common approach is for the trustees or directors to hire an independent advisor on a fee basis to manage the REIT's assets. Finally, the entity desiring to be taxed as a REIT must make an election to have the REIT rules apply to it.

2. *Ownership.* The ownership interests in a REIT must be evidenced by transferable shares. If the entity electing REIT status is a corporation, these shares will be stock certificates. If the entity is a trust, the units will be shares of beneficial interest. From an investor's viewpoint the difference will generally be a mere technicality. However, all of these ownership shares must be freely transferable.

The ownership interests must generally be widely held. A number of mechanical tests have been devised to assure broad ownership. At least 100 persons must own a REIT's shares for at least 335 days during the year. In addition, to assure that the diversified ownership is substantial, the REIT must also meet an anticoncentration test. More than 50% of the REIT's shares cannot be owned by five or fewer persons. Tax reform has slightly liberalized these ownership requirements. In order to make it easier to organize a REIT without running afoul of these strict rules, these closely held ownership requirements are not applicable for the first tax year for which a REIT election is made.

3. *Tax Year.* Most REITs are required to use a calendar year ending December 31 for determining income and expense for tax purposes. A fiscal year (a tax year ending on the last day of any month other than December 31) is generally not permitted.

Tax reform made this requirement less burdensome for newly organized REITs. The problem many new REITs had previously was that when they were first organized they could not immediately elect REIT status. For example, the proceeds the entity received from selling shares might have been invested in short-term securities until suitable real estate investments could be located. This type of investment is not suitable for a REIT (see

Assets, below). Later in their initial year, when acceptable REIT investments were made, they could elect REIT status. A REIT in this situation would want to elect a fiscal year ending on the last day of the month before it elected REIT status. This would enable the entity to cut off the period for which it couldn't be taxed as a REIT, and let it start fresh as a REIT for the remainder of that year. Once REIT status was elected the REIT would want to change to a calendar year-end as it is required to do. However, since it would have already elected a fiscal year (for its non-REIT period) it would require IRS permission to change to a calendar year. Seeking IRS approval can be a burdensome process. Thus the Tax Reform Act of 1986 provided that a newly electing REIT, which hasn't engaged in an active trade or business, can elect to be taxed on a calendar-year basis without seeking IRS approval.

4. *Assets.* To maintain REIT status, a number of strict mechanical tests must be met. Fully 75% of a REIT's assets must be invested in cash, government securities, and real estate. This test must be met at the end of each quarter of the REIT's tax year. In addition, other requirements are imposed to assure that the REIT's nonreal estate assets are diversified. Thus no more than 10% of the stock of any single corporation can be held and no more than 5% of the REIT's total assets can be invested in the stock of any single issuer. Given the vagaries of the securities markets, a number of safety valves, to which tax reform adds, are available in case these tests are not met. If the REIT finds itself with certain nonqualified assets, they may, under certain conditions, be disposed of within 30 days after the quarter-end. Also, a REIT won't be treated as failing this test solely due to the change in the market value of its holdings.

Tax reform provides additional relief from these tests in the case of a REIT which has just received a capital infusion. Recognizing that after receiving a capital infusion from raising new equity capital or from a public debt offering the REIT will need time to locate suitable qualifying real estate investments, tax reform provides some leniency. Thus the proceeds from such a capital infusion are treated as if invested in qualifying assets for a period of one year, no matter how they are invested.

5. *Income.* To assure that a REIT invests in passive real estate holdings, a number of strict income requirements must be met. Tax reform relaxed these restrictions somewhat, but the require-

ments nevertheless remain stringent. If a REIT doesn't meet these requirements, its status as a REIT can be terminated.

To assure that a REIT is primarily a vehicle for passive real estate investments, fully 75% of a REIT's income must be from the following sources: rents from real property, tenants' reimbursements for property taxes and other expenses, real estate tax abatements and refunds, interest on real estate mortgages, distributions from other REITs in which it has invested, and gains on the sale of real estate and real estate mortgages it has held for a required time period. Tax reform added income from shared appreciation mortgages to the list of qualifying incomes. Under prior law income received from shared appreciation provisions in debt instruments secured by real estate could have been treated as income from prohibited transactions (see Taxation of REITs, below).

Tax reform relaxed this 75% requirement in one case. If a REIT raises additional capital from issuing stock or from offering debt securities, the income generated on these funds will automatically be treated as qualified income for a period of one year. This rule is intended to give the REIT time to locate suitable investments.

Also, 95% of the REIT's gross income must be derived from the sources which satisfy the 75% test and from dividends, interest, and gains on the sale of stocks and securities. Finally, less than 30% of the REIT's gross income must be from the sale of stocks and securities held short term, from prohibited transactions (see below), real property held less than four years, and interests in mortgages on real property held less than four years.

The types of real estate rentals a REIT may receive are also restricted in order to assure that the REIT's rental activities are passive. Thus a REIT cannot receive rentals which are based on the net profits of a tenant. If any such rent is received, then all of the rentals from that tenant will be treated as disqualified rentals.

Planning Tip. Care must be exercised in negotiating and drafting leases, particularly those with percentage rental clauses. Percentage rentals are based on a percentage of the tenant's sales above a certain base or trigger amount. Sales, however, are usually reduced by returns and other items. If the adjustments to sales become too extensive, a rental based on the tenant's net income may be approached.

Percentage rental terms should be negotiated at the inception of the lease and should not be changed during the term of the lease in a manner which suggests that they are based on net income of the tenant. Percentage rental terms should also conform to normal business practices.

Tax reform has relaxed the restrictions on receiving rentals based on a tenant's net income in one case. If the tenant receives its income from subleasing the premises and the sublease income would be qualified income if received directly by the REIT (i.e., it's not based on the net income of the subtenant), then the REIT can receive a rental from the tenant (i.e., the sublessor) based on the tenant's net income.

A REIT is not allowed to have a 10% or greater ownership interest in a tenant. If it does, the income the REIT receives will be nonqualified.

In the past, a REIT couldn't render any services to tenants. Instead, the REIT's properties had to be managed through an independent contractor from whom the REIT didn't receive any income or payments. The purpose of these restrictions was to assure that the REIT was only passively involved in its real estate holdings. These restrictions presented a number of practical difficulties because many of the types of real estate which REITs own, such as shopping centers and large office buildings, require at least some management services. Tax reform has somewhat reduced the restrictions on the rendition of services by a REIT. A REIT is now allowed to render the same services for its real estate holdings which a tax-exempt entity is allowed to render without producing what is technically referred to as "unrelated business income." Thus a REIT can render certain services which are customarily rendered in the geographic market in which it is located. Prohibited services are those considered rendered primarily for the convenience of the tenant. Furnishing heat and light, cleaning public or common areas, and providing for trash removal are not prohibited. Operating a warehouse, hotel, or storage garage is prohibited. However, a REIT can now operate a parking lot for the convenience of its building's patrons so long as the parking spaces are not reserved and no fees are collected. If parking spaces are reserved or fees charged, then the parking lot will have to be maintained, as under prior law, by an independent contractor.

The rentals which the REIT receives must be earned on the rental of real property (land, buildings, and their structural components). Only a minimum amount of the rental may be from the rental of personal property (fixtures, equipment, movable partitions, etc.). If more than 15% of the rentals are attributable to the rental of personal property, the rental income will not be qualified rental income for purposes of meeting the 75% test noted previously.

6. *Subsidiaries.* Tax reform relaxed the rules concerning REIT subsidiaries. Under prior law, if a REIT owned stock in a corporation that was not a REIT, it could not treat that investment as a qualified real estate asset. The effect was to prevent a REIT from setting up a subsidiary to hold a specific property which the REIT deemed prudent to isolate in a separate corporate entity because of liability concerns. Tax reform will now allow a REIT to put property in a 100% owned subsidiary. The REIT treats the income and assets of the subsidiary as its own for purposes of the income and asset tests.

7. *Distributions.* A REIT must meet strict distribution requirements, which are directed at assuring that the REIT serves as a conduit for the income earned on its real estate investments. Thus a REIT must distribute at least 95% of its taxable income to its shareholders. Since it may be difficult to calculate or distribute the correct amount, a numer of safety valves are provided. Distributions may be made in certain cases after the REIT's year-end and treated as if made on account of that year. To qualify, the REIT must declare the dividends before the extended due date of its tax return for the year in question. An election must also be made on that tax return to treat the distribution as relating to the prior year. A further safety valve exists in the form of a deficiency dividend procedure which permits a REIT to make distributions if the IRS determines that the dividends made were insufficient.

Tax reform relaxed these distribution requirements with respect to distributions when rules which require that income be imputed in certain cases affect the REIT. The tax laws require in certain situations that taxpayers must recognize income even if the income was not received. Realizing the hardship these imputed income rules could have on a REIT (unexpected imputed income could cause a REIT to violate the distribution test and lose its REIT status), Congress modified the REIT rules. Now if a REIT must recognize income for tax purposes as a result of the imputed interest rules (see Chapter 5) or the deferred rental rules, or as a result of a like-kind exchange (see Chapter 10) which did not qualify, these amounts can be excluded from the calculation of the 95%-of-income-distribution test. These amounts are not, however, excluded from the REIT's calculation of taxable income. Therefore the REIT will still have to pay tax on these amounts. The important advantage, however, is that the REIT will not be disqualified for failing to meet the distribution tests.

Finally, tax reform imposes a nondeductible excise tax of 4% of the excess of the amount which a REIT is required to distribute during the year over the amount it actually distributed. For this calculation the amount required to be distributed is 85% of the REIT's ordinary income plus 95% of the REIT's capital gain income. A number of other technical adjustments must be made for this calculation.

8. *Record Keeping.* In order to demonstrate that it has met all the preceding requirements, a REIT must also meet strict record-keeping requirements.

Taxation of REITs

Generally REITs are taxed in the same manner as any corporation. However, if a REIT meets all the requirements described above, it will qualify to deduct the distributions made to its shareholders in determining its taxable income. This deduction, which must at least equal 95% of the REIT's taxable income, will effectively eliminate almost all the tax a REIT would otherwise have to pay. The distributions which the REIT makes and deducts are then taxed to the recipient shareholders as dividend income.

A REIT can also be subject to severe penalty taxes. A 100% penalty tax is imposed on income received from the sale of property held primarily for sale in the ordinary course of the REIT's business, other than foreclosure property. The purpose of this test is to prevent the REIT from actively and regularly engaging in the sale of real estate. This is consistent with the objective that the REIT be a mere conduit for passive real estate investments. A safe harbor is available which enables a REIT to avoid this 100% penalty tax. Tax reform further liberalized this safe harbor. If a REIT sells real estate subject to the following conditions it will not be subject to the 100% penalty tax:

The property sold is a real estate asset.

The property sold must have been held for at least four years.

The total expenditures the REIT made to the property during the four-year period before the sale cannot exceed 30% of the net sales price (the limit had been 20% before tax reform).

During the year in which the property was sold, the REIT could not have made more than seven property sales (it had been five properties before tax reform). Foreclosure properties are not included in this calculation. Tax reform has also added an alternative to this test. Under this alternative test the REIT can sell any number of properties during the year so long as the income from the sales does not exceed 10% of the REIT's investment (adjusted basis) in all its assets.

When calculating the taxable income of a REIT, adjustments are made for the transactions subject to this 100% penalty tax.

Types of REITs

Real estate investment trusts may be categorized according to a number of different characteristics. Some REITs have been organized as single-project REITs to develop a single real estate investment. Another type of REIT which has become common is a finite-life REIT. After a specified number of years a finite-life REIT will be liquidated and the proceeds distributed to its shareholders. For example, a finite-life equity REIT may be liquidated after 5 to 10 years. A finite-life mortgage REIT will usually be liquidated after a longer period, often about 12 years. One of the purposes of finite-life REITs is to force Wall Street to more fairly value the REIT based on the value of the REIT's underlying assets. This valuation issue has been a persistent problem for the REIT industry. The stock market has often valued REITs at a discount from the value of their underlying assets. If the assets will be sold at a definite date, according to the finite-life REIT theory, then the market will have to more fairly value the REIT shares.

Real estate investment trusts are also distinguished according to the types of real estate investments they make: (1) REITs which invest solely in real estate properties are known as equity REITs,

(2) REITs which invest solely in mortgages are known as mortgage REITs; and (3) REITs which invest in both equities and mortgages are known as hybrid REITs.

A final method of distinguishing REITs is based on the approaches to the sale and issuance of ownership shares. Closed-end REITs issue shares to the public once. They can't issue additional shares (which would dilute the interests of the current holders) unless the current shareholders approve it. An open-end REIT can issue new shares at any time. In addition, the trustee can redeem the shares in an open-end REIT at any time, at their market value.

Once you've determined which type of REIT you may want to invest in, you must evaluate the REITs available to determine which are the best opportunities. The following section should help in this task.

Choosing a REIT for Investment

A number of factors must be analyzed in determining which REIT to invest in. Factors to consider include the following:

What is your personal tax situation? Do you need additional passive income to offset otherwise unusable passive losses? (See Chapter 9.) If you do, then limited partnerships, or master limited partnerships, may be the preferred form of investment. If not, then you can evaluate REITs, partnerships, and other competitive investments based solely on their investment merit.

Does the REIT have a discernible investment policy? Do you feel that policy is appropriate for today's real estate investment environment?

What is the REIT's track record? How has the REIT fared in both good and bad real estate markets?

How are the trustee, director, and management compensated? Does the compensation motivate management to maximize the long-term benefits to the shareholders? Is the compensation structured as an incentive to encourage performance?

How has the market valued the REIT? How does the share price compare with the true market value of the underlying assets?

How regular have the REIT's dividends been? What is the source of the dividend distributions and income? Has the REIT consistently generated the necessary cash from ongoing operations or have distributions come from sales or property which may not be repeated in the future?

Has the REIT's cash flow ever exceeded its income (e.g., as a result of depreciation deductions)? This could be important because it could indicate that the REIT has been able to accumulate reserves for repairs or further investment. It is also possible that the REIT will use cash flow in excess of taxable income to make tax-free distributions to investors.

If you are investing in a REIT which is raising new capital, how will that capital be spent? Has the REIT identified specific properties which it will invest in, or at least specific types of properties which it will seek? Or is the money merely going into a blind pool which the REIT will invest in any manner its management chooses?

Conclusion

Tax reform has had a number of direct and indirect effects on REITs. These changes generally make REITs better real estate investment vehicles. However, the extent to which these changes will stimulate more REIT activity will depend on the market's perception of REITs.

CHAPTER SUMMARY

One of the most important decisions to be made by a real estate investor is how an investment will be structured. The ownership form used will have important implications to the legal and tax consequences an investor can face. Tax reform has made this decision more complicated to make. Carefully review the considerations outlined in this chapter, and any other factors affecting your personal tax situation, with your tax advisor.

2 FINANCING REAL ESTATE INVESTMENTS

GENERAL EFFECTS OF TAX REFORM

Tax reform will greatly change the way real estate is financed. In most cases, tax reform will significantly reduce the tax benefits available from the financing that is used. The bias which the tax laws have had in favor of debt financing over equity will still exist to some extent, but the bias will be dramatically reduced. Deals will often be structured with less debt and more equity than in the past. The changes, however, are far more complicated and far-reaching than this generalization indicates. Consider the following direct and indirect changes tax reform will have on real estate financing:

Tax rates will be much lower. Thus the value of deducting interest incurred on financing real estate investments will be reduced, often significantly.

Example. An investor purchases a $2 million building and obtains a $1.8 million mortgage. If 10% simple interest is paid, he will incur $180,000 in annual interest charges. Under prior law this deduction would have provided a tax benefit of $90,000 at the maximum 50% tax rate. When the new tax reform rates are effective in 1988 the maximum tax rate will be only 28% (see Chapter 8). Thus the value of the tax benefit of deducting the interest expense will be only $50,400 ($180,000 × 28%). This is a reduction of 44%. Clearly the tax subsidy for debt financing, and hence the incentive to favor debt financing, have been reduced. But this is only part of the story. The question

after tax reform may often be when, or even whether, this re-
duced-interest benefit will be available.

The investment interest limitation, which can limit the amount
of interest expense which can be deducted in any given tax
year, has been made even tougher.

The new passive loss limitations can limit all deductions from
certain passive investments—including interest expense (see
Chapter 9). The passive loss limitations also add tremendous
complexity to the process of planning interest deductions. The
interplay between the passive loss and investment interest
limitations is very complicated.

Consumer interest deductions (home appliances, department
store charges, auto loans, etc.) are being eliminated (see Chapter 8). This will provide an incentive to characterize what
would have been consumer interest as something else, including home mortgage interest or investment interest. This
will further complicate the planning process for individual
investors.

The deductibility of mortgage interest on second homes has
been complicated by the interplay between the vacation home
limitations continued from prior law and the new limitations
on deducting mortgage interest and passive losses.

Home mortgage interest deductions are the subject of their
own set of complicated and confusing limitations (see Chapter
7).

The minimum tax will require separate calculations for its
own limitation on the deductibility of investment interest and
home mortgage interest. Since the rules differ for both the
regular and minimum tax calculations, the planning process
is complicated even more (see Chapter 11).

The rules for using the installment method of reporting gain
from the sale of real estate (i.e., reporting profits as the sales
proceeds are received) have been changed. Now, portions of
the deferred profits on installment sale may be triggered by
changes in the debt structure of a taxpayer's balance sheet (see
Chapter 5). Thus additional debt financing could have an additional indirect cost of accelerating tax liability on prior unrelated sales. These new rules add yet another new and
complicated dimension to the financial planning process.

Tax reform has extended the at-risk limitation to real estate. This rule could further limit the deductions which can be claimed for certain mortgaged real estate. Also, these rules will change the types of financing used.

The tax consequences of restructuring debt have become much more costly. If a lender agrees to forgive a portion of a loan, taxable income will be triggered.

Tax-exempt bond financing (industrial development bonds, etc.) has been greatly restricted. This will limit the availability of what had been an important financing source for many real estate projects. Also, interest on certain tax-exempt bonds will be subject to the minimum tax. This could increase the costs of using this type of financing (see Chapter 11).

REIT rules have been somewhat liberalized. Thus these entities could become a more viable source for financing real estate (see Chapter 1). The problem with REITs, however, often appears to be more one of market valuation and perception rather than tax law considerations.

A new real estate mortgage financing vehicle designed specifically to meet the needs of the mortgage-backed securities industry has been created—REMIC. This vehicle could channel more dollars to the real estate mortgage market, make those markets more efficient, and lead to the development of new types of mortgage financing (see Chapter 1).

Syndications should continue to remain a viable method of raising capital for real estate investment. Syndications, however, will be structured differently in order to respond to the changes noted, as well as many other tax reform changes.

The many changes to corporate taxation, including the new minimum tax preference item based on income reported for financial statement purposes, may change the way larger corporations view their real estate investment and financing activities (see Chapter 1). This preference item could make all municipal bond income taxable to some corporations. This could increase the cost of municipal bond financing.

A number of changes were made to the tax treatment of financial institutions; these concern tax rates, bad debt reserves, net operating losses, accounting methods, tax-exempt obligations, and so forth. Although these changes are not discussed further, they could have an impact on real estate transactions financed through the institutions affected.

Finally, many of the rules described above are subject to various transition rules, exceptions, and phase-in procedures.

The balance of the chapter will review many of the changes outlined above which are not discussed elsewhere in this book.

AT-RISK RULES

Most investment activities have been subject to the at-risk rules for some time. Real estate, however, has enjoyed favored status, at least until now. Tax reform has extended these at-risk rules to real estate investments. Therefore, real estate investors (including individuals, partners, S corporation shareholders, and certain closely held regular corporations) must now acquaint themselves with this concept and plan accordingly.

The at-risk rules limit the amount of tax losses you can deduct, and credits you can claim (subject to some special rules not reviewed here), from any activity to the amount that you are economically risking in that activity. Cash and property which you invest are considered to be amounts at risk.

Example. Assume that in 1988 you invested $100,000 in cash, and land which cost you $250,000, in a real estate partnership. The amount for which you are economically at risk is $350,000 ($100,000 cash + $250,000 adjusted tax basis of the property). Thus you could deduct no more than $350,000 in losses from the partnership. If your share of the partnership's tax losses exceeded the amount at risk you would not be entitled to deduct them.

As you deduct losses incurred, you must reduce the amount you have at risk in the investment. This is because the losses are treated as reducing the amount for which you are economically at risk—that is, as if you lost that amount. What happens if you incur losses in excess of your amount at risk? You can deduct the portion of the loss exactly up to your remaining amount at risk. This will necessarily reduce your amount at risk to zero. The remaining undeducted losses are carried forward to future years. They can be deducted in future years to the extent that you increase your amount at risk. This can be done, for example, by investing more cash or contributing more property to the activity.

Example. Let's continue the example above. Your amount at risk in 1988 is $350,000. The real estate investment generated a $250,000 loss to you. You can deduct the entire amount (subject to the passive loss and other limitations) in 1988 since it is less than your amount at risk. In 1989 the investment generates a $135,000 loss. This loss exceeds your $100,000 amount at risk by $35,000. You can deduct up to the $100,000 you still have at risk. This reduces the amount you have at risk to zero. The unused $35,000 loss is carried forward to future years. If you make an additional $50,000 cash investment in the real estate activity in 1990, this would increase your amount at risk from zero to $50,000. You could then deduct the $35,000 unused loss in 1990. Your amount at risk is then $15,000.

There is an important third common component to most taxpayers' amount at risk—debt. When you personally obligate yourself on a loan (i.e., the loan is "recourse" so that the creditor may proceed against your personal assets in the event of a default), you may include the amount of such a loan in your amount at risk. Nonrecourse debt, since you are not personally obligated, has generally not been includable in the amount for which you are considered at risk. When Congress extended the at-risk rules to real estate, it realized that most real estate financing is done on a nonrecourse basis. In response to this, special exceptions were provided to allow certain nonrecourse real estate financing to be includable in the amount at risk in a real estate activity. Importantly, real estate activities are defined broadly to include both holding personal property and providing services which are incidental to making the real property available as living accommodations. This is important since these ancillary activities will receive the benefit of the special exception made only for real estate. This is important for hotels (see Chapter 9).

Thus, for real estate activities, in addition to the cash and property you contribute and recourse loans you sign, you will also be at risk for qualified nonrecourse financing. This is generally financing from a person regularly engaged in the business of lending money. This will include, among others, insurance companies, pension funds, banks, savings and loan associations, and credit unions. Loans from federal, state, and local governments and their instrumentalities are also qualified. Newly formed lenders and private groups organized to lend on a specific project may have difficulty qualifying. In addition, the following requirements must be met:

The debt can't be convertible into an ownership (equity) position.

The debt must secure the real estate in question.

There can't be any guarantees against losses, stop-loss arrangements, and so forth.

No person may be personally liable on the debt (except as may be allowed for in future regulations).

The lender can't be the person from whom you acquired the property (or anyone related to the seller). Thus seller financing (purchase money debt) will no longer be advisable if the at-risk rules could significantly limit your deductions.

The lender can't receive any fee based on your investment in the property. In addition, anyone related to a person receiving such a fee can't be a qualified lender. Common examples of the types of financing sources this rule may preclude are promoters and their related finance companies. A "related person" for these rules includes members of your family, corporations which are members of the same controlled group, a corporation and a partnership if the same person owns more than half the corporation's stock and partnership's capital, and so forth.

Planning Tips. Carefully evaluate the structure of and parties to any financing before consummating a real estate acquisition. If the at-risk limitations could be costly, evaluate alternative sources to seller or promoter financing. Don't necessarily assume that they will. If you are preparing an economic deal and are confident that no tax losses will result, the at-risk rules may not be important. If the at-risk limitation is important, have your tax advisor carefully review the terms of all third-party financing to be sure that the fee structure won't run afoul of the prohibition of a lender receiving fees based on your investment in the property.

Finally, with all the other limitations discussed in this book, particularly the passive loss rules (see Chapter 9), don't jump the gun. Seller or promoter financing may still be advantageous if the terms are better than you can get elsewhere. The passive loss and other limitations may so limit the benefit of the tax losses the prospective investment will generate that any additional harm caused by violating the at-risk rules will not outweigh the economic advantages offered by favorable seller or promoter financing.

To prevent abuses by related parties, additional restrictions apply to nonrecourse loans from related lenders. A loan from a related party must be on terms which are commercially reasonable and substantially similar to the terms to which an unrelated borrower would be entitled. Among other requirements, the interest rate charged must be reasonable in light of the maturity date of the loan. The term of the loan can't exceed the life of the property.

If an investor actively participates in a number of real estate projects, these projects may qualify to be treated as a single activity for purposes of the at-risk rules. This can be a significant advantage since the amounts invested (at risk) in all the projects can then be aggregated for purposes of determining the limitation on deducting losses. This favorable treatment is not afforded to many other types of investments.

When a real estate investment is structured in partnership form (see Chapter 1) the at-risk tests are applied first at the partnership level. Thus the loan must meet all the requirements discussed above (e.g., it can't be from a person related to the partnership), at the partnership level, in order for each partner to include his share of the loan in his amount at risk.

These new real estate at-risk rules only apply to real estate put in use ("placed in service") after 1986. Therefore, real estate put into use before this date is exempt. It appears that real estate which was in use before 1987 can even be refinanced without being subjected to these rules.

Caution. If an investor acquires an interest in an S corporation or partnership after 1986 the at-risk rules will apply. This is true even if the S corporation or partnership purchased the real estate before 1987.

Conclusion

The at-risk rules still afford real estate investments preferential treatment as compared with other investments. Tax reform, however, has significantly reduced this preferential treatment. These changes must be carefully considered in structuring the financing and acquisition of real estate.

TAX-EXEMPT BOND FINANCING

The interest paid on bonds issued by state and local governments for traditional governmental purposes has generally been, and will generally continue to be, exempt from federal taxation. Many state and local government bonds have been issued to finance activities other than traditional governmental functions. These private activities have included such things as sports facilities, convention and trade show centers, industrial parks, and parking facilities.

The tremendous advantage to real estate developers has been the ability to benefit from such tax-exempt bonds in financing these and other private projects. Since the interest on these bonds was tax exempt, the real estate developer was able to lower the overall cost of financing. This has made viable projects which otherwise may not have been undertaken. It has also increased the profitability of projects. To the extent that tax-exempt bonds can still be tapped as a source of financing, similar benefits can be realized. Tax reform, however, has added a number of restrictions and limitations to the use of tax-exempt bonds to finance private activities. In addition, it has imposed a number of other restrictions on the use of tax-exempt bonds that can affect real estate activities. The following discussion will present an overview of the changes which should be of the most interest to real estate investors and developers.

Private Activity Bonds (Formerly IDBs)

The Tax Reform Act of 1986 places a number of additional restrictions on bonds which can be used for private (i.e., nongovernmental) purposes and still qualify as tax exempt. If tax-exempt bonds are used more than a specified amount in private activities, they will be characterized as private activity bonds (previously called industrial development bonds, or IDBs). As private activity bonds, a number of additional requirements must be met in order for the interest paid on the bonds to remain tax exempt.

If tax-exempt bonds have the following characteristics they will be tainted as private activity bonds:

Ten percent or more of the bond proceeds are used by a non-governmental person in that person's trade or business. Use of bond proceeds or bond-financed property includes direct ownership of the property, or beneficial use of the property through a lease or incentive payment contract. This also includes use by certain exempt organizations (Internal Revenue Code Section 501(c) (3) organizations) and use by certain power facilities.

Ten percent or more of the payments on the bond issue must be directly or indirectly made by nongovernmental persons (i.e., the payments are related to the nongovernmental use).

Bond issues which fail these tests are tainted as private activity bonds. These tainted bonds must generally meet the following additional requirements in order for the interest on them to remain tax exempt:

1. *Application of Proceeds. Ninety-five percent or more of the proceeds must be used for the exempt purpose of the borrowing.* Less than 5% of the bond proceeds can be used directly or indirectly in a trade or business which is not related to the government function being financed. For example, if $20 million is raised for a school, this limitation won't apply to the use of moneys to construct a school cafeteria owned and operated by a private investor. This is because the cafeteria is related to the exempt purpose of the school being built. If, however, a portion of the proceeds were applied to finance adjacent public tennis courts, this rule would apply. In this latter situation if $1 million or more of the proceeds ($20 million total × 5% rule] were applied to the construction of the tennis facility, the interest paid on the bond issue would not be exempt from federal tax.

2. *Costs of Issuance. No more than 2% of the proceeds of the bond issue may be used to finance certain costs of the issuance.*

3. *Qualified Purpose. The bond issue must be issued for one of the uses listed below, or must qualify as a small-issue bond:*

a. The proceeds of the bond issuance can be used to finance a qualified exempt facility. This includes certain multifamily residential rental projects (these must generally meet the same requirements as projects qualifying for the low-income housing credit—see Chapter 6), airports, docks and wharves (including certain storage facilities, but excluding hotels, retail, and office facilities if used in private businesses), mass commuting facilities, sewage disposal facilities, solid waste disposal facilities, facilities for the local furnishing of electric energy or gas, facilities for the furnishing of water (including irrigation systems), local district heating or cooling facilities, and certain hazardous waste disposal facilities. Tax reform also requires that the property in a number of these exempt facilities must be owned by the government.

b. The proceeds of the bond issue can be used to finance a qualified redevelopment activity, which means the proceeds of such an issue must be used to redevelop a locally designated blighted area. The bonds must be repaid by (or their repayment secured by) general tax revenues and incremental tax revenues. Taxes in the designated blighted areas must be imposed at the same rates and using the same assessment methods applicable to comparable properties elsewhere in that government's jurisdiction. Detailed criteria have been established for determining what is a blighted area for purposes of this exception.

c. The bond issue must meet the requirements of small-issue bonds. Small-issue bonds must be part of an issue of bonds not exceeding $1 million, the proceeds of which are used to acquire land or depreciable property. In certain instances the amount of the issue may be increased to $10 million. Small-issue bonds which will be used to acquire manufacturing facilities may be issued until the end of 1989.

Qualified Mortgage Bonds (Formerly Mortgage Subsidy Bonds)

The general rule is that tax-exempt bonds must be used for a traditional governmental purpose in order to remain tax exempt. There are a number of exceptions to this rule. The major exceptions—that private activity bonds may be used in certain situations which are not for traditional governmental functions without losing their tax-exempt status—was discussed above. Another exception to this general rule, which is important to real estate investors, is the exception for qualified mortgage bonds.

Qualified mortgage revenue bonds are bond issues the proceeds of which are used to finance low-interest loans for certain (generally first-time) buyers of single-family homes. Home buyers will have to have income within certain prescribed levels. These limitations, however, are relaxed considerably if the homes are in targeted areas. Similar to the requirement for private activity bonds, 95% of the proceeds must be used for the intended purpose.

In lieu of issuing qualified mortgage revenue bonds, the government may issue mortgage credit certificates of up to 25% of the amount of bonds not issued. For example, if the issuing government could issue $100 million in mortgage revenue bonds it will be permitted to issue $25 million of mortgage credit certificates instead. The mortgage credit certificates enable the recipient homeowner to claim a credit on his tax return based on a percentage of the home mortgage interest paid.

State Volume Limitations on Private Activity Bonds

Limitations on the dollar amount of private activity bonds are imposed on a state by state basis. The Tax Reform Act of 1986 replaces the multiple-volume limitations existing under prior law with a single-volume limitation. Under this new limitation each state may issue, until the end of 1987, private activity bonds up to the greater of: (1) $75 for each resident or (2) $250 million. After 1987 the limitation is reduced to the greater of: (1) $50 for each resident or (2) $150 million. These volume limitations will generally apply to certain exempt-facility bonds (excluding airports, docks and wharves, etc.), (2) qualified mortgage revenue bonds, (3) small-issue bonds, (4) qualified redevelopment bonds, and (5) certain other bonds. Rules are provided to allocate the volume limitations among state and other governmental units. In addition, carry forwards of unused amounts are provided for in certain instances.

Additional Requirements Affecting Tax-Exempt Bond Financing

A number of additional changes made by tax reform are important to note. Depreciation of property financed with tax-exempt bonds must be depreciated using the alternative depreciation system (see Chapter 10). Thus real estate financed with tax-exempt bonds must be depreciated over a 40-year period, using the straight-line method.

Interest on private activity bonds issued after August 7, 1986, will be treated as a tax preference item for purposes of the alternative minimum tax paid by individuals (see Chapter 11) and corporations (see Chapter 1). In addition, for corporations paying the corporate alternative minimum tax, tax reform has created a new preference item based on one-half of the excess of financial statement (book) income over a tax income figure. To the extent that any tax-exempt bond interest is included in book income it could be taxed under this rule (see Chapter 1). Banks and insurance companies will be taxed on certain tax-exempt bond interest for the first time. These changes could adversely affect the market for some of the bonds which real estate investors had used in the past.

Conclusion

Tax-exempt bond financing has been severely restricted by tax reform. In some situations, however, it will remain an important financing source. In these situations, plan carefully to meet all the new requirements.

CANCELLATION OF DEBT

Tax reform has significantly changed the rules concerning the discharge (cancellation) of debts. This change can be very costly. A general rule has been that when a lender forgives a debt you owe, you realize taxable income in the amount of the debt forgiven. There have been a few exceptions to this rule of recognizing income. If you are in bankruptcy, or are insolvent when the debt is forgiven, no income need be recognized. Tax reform has not changed these rules. There was, however, a very important third exception from the requirement to recognize income.

If a taxpayer incurred a debt in financing his trade or business, or the taxpayer was a corporation, a lender's forgiveness of a debt would not have to result in income. To avoid reporting taxable income the taxpayer had to elect to reduce the investment (adjusted tax basis) in depreciable property or real estate.

Example. A developer owns a building in which his tax basis is $500,000. He is in dire financial straits and cannot meet his payments on a $400,000 loan. The lender agrees to restructure the loan and forgive $100,000 of the debt. The developer elected to reduce his basis in his building from $500,000 to $400,000. No income has to be recognized.

Tax reform has repealed this rule. A taxpayer, other than one in bankruptcy or who is insolvent, will now have to report income when a debt is forgiven.

Planning Tip. Carefully factor in any potential tax cost when negotiating to reschedule loans due. Don't get caught short of cash due to an unexpected tax liability.

ORIGINAL ISSUE DISCOUNT RULES AND IMPUTED INTEREST

The tax laws require that certain minimum rates of interest be charged on deferred payment transactions, such as installment sales. The concern is that if less than an adequate interest rate is charged, taxpayers could manipulate the purchase price and interest payments to their advantage.

Example. Assume you sell a parcel of undeveloped land for $100,000. The buyer convinced you to take a note for the full purchase price of $100,000, which he would pay in one year with interest at the prime rate of 10% simple interest. In one year the buyer should pay you $110,000 ($100,000 in principal + (10% × $100,000 = $10,000) in interest).

If you will receive $110,000 in one year, it may not appear to matter whether you call a portion of the proceeds interest, at a fair 10% rate, or whether you call the entire amount principal. From a tax standpoint, however, the classification between interest and principal could have been very significant. This is because amounts allocated to the sale of land, for example, would have been taxed as capital gains at a tax rate of only 20%. Amounts allocated to interest income would have been taxed as ordinary income at tax rates of up to 50%. Thus as a seller you may have been willing to give the buyer his one-year-no-money-down request in exchange for his agreeing to let you call the entire amount "principal." This would have enabled you to save $3,000 in taxes ($10,000 called principal instead of interest × (50% − 20% tax rate savings)).

The solution to this potential manipulation was to require that a minimum interest rate be used in most sales transactions. If less than the minimum interest rate is charged, then the tax laws will impute a minimum rate. These concepts are illustrated in the latter portion of Chapter 5 in the discussion of installment sales.

Tax reform, by generally eliminating the distinction between capital gain income and ordinary income (i.e., interest income in this instance), has eliminated the result illustrated in this example, which encouraged sellers to understate the interest rate on a real estate sales transaction. Thus, when the new tax rates are fully effective, the seller would owe $2,800 in taxes on the $10,000 interest payment no matter what he called it ($10,000 payment × 28% tax rate).

In fact, the bias after tax reform may be the opposite of that under prior law. The incentive now may be to overstate the interest portion of the allocation. The seller may be indifferent to receiving interest or principal since both will probably be taxed at the same 28% rate. The buyer may strongly prefer the allocation to interest. This is because amounts allocated to principal (i.e., purchase price for the real estate) might have to be depreciated over 31.5 years (or 40 years if the buyer is subject to the minimum tax). The interest deduction, however, may be available sooner.

Caution. The parties, however, could have a different result in some situations because of the interplay of the various investment interest and passive loss rules. The parties should consider the effects of the investment interest and passive loss rules. For example, the capital gain may be treated as passive income whereas the interest may be characterized as portfolio income. If the seller has unused passive losses he would prefer an allocation to land since the gain on the sale of the land will be sheltered by his excess (suspended) passive losses. The interest income, however, could be taxed currently. Any such artificial allocation faces substantial risks. If the transaction is successfully challenged by the IRS, not only could taxes and interest be assessed, but substantial penalties could also be levied (see Chapter 12).

LIMITATION ON THE DEDUCTIBILITY OF INVESTMENT INTEREST

For many years the tax laws contained a limitation on the ability to deduct interest expenses incurred to own investments (e.g., interest paid on a mortgage taken to buy raw land). Tax reform has significantly changed these rules and the way they affect real estate investors.

The most important change for real estate investors is that the interest expense incurred to carry most real estate will no longer be subject to the investment interest limitation. Instead, interest paid on most real estate mortgages will be subject to the new passive loss limitations (see Chapter 9). The complicated rules for determining which real estate projects would be subject to the investment interest limitations, and which would not, have all been eliminated (the net leased property rules and 15% test and all the related complications are gone!).

Caution. Real estate investors should still be familiar with the investment interest rules because they can still affect the overall planning for real estate, and financing for related investments as well. Also, the interplay between the investment interest rules and the new passive loss rules (which will affect all real estate investors) is important to understand.

Overview of the Investment Interest Limitation

The basis calculation of the investment interest limitation is relatively simple and will provide an understanding of how the limitation works. It will also provide a good framework within which to explain the rules. The basic calculation is: interest paid to carry investments is deductible up to the amount of investment income:

> | Investment income |

minus

> | Investment expenses
> (excluding investment
> interest expense) |

equals

> | Net investment income
> (adjusted for certain
> phase-in rules) |

With this overview, each of the components of the calculation can be discussed.

Which Interest Expense Is Subject to the Limitation?

The first step in determining the amount of investment interest expense which can be deducted is to determine your investment interest expense for the year. This task is complicated by the many changes, restrictions, and limitations tax reform and prior law place on deducting interest expense. The best approach is to describe what is included in investment interest expense and what is not.

Investment interest expense includes any interest paid or accrued on debt incurred, continued to purchase, or hold property for investment. The simplest example is the one given in the beginning of this section: interest paid on a mortgage taken to buy raw land. In addition, interest expense allocable to portfolio income (interest on certificates of deposit, dividends, etc.) under the passive loss rules (see Chapter 9) is treated as investment interest expense. An example of this can be provided in the context in which it will affect many real estate investors.

Example. A partnership owns a garden apartment complex. The project is doing well and has a respectable cash flow. These funds are kept temporarily in a money market account pending payment to a contractor for reroofing the buildings. The partnership earns interest on this account. The passive loss rules require the partnership to classify this interest income as portfolio income, rather than as passive income from the rental activity (see Chapter 9). This interest income will thus be treated as investment income. Importantly, a portion of the interest expense paid on the borrowings used to invest in the partnership will now have to be allocated to this portfolio (i.e., interest) income which was earned. The interest expense allocated to the interest earned on the money market account will then be subjected to the investment interest limitation. NOTE—The remaining interest expense on the project (i.e., the interest allocable to carrying the investment in the buildings) is not subject to the investment interest limitations (under prior law it had been). Rather, it is subject to the passive loss rules.

Caution. This rule treating some interest expense as subject to the investment interest limitations and some to the passive loss limitations will make planning and bookkeeping extremely difficult. Even if you or the partnership pay the same amount of interest expense each year, the amount of that interest expense which will be subject to the investment interest limitation each year (rather than the passive loss rules) could still fluctuate dramatically. These fluctuations will depend on how much working capital is generated, when distributions are made to partners, the income earned on investments, and so forth. Be cautious when projecting interest deductions; this rule could result in a costly oversight.

Planning Tip. If the passive loss limitations will severely limit your deductions (including interest expense), it may prove advantageous to leave working capital in the partnership rather than distribute it. The interest and dividend income which the partnership will earn on its investments could result in allocating interest expense to this income. This will remove some of the interest expense from the passive loss limitation rules and instead subject it to the investment interest limitations, which in some situations will be more favorable. This planning possibility demonstrates how complicated planning can become under tax "simplification." Don't attempt this without first having your accountant project the results with and without this planning.

All interest payments are not subject to the investment interest limitation. As illustrated above, interest expense incurred on a passive activity, such as most real estate rental activities (see Chapter 9), will not be subject to the investment interest limitation. Interest expense subject to one of the many other Internal Revenue Code limitations will also be excluded. This is important since each type of interest must be planned for separately. This includes interest incurred during the construction of a building which must generally be added to your investment in the building and depreciated over the life of the building (see Chapter 3). Interest expense incurred on a personal residence (qualified residential interest) is subject to its own special rules (see Chapter 7). Personal interest expense, such as on automobile loans, and so forth, is excluded from the investment interest limitations because it will generally not be deductible (see Chapters 7 and 8). Finally, interest incurred to carry tax-exempt bonds is not deductible (under the theory, not always true after tax reform, that if the interest earned isn't taxable the interest paid to borrow money to buy the bonds shouldn't be deductible). Now that your investment interest expense has been determined, the limitation to which it can be subjected should be calculated.

Investment Income
The next step in calculating the limitation on investment interest expense is to determine your total investment income. Investment income includes interest, dividends, royalties, and gains (in excess of losses) on sales of investment property. If any of this income is from an active trade or business (such as real estate mortgage lending) it is generally not included. Tax reform has also added another complicated category of income, namely income from a trade or business in which the taxpayer doesn't materially participate, but which isn't subject to the passive loss rules. This could include dividends paid by an S corporation which is involved in an active business to a shareholder who is not a material participant in that activity. Future regulations should clarify which types of income the IRS will include in this category. Remember, the more income included in the investment income category, the higher the limitation on how much investment interest you can deduct.

Investment Expenses
In calculating net investment income, which will be the ceiling on the investment interest you can deduct, the next step is to reduce investment income by certain expenses. Investment expenses are all the expenses directly connected with the production of the investment income described above. This may include legal, accounting, and financial planning fees, and so forth. Tax reform only permits a deduction for many of these expenses (miscellaneous itemized deductions on your Form 1040, Schedule A) to the extent that they exceed 2% of your income (see Chapter 8). Therefore you need only reduce your investment income for purposes of the investment interest limitation calculation by the amount of expenses allowed (i.e., those in excess of the 2% floor). Interest expense is specifically excluded from investment expenses for this calculation.

Net Investment Income—The Limitation
Net investment income is your investment income less any investment expenses. This amount will, subject to two complications discussed below, be the limit on the amount of investment

interest expense which you can deduct in any tax year. Investment interest expense which can't be deducted in the current year due to this limitation is carried forward to future years when it can be deducted to the extent of any investment income in those years.

Example. An investor pays $45,000 in investment interest in 1990. His net investment income, however, is only $26,000. He can only deduct $26,000 of his investment interest expense. The remainder, $19,000, is carried forward to the next year. In 1991 the investor pays $32,000 in investment interest expense but has no investment income. He can't deduct any of his investment income in 1991. His carryover to 1992 is now $51,000 ($19,000 carryover from 1990 + $32,000 carryover from 1991). In 1993 he doesn't pay any investment interest expense. His investment income was a significant $124,000 due to the sale of appreciated bonds. He can deduct the entire $51,000 of investment interest expense carryover amounts in that year.

Two complications to the general rule of deducting investment interest expense up to net investment income must be noted. Any passive losses which can be deducted during the five-year phase-in period of the passive loss limitation (see Chapter 9) must be used to reduce your net investment income for purposes of the investment interest expense limitation. Thus, what Congress gave through a phase in of the new passive loss rules, it will often be taking back through this cumbersome mechanism.

The second complication is more positive. Under prior law, investors could generally deduct investment interest expense up to the amount of their net investment income plus $10,000. A rather complicated transition rule will permit investors to obtain some benefit from this $10,000 amount as it is phased out. The mechanics of this phased-out benefit are unnecessarily complicated. Since they can't be planned for, your accountant will simply calculate what portion of the phaseout you're entitled to when he completes your tax return.

Conclusion
As a result of the new passive loss rules the investment interest limitation will be less important to real estate investors than it had been in the past. Nevertheless it remains an important limitation to consider in many tax planning scenarios.

REAL ESTATE SYNDICATIONS

Real estate syndications have been, after mortgages, the most popular way to raise capital to finance the acquisition of real estate. Tax reform will have a significant impact on real estate syndications. Real estate investors should understand what syndications will be like in order to better evaluate an investment in a syndication, or how to structure a syndication in order to finance a real estate project.

The term "real estate syndication" has been almost synonymous with "tax shelter." Although this will no longer be true, syndications will continue—but in a rather different style. The almost generic means of syndicating real estate has been to package a real estate project in a limited partnership and sell the partnership interests to investors. This technique had no natural leaning toward tax benefits. Deals were simply done with a tax emphasis because the tax laws encouraged it and the marketplace loved it.

Real estate syndications will continue to be formed because they are still the most common means of enabling investors who can't or don't want to be actively involved to invest in real estate. The partnership form of owning real estate has been the most common form of ownership (see Chapter 1). Thus many investors and syndicators will continue to favor the real estate limited partnership as an investment (or financing) vehicle.

How will these post tax reform syndications differ from their tax-oriented predecessors? The objective of syndications is now to make money by investing in good quality real estate and, more often than in the past, managing that real estate to increase its value. Tax planning is still very important, but the goals will differ. Tax planning (such as improving depreciation benefits, etc.) will be important to help the partners shelter the cash flow the syndication earns from taxes. The "deep shelters" of the past (two-to-one and higher write-off ratios) will no longer be sought. This is because any tax shelter (i.e., tax deductions) greater than the income produced from the property may be useless because of the new passive loss rules (see Chapter 9).

A second goal of many real estate syndications will represent a complete change from prior law. Many deals will intentionally be structured to generate taxable income (and hopefully cash flow along with it). The income earned on an investment in one of these real estate limited partnerships will be treated as passive income for purposes of the new passive loss limitation rules. The general rule of the new passive loss limitations is that losses generated by an investment in a passive activity (such as a real estate limited partnership) can only be used to offset passive income. Because of this, investors are now seeking passive income to absorb the passive losses being generated by the more tax-oriented deals they purchased in the past few years.

Caution. Although everyone is touting income-oriented real estate deals as the answer to unusable passive losses, they're not always the panacea claimed. Many tax shelter investments turn around or burn out after a period of about eight years or so. This means that the "shelter" they provided (i.e., the excess of tax deductions over taxable income) is gone.

This can happen, for example, in a real estate deal which used accelerated depreciation and claimed investment tax credits in early years. After a few years the investment tax credits are gone. After a few more years the accelerated depreciation benefits are used up. Accelerated depreciation doesn't provide additional depreciation deductions, it just pushes (accelerates) deductions from later years into earlier years. Thus, after some point the depreciation benefits are much lower for an investor using accelerated depreciation than for an investor using the straight-line (ratable) method (see Chapter 10). As a result, passive tax losses won't be generated by many of these older deals. In many cases the income they begin throwing off after they burn out is only phantom income. This is income for tax purposes (because that's how the numbers often work out when depreciation deductions decline) even though there is no cash available for distribution.

Planning Tip. Before buying an interest in a real estate syndication because "you need the passive income to absorb passive losses," make sure your old deals aren't about to burn out. You could be left with a lot of passive income and no cash in hand to pay the tax due. Remember, the person flouting the new "passive income deal" may be the same one who last year sold you the tax shelter that's generating the losses you can't use. The moral is simple: If you want to invest in real estate, find a good investment that is suitable for your financial and risk profile. Don't buy into an investment just because it will provide passive income.

Another change that has been evident in many of the real estate syndications formed since late 1986 is the much more reserved use of leverage. It is simply not as advantageous to leverage real estate investments as it had been. The interest on all the debt may not even provide a deduction, as illustrated throughout this chapter. Even when a deduction is available, it will be worth much less because of the lower tax rates.

A major incentive to the use of leverage in pretax reform deals was to help magnify the deductions relative to the investment being made. This was usually structured with the investor making his capital contribution over a number of years. With a bit of planning, the high leverage and timed capital contributions could assure investors of tax deductions sufficient to offset the investment made in each year. The passive loss, at risk, and many other limitations on deducting real estate losses have eliminated these tax benefits of high leverage and phased-capital contributions. Syndications are being structured with more cash contributions, and those larger contributions are being made over a shorter time period, often in the initial year.

Leverage in many syndications has also included borrowing on limited partner notes to finance a portion of the investment each limited partner makes in the partnership. It is not clear how this interest expense will be treated for purposes of the new passive loss rules (see Chapter 9). If this interest expense is treated as passive it will be subject to the passive loss limitations. If, however, it is treated as investment interest expense it will be subject to the investment interest expense limitation.

Zero coupon and other bond instruments have often been added to real estate deals. The sales benefit is that the sponsor can then claim that you will be guaranteed to get your money back in 10 years. All that really happens is that a portion of your contribution is diverted and used to buy a zero coupon bond which matures in, for example, 10 years at a value equal to your original investment. This had been a sales gimmick in the past, and is a gimmick some syndicators may still use, but tax reform will create a problem for it. The interest earned on a bond can no longer be offset by the losses generated by the depreciation and other deductions on the rental property. This is because, under the new passive loss rules, the interest on the bond must be treated as portfolio income, not passive income. Zero coupon bonds have also been used as a financing device. With investors focusing on income and cash flow many syndicators will be tempted to use zero coupon financing. This will lower interest deductions in early years permitting the sponsor to project a greater cash flow. The obvious drawback, however, is that this approach will significantly reduce any back end (appreciation) potential from the investment.

Planning Tip. If you want to invest in a good real estate project, invest. If you want to buy a zero coupon bond or any other type of portfolio investment instrument, call your banker or securities broker and buy one. Don't buy bonds from a real estate syndicator when what you really want is real estate.

The fee structures in many syndications will also change in response to tax reform. The large fees which promoters and sponsors often took in the first year of a syndication (rent-up fee, negative cash flow guarantee fee, etc.) are likely to decline. Investors will become less willing to pay large fees up front if they aren't getting a sizable tax benefit to offset them. And in many cases they won't. Also, as syndications have become economic deals designed to make profits, many of these large up-front fees simply can't be supported. What will happen in many instances is that the promoters and sponsors will take a larger percentage of the profits on the eventual sale of the project (back-end fees). An advantage to this approach is that it encourages the promoter and sponsor to keep the investors' interests paramount—appreciation.

Real estate syndications will continue to be a viable investment approach. The structure and objectives have changed, but these changes are for the best. Real estate investment should be made for cash flow and appreciation, not just tax benefits. To this extent one of the objectives of tax reform has been achieved.

Example. The following example illustrates: (1) how a real estate syndication fared under the old tax laws, (2) how the same syndication will fare under the new tax laws, and (3) how a new syndication, structured after tax reform, will fare when all of the new rules are effective. The example also illustrates the effect of planning to use passive losses to offset passive income under the new rules. Losses from real estate syndications can only be used to offset income from other passive investments. They can no longer be used to offset other income, such as salary. Because of this taxpayers will have to plan to use these losses if they are to realize any tax benefit.

Hypothetical Real Estate Investment

	Old Deal Old Law	Old Deal New Law	New De New La
Rent	$250,000	$250,000	$250,00
Administration management (at 15% of rent)	52,500	52,500	52,50
Amortization	20,000	20,000	20,00
Depreciation:			
$2.5 million divided by 19 years	130,000	130,000	130,00
$2.7 million divided by 31.5 years	—	—	85,70
Interest and taxes during construction ($200,000 divided by 10 years)	20,000	20,000	N/A
Debt service (interest only)	150,000	150,000	150,00
Total deductions	$372,500	$372,500	$308,20
Tax loss	(122,500)	(122,500)	(58,20
Tax rate	50%	28%	28%
Tax benefit—unplanned	$ 61,250	None	None
Tax benefit—planned	Same	$ 34,300	$ 16,29
Return On Investment[a]:			
Unplanned	18.13%	7.92%	7.92%
Planned	Same	13.63%	10.63%
Cash Flow—Unplanned (i.e., without passive income to offset):			
Tax loss	$(122,500)	$(122,500)	$(58,20C
Add back:			
Tax benefit	61,250	None	None
Depreciation	130,000	130,000	85,70
Amortization	20,000	20,000	20,00
Construction interest and taxes	20,000	20,000	N/A
Cash flow	$108,750	$ 47,500	$ 47,50

Hypothetical Real Estate Investment *(Continued)*

	Old Deal Old Law	Old Deal New Law	New Deal New Law
Cash Flow—Planned (i.e., with passive income to offset):			
Tax loss		$(122,500)	$(58,200)
Add back:	Same as unplanned		
Tax benefit		34,300	16,296
Depreciation		130,000	85,700
Amortization		20,000	20,000
Construction interest and taxes		20,000	N/A
	Same	$ 81,800	$ 63,796

Cash flow divided by the $600,000 cash investment made by the limited partners.

Rules Applicable Under Each Scenario

	Old Deal Old Law	Old Deal New Law	New Deal New Law
Depreciation	19 years straight line	19 years straight line	31.5 years straight line
Interest and taxes during construction	10 years straight line	10 years straight line	N/A—under tax reform must include in cost of building (depreciates over 31.5 years straight line
Tax loss—unplanned	Used to tax at 50% maximum rate	Tax loss unavailable because of passive loss limitations	Tax loss unavailable because of passive loss limitations
Tax loss—planned	Not necessary loss usable without special planning	With planning, tax loss used to save tax at 28% maximum rate[a]	With planning, tax loss (much less than prior law) used to offset tax at 28% maximum rate[a]

[a]Assumes the new tougher minimum tax does not apply.

Planning Tip. When evaluating an investment in a real estate syndication after tax reform consider the following factors:

1. What is the track record of the promoter? Have many prior real estate deals been done? How well have they done? Ask for details of prior deals.

2. Does the promoter have the expertise to manage the property. If the promoter is also involved in equipment leasing, research and development, cable television, and other types of deals his expertise may not be in real estate management. What experience does the management team have? Are there capable leasing personnel? If the promoter plans to use outside companies to perform these tasks ask additional questions. Are theses companies related to the promoter? What kind of experience do they have? Are the prices reasonable?

3. Is the location of the property good? Are there adequate entrances and exits from major roadways? If it is a commercial project, is there adequate visibility? If a shopping center has ready access to a major highway, but is not visible because of a hill or other development this could hurt sales.

4. What is happening in the region where the building is being purchased or built? Is the population growing? What has happened to income levels in the past and what is likely to happen in the future? What is the economy of the region based on? Do these economic activities appear that they will prosper in the future?

5. What is the financing like on the project? Will a large balloon payment be due after a certain period or will most of the mortgage principal be amortized by principal payments? If refinancing is projected are the assumptions reasonable? Will the at-risk rule pose a problem in light of the financing used?

6. Review the appraisal of the property very carefully. Does it sound reasonable? Does it raise any new issues of concern? Does it address all the issues you believe are important to the success of the real estate project? If not, ask the sponsor the questions. If an appraisal isn't offered ask for it. If one is not available, find out why.

7. If the deal projects a credit for rehabilitating an old or certified historic structure, review the requirements discussed

in Chapter 3. Does the deal appear to meet the requirements? Are the problems in meeting the requirements adequately addressed in the risk discussions of the offering materials? Has the architect considered the requirements in his plans? Will the rehabilitation tax credit provide you any value in light of the passive loss limitations (see Chapter 9)? Does the deal project a donation of a conservation easement? If it does, is there a legal opinion addressing the problems which could arise? Has the allocation of the amount donated been made in a reasonable manner between the land and building? Does the appraisal support these allocations?

8. If the deal projects a credit for an investment in a low income housing project, review the requirements discussed in Chapter 6. Does it appear that the deal will meet the requirements? Has adequate credit authority been obtained from the local government? Will you benefit from the credit or will the passive loss limitations prevent you from claiming it?

9. Are any sales gimmicks, such as zero coupon bonds, being used? If they are, ask why. How do they really affect the deal? Many legitimate syndicators may use sales gimmicks because the marketplace demands them; the presence of "gimmicks" may not always indicate the worth of the deal.

10. How will an investment in the syndication affect your alternative minimum tax situation. The projections and tax discussions in syndication offering materials can't comment on this specifically, since the results will vary depending on the tax position of each investor. Review this matter carefully with your tax advisor. If you're subject to the minimum tax you could have to calculate depreciation using a 40-year period instead of the 27.5- or 31.5-year periods projected. (See Chapter 11.)

11. How do the results projected for the deal fit into your own personal passive loss situation? If you have unused passive losses consider a deal generating passive income. If you have passive income consider a deal generating passive losses. If you are indifferent you will probably prefer a deal which shelters its cash flow to the maximum extent possible and generates minimal income or loss.

12. What is the fee structure like? How is the sponsor being compensated? Is the sponsor taking fees for services actually

performed and which are important to the success of the project? Or, do the fees sound more like fancy accounting? Is the sponsor's success contingent on the project's success? If a sponsor will earn most of his profit only after the investors receive a reasonable return and only if the project succeeds, then the sponsor will be motivated to make the project work.

13. Since deals should be done for economic reasons, do the economics of the project make sense? The heart of any real estate deal is the tenants. Are tenants already committed? If so who are they, how good a credit risk are they, and how much space have they committed for? What are the prospects regarding the leasing of the remaining space in the building? Has a leasing program been formulated? Is an advertising campaign in place? Are the projected rents reasonable? Has an adequate vacancy factor been allowed for?

14. Have there been any recent sales of the property? Find out to whom and at what price. Are the parties to this sale related to the sponsor? Has a ground lease interest been carved out?

Each deal will have its own unique factors which should be reviewed. The above list should only be used as a starting point of the more common factors. If you're considering investing any significant sum it is advisable to have your tax and investment advisor review the offering materials. The cost of a professional review should be nominal relative to the minimum investment in many deals.

Conclusion
Real estate syndication will probably continue to be the most favored investment for many investors. As such, syndications will continue to provide an important source of financing for real estate investment. As illustrated in the discussions in this chapter, however, the nature of syndications will change in response to tax reform.

Chapter Summary
As this chapter has illustrated, financing real estate has become a far more complicated, and often costly, task after tax reform. Investors must reconsider the way many real estate transactions are structured to adapt to the many changes made by tax reform.

3 DEVELOPING AND OPERATING REAL ESTATE

GENERAL EFFECTS OF TAX REFORM

Real estate development is driven by a number of forces, in-cluding interest rates (cost of funds), demand, and tax benefits. Tax reform has had an important effect on the net cost of funds (as analyzed in Chapter 2). The impact of tax reform on demand is difficult to predict. Clearly the demand created by the tax shelter industry has been eliminated to a significant extent. However, the overbuilding which tax shelter benefits helped to stimulate in many markets may continue to affect supply and demand for some time.

The impact of tax reform on demand for space will depend in part on the impact which tax reform will have on different sec-tors of the economy. Tax reform has hit the heavy manufacturing sector the hardest. The prized depreciation and investment tax credit benefits which had helped this sector reduce its tax costs for years have been curtailed. Service businesses which had often borne the highest tax burdens should benefit under tax reform. Thus development in regions with service-oriented economies which weren't plagued by significant overbuilding could benefit the most. Regions whose economies are dominated by manufac-turing industries and which have experienced heavy overbuild-ing may fare the poorest under tax reform. However, tax reform is only one part of the analysis. The economy, interest rates, government regulation, union developments, highway construc-tion, and numerous other factors can significantly affect demand for construction.

Since the direct tax benefits and costs of real estate development and operations are very important to consider, this chapter explores many of the changes tax reform made to these areas.

LIMITS ON CONSTRUCTION EXPENSES

When a developer is constructing a building the costs of laying the foundation, brickwork, roofing, drywall, and so forth, cannot be deducted currently. Instead, these costs must be added to (i.e., "capitalized" as part of) the investment ("tax basis") in the building. The total cost of the building will then be depreciated as described in Chapter 10. Many costs are incurred during construction which don't relate so obviously to the investment in the building. In the past many of these less obvious costs were often deducted currently as paid or incurred. For example, the salary for the president of a development firm, general and administrative costs of a development firm's office, and so forth, may have all been deducted currently without regard to the extent to which they related to the new construction undertaken during the year. Tax reform will change this.

Tax reform has added new rules governing which costs must be capitalized during the construction period as part of the investment in the building. These new rules are called "uniform capitalization rules." They will apply to a number of activities including real estate development. Thus rebuilding a warehouse or plant, and even undertaking major capital repairs or improvements, would be subject to these new rules. The thrust of these rules is to require that most expenditures directly or indirectly relating to the construction of a building be capitalized.

The portion of the following costs which relate to the building being constructed (or the renovation, rehabilitation, or improvement of an existing building) will have to be capitalized:

Repair and maintenance of equipment and facilities.

Heat, light, gas, electric, water, and any other utility costs, including related equipment.

Rental of equipment and facilities.

General administrative and overhead costs, including all head-office-type functions such as personnel, administration, accounting, legal, planning, and the like. These costs may have to be allocated from different corporate (or other) entities to the entity actually undertaking the construction. This could be done through charging a management or consulting fee.

Pension, profit sharing, stock bonus, and other employee benefits for employees working directly or indirectly on the construction project.

Indirect labor costs.

Holiday pay, vacation pay, sick leave, payroll taxes, unemployment taxes, workers' compensation, supplemental unemployment benefits, overtime pay or shift differential pay, and other related labor costs for persons working directly or indirectly on the project.

Direct materials costs including all materials which become an integral part of the building, and those materials, consumed in the ordinary course of building, constructing, and installing the building and its component parts.

Contract supervision wages.

Indirect materials and supplies used in the performance of the construction.

Tools and equipment used or consumed in the construction process.

State and local real property taxes, personal property taxes, sales taxes, use taxes, to the extent attributable to labor, materials, supplies, equipment, or facilities used in the construction process. NOTE—the inclusion of taxes incurred during the construction period in these uniform capitalization rules replaces the rules under prior law which enabled construction period interest and taxes to be deducted ("amortized") over a 10-year period. The treatment now available is much less favorable since taxes will now be written off over as long as 31.5 years.

Compensation paid to officers.

Insurance incurred during the construction project including insurance on the equipment and machinery used in the construction process.

Depreciation and amortization of equipment and facilities currently being used to the extent it exceeds depreciation and amortization reported for financial accounting purposes.

Rework labor, scrap, and spoilage costs.

Although this listing is comprehensive, it doesn't include all costs likely to be incurred during the construction period. Some costs will still be deductible on a current basis in the year incurred ("period costs"), or are subject to their own special rules. These include:

Any costs not properly allocable to the construction, renovation, rehabilitation, or improvement of the building.

Pension and profit-sharing costs to the extent they relate to past service costs.

Interest (see the next section for special rules for interest, which replace the construction period interest and tax rules of prior law).

Marketing, selling, and advertising costs. (Some of these costs, however, may have to be capitalized as lease acquisition costs and deducted over the lease term, as described in Chapter 4.)

Costs attributable to strikes.

Losses (e.g., due to fire or tornado).

Depreciation for idle facilities.

State, local, and foreign income taxes.

The listing of costs which must be included is very comprehensive. These rules will probably result in taxpayers' capitalizing many more costs than they had in the past. These costs will then be depreciated as part of the cost of the building over 27.5 years for residential property and 31.5 years for nonresidential property. The difference in the tax result due to longer depreciation periods is significant.

In addition to this unfavorable tax result, developers will be forced to incur considerable expense to revise many of their accounting systems to track the additional costs required.

The most difficult task in implementing these new rules, and probably the most fruitful ground for planning to minimize some of their harsh impact, is determining which costs relate to the construction process and which do not. The forthcoming discussion describes a number of planning considerations. Since the Treasury Department is supposed to issue regulations providing some guidance on how these rules should be implemented, check with your tax advisor before proceeding.

The key to planning is to identify the most favorable of the reasonably available methods for allocating costs between the building being constructed (which must be capitalized) and your ongoing operations (which may be deductible currently).

Direct costs should not pose a significant problem. The steel used in the construction of an office building is clearly a cost of that building. This cost should not be difficult to trace. An invoice from the steel wholesaler should suffice.

Indirect costs are where the difficulties and planning benefits will be found. What about the bookkeeper (or accounts payable clerk) who pays the bill from the steel company? In the past the salary and other costs associated with the bookkeeper would have been deducted immediately as a part of the costs of your ongoing operations (such as renting and operating other buildings which are already in use, management and leasing operations, etc.). This is probably not allowed under the new capitalization rules. A portion of the cost of the bookkeeper must now be allocated to the construction of your new office building (and any other new construction your firm is involved with). The remaining costs associated with the bookkeeper can probably be deducted currently.

Planning Tips. Does it pay to bother allocating costs for a bookkeeper? Maybe not. If the costs involved are insignificant, or if the vast majority of an employee's time is spent on the new construction, it may be easier administratively to allocate the entire cost to the new construction. In many instances, however, planning will be worthwhile. The amounts involved will probably entail much more than the cost of a single bookkeeper particularly for a larger development firm also involved in leasing and management. Even if the individual costs are relatively small (such as the bookkeeper's salary), the sum of all the allocations away from the construction project may be significant in the aggregate.

How can you allocate a portion of an employee's cost to the construction project and a portion to ongoing operations? The most obvious method is via a time analysis. Have each employee maintain a daily log of which projects his time was spent on.

For secretaries, bookkeepers, accounts payable clerks, and other administrative-type employees who may spend their day working on dozens of different projects, it may be more cost effective to require them to perform time analysis on a sample basis. Pick a number of representative days during which the employees are working on both the construction project and ongoing operations. Have each employee log his time for the sample days. Use the ratio of the number of hours spent on the new construction to the total hours worked as a guide for allocating costs.

Example. A developer has three office buildings which are rented and being managed. A fourth office building is in the construction process. A decision must be made as to what portion of the cost of maintaining a headquarters staff must be allocated to the construction project to comply with the new uniform capitalization rules. The following costs are incurred:

Secretarial staff	$140,000
Bookkeeping staff	65,000
Other personnel costs	34,850
Rent	85,000
Supplies, equipment rentals	32,400
	$357,250

The simplest approach may be to allocate one-fourth ($89,313) of the overhead costs to the building under construction and to deduct the remaining three-fourths ($267,937) currently as relating to the ongoing operations of managing the three rental office buildings and other affairs. The time-analysis approach may, however, be more beneficial.

The president had each secretary and bookkeeper maintain a log, like the one in Figure 3.1, of where their time was spent on the 4th, 13th, 19th, 23rd and 29th of the month.

The reason for the divisions in the log is that it may be possible to exclude training and similar costs which would be necessary whether or not a new building was being constructed. Similarly, advertising, marketing, and selling-related expenses need not be capitalized. Thus the time your headquarters office spends on such things as billing, resolving tenant and promotional grievances, and answering letters regarding these matters should not have to be allocated to, and capitalized as part of, the cost of the new building.

Employee name:_____

Department:_____

Job description:_____

Date of time analysis:_____,198___

Time	Project Code*	Work Code**
8:00–8:30	_____	_____
8:30–9:00	_____	_____
9:00–9:30	_____	_____
9:30–10:00	_____	_____
10:00–10:30	_____	_____
10:30–11:00	_____	_____
11:00–11:30	_____	_____
11:30–12:00	_____	_____
12:00–12:30	_____	_____
12:30–1:00	_____	_____
1:00–1:30	_____	_____
1:30–2:00	_____	_____
2:00–2:30	_____	_____
2:30–3:00	_____	_____
3:00–3:30	_____	_____
3:30–4:00	_____	_____
4:00–4:30	_____	_____
4:30–5:00	_____	_____
Total Hours		

*Project Codes: NB = New office building project
                B1 = Building at 100 Pine Street
                B2 = Building at 140 Main Street
                B3 = Building at 122 South Street
**Work Codes: Lease = Leasing work (tenant relations)
                Adv. = Advertising and marketing
                A/P = Accounts payable and other billing matters
                Train = Training, development of new staff, seminars, reading
                      manuals, etc.
                Other = Any activities not in the above categories (describe on
                      reverse side of sheet)
Do not record lunch and coffee break periods

Figure 3.1 Estimated employee time allocable to new office building

Once the time breakdown is available for each employee on the sample days, two approaches may be acceptable. The more accurate approach would be to multiply each employee's wages for the period during which the building was constructed by the following ratio:

Hours worked relating to new building
Total hours worked during sample days
= Allocation percentage

If the employee reported four hours on assignments relating to the new building, out of 35.5 hours of total time, then the allocation percentage would be 11%.

If the new building was in the construction phase during 10 months of the year and the employee's compensation for the year was $22,000, the portion allocable to the new building would be:

$$\frac{10 \text{ months}}{12 \text{ months}} \times 11\% \times \$22{,}000 = \$2{,}017$$

Thus only $2,017 of the employee's wages should be allocable to the new construction. If the initial estimate of one-fourth were used then $5,500 of the employee's wages would have been allocable. Although this difference is not material, this is just one component of the total general and administrative costs. Let's say the average time allocable to the new building for all the employees was 13%. This low percentage could be due in part to the fact that a subcontractor is used for certain functions so the burden on the office isn't great. Rather than having to go through detailed, individual calculations for each employee, it should hopefully (only final regulations will tell) be reasonable to apply an average time analysis to all the head office payroll costs. In addition, in many situations it should be reasonable to allocate all the other overhead costs by the same ratio.

Thus for the headquarters office as a whole only 13%, or $46,442 of the total cost of $357,250, must be allocated to the new building. This compares rather favorably to the initial rough estimate of one-fourth which would have resulted in $89,313 being allocated. Importantly, this additional benefit of $42,871 in costs which don't have to be allocated to the new building can be deducted immediately, rather than being depreciated over the 31.5-year depreciable life of the building.

The benefit of having employees keep logs for a few days can be much greater than noted. If the IRS were to audit the development company, the audit may not occur until years after the costs were incurred. It may be impossible to reconstruct records or support any allocation that long after the events occurred. The result may be the IRS advocating and succeeding with an even less favorable allocation. The notes and log sheets from the time study, kept with the tax return data for the year, could prove invaluable, at the time of a later audit, to substantiate the position taken.

Planning Tip. The most important time sheets to maintain will be those for the senior management of a development company. The president may draw a tremendous salary, particularly if the development company is a closely held business he founded. It may be advisable to keep a log on a daily basis, not merely on a test basis, which may have been sufficient for clerical and similar employees.

A number of other methods may be appropriate for allocating costs. The method chosen must, however, be both reasonable and permitted by the future regulations. Once the calculations for each cost are determined, have your accountant and tax advisor determine which method will provide you with the most favorable results. Consider some of the following methods:

1. *Specific Identification.* If an employee works solely on the new project then his wages and benefit costs should be allocated solely to the building being constructed. If an employee's time is spent solely on projects other than new construction then don't allocate any costs to the new construction. When regulations are eventually issued they should permit an employee to work a minimum amount of time, say 10%, on new construction related matters without requiring any allocation to the construction project. This will provide some planning flexibility.

2. *Direct Material Costs.* If you have a plumbing crew on payroll it may be reasonable to allocate their wage and benefit (and other) costs based on materials costs. For example, if you purchase $352,928 in materials and parts from a plumbing supplier and $147,390 of the parts were shipped to the new building's job site, then allocate the plumbing crew's wages in the same

ratio: $147,390/$352,928, or 42% of their labor costs to the new building.

3. *Regression Analysis.* This may be an appropriate method of allocating costs. Regression is a method of breaking certain costs down into their fixed components (the portion which won't change from year to year no matter how the volume of new construction changes) and variable components (the portion of costs which will vary from year to year depending on how the volume of new construction varies).

For example, assume a development company builds garden apartments. Regression analysis could be used to help allocate costs to the new construction in the following manner:

STEP 1. Set up a graph with the horizontal axis being the number of new apartment units under construction in any given year. The vertical axis is the total dollar costs of running the development company's head office.

STEP 2. Plot on the graph the points at the intersection of: (1) the number of new units built in each of the last five years; and (2) the costs incurred in running the head office.

The graph could appear something like the one in Figure 3.2.

STEP 3. Visually fit a line to the points in the graph in a manner which will minimize the distance from each point in the graph to the line. Extend the line so that it intersects the vertical axis of the graph. Note that this technique can be done precisely on many hand-held calculators. The less precise visual approach is used here since it better illustrates the concept. The graph will now appear something like the one in Figure 3.3.

The point at which the line intersects the vertical axis indicates a dollar amount of overhead costs which will be incurred even if no new construction is undertaken. This component of your overhead and administrative costs is arguably fixed and should not be allocable to the cost of new construction. Since this cost will be incurred even if no new units are built, then it is not really an incremental cost of construction. The relationship between new construction of apartment units and the general and administrative costs which must be incurred will be defined by the graph. This relationship is the slope of the line which was fitted to the points plotted on the graph. This can be used as a variable cost rate. Multiply the number of units constructed in a given year by this figure to estimate the portion of

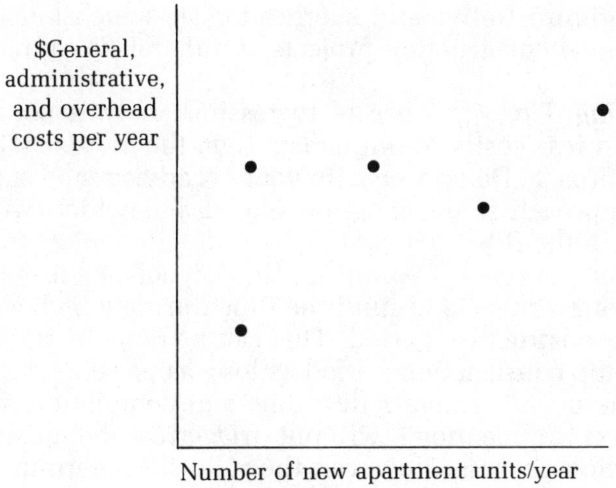

Figure 3.2 Sample graph

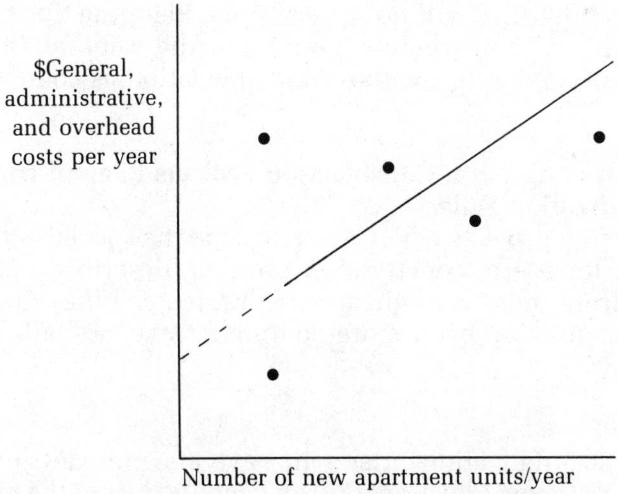

Figure 3.3 Sample graph with line drawn in

general administrative and overhead costs which must be allocated to new construction projects and therefore capitalized.

Planning Tips. The use of regression analysis could be far easier and less costly to implement than the more detailed time study approach. Determine with your tax advisor and accountant which approach is the most beneficial and which will be acceptable to the IRS.

Another approach to limiting the impact of the harsh new capitalization rules is to limit the time during which a building is in the construction period. This can be done by delaying the onset of the construction period as long as possible without delaying the overall construction time and completion date. Certain work can be done without triggering the onset of the construction process. However, the rules for determining when construction begins appear to be much stricter than under prior law. If the capitalization rules will prove costly, review the proposed construction process with your tax advisor. Determine which activities can and can't be done before triggering the onset of the construction process. Complete all activities possible before triggering the onset of the construction period. The PERT/ CPM type of analysis discussed in Chapter 10 may be helpful in executing this type of planning. A complementary planning idea is to complete the construction process as soon as possible. Once the construction period can be said to have ended, these tough capitalization rules will no longer apply. Planning tips to hasten the end of the construction period are the same as those discussed in Chapter 10 for starting depreciation as soon as possible.

Certain Long-Term Construction Projects Exempt from New Capitalization Rules

Construction projects which are subject to the special accounting rules for long-term construction projects (described below) are exempt from these capitalization rules. Instead they are subject to what can be an even more comprehensive capitalization requirement.

Conclusion

The new capitalization rules will have a significant impact on many, if not most, developers. Tax benefits during the construction period will decline, hurting cash flow. Accounting and bookkeeping costs will increase to cope with the new rules. Many new records will have to be kept. Also, financial statement reporting may differ from tax reporting if costs required to be capitalized under the new tax rules are to be deducted under generally accepted accounting principles (GAAP). Planning can be done, but as illustrated, it can be complicated and take some real pencil pushing.

NEW RULES REQUIRING CAPITALIZATION OF INTEREST EXPENSE

Interest expense paid during the construction of a building (construction period interest expense) can be a major out-of-pocket expense. Unfortunately, the tax laws have not permitted an immediate deduction for construction interest costs. Under prior law, interest expense incurred during the construction phase of a building couldn't be deducted. Instead, it had to be capitalized to a separate account which included all the interest (and taxes) paid or incurred during construction. The balance in this account was then deducted ratably ("amortized") over a 10-year period. Tax reform replaced these tough rules with much tougher rules. Taxes paid during the construction period are now subject to the new capitalization rules discussed in the preceding section. Interest expense is subject to its own similar rule described below.

Tax reform made two fundamental changes to the requirement to capitalize, instead of deduct, construction period interest expense. The interest expense which must be capitalized is no longer added to a separate account and deducted over a 10-year period. Instead, interest is added to (capitalized as part of) the investment (tax basis) in the building being constructed. Thus the interest will now be written off over the depreciation period for the building: 27.5 years for residential buildings, 31.5 years for nonresidential buildings, and 40 years if subject to the minimum tax (see Chapters 10 and 11). This dramatically reduces the value of deducting construction interest costs.

The second change tax reform made to the treatment of construction period interest expense concerns the determination of what interest must be capitalized under this rule. Tax reform has made the rule much broader.

Under prior law, interest relating to the construction project had to be capitalized. This included interest paid or accrued on debt incurred, or continued, to carry and construct the real property. This would have included a mortgage taken out specifically on the building under construction as well as an existing line of credit which was continued in order to help fund the property's construction. Other interest expense incurred by the taxpayer was not affected.

The new rules can reach much further. Any interest expense capitalized under the old rules is still capitalized under the new rules. However, interest on any other loans will also be subject to the new capitalization rules if those loans could have been reduced had the construction project not been undertaken.

Example. Assume that you can only obtain 80% financing on a $2.5 million office building you are constructing, at 10% simple interest. This means that you must cover the remaining 20%, or $500,000 of the construction and related costs, from your own capital. Let's say you built an apartment building last year and have a $1.8 million, 12% (simple interest) mortgage outstanding on it. How much interest must be added to your investment in the new building (capitalized) and depreciated over a 31.5-year period? The answer consists of two components:

1. The first component is the interest on the mortgage on the new building of $200,000 ($2.5 million building × 80% mortgage ratio × 10% simple interest).

2. The second component which tax has added is the amount of interest on other debt which could have been reduced if the new construction had not been undertaken. If you hadn't built the new office building you could have used the $500,000 of your capital to reduce the outstanding balance on the mortgage on your apartment building. Since you didn't, it's as if the interest paid on $500,000 of the mortgage on your apartment building was paid to carry the new office building. This means that an additional $60,000 of the interest paid on the mortgage on the apartment building must be added to your investment (tax basis) in the new office building ($500,000 mortgage which could have been reduced × 12% interest rate on the apartment building mortgage). If a number of loans were outstanding, an average interest rate would be used for this calculation. The accounting, however, would be very tedious and time consuming.

Thus you will have to add (capitalize) $260,000 [($200,000 direct + $60,000 imputed)] of interest expense to your investment (tax basis) in the new building.

Planning Tips. When analyzing the impact of this new rule consider the following:

1. *Loan Prepayment Prohibition.* What if the loan on the apartment building in the above example contained a clause prohibiting any prepayments on principal? If you couldn't make them even if you wanted to, then the logic of the new interest capitalization rule is destroyed. The $500,000 of your own capital put into the construction of the new office building couldn't be used to reduce your debt. In this case it could be argued that the rule shouldn't apply and the $60,000 of interest expense should be currently deductible (to the extent otherwise allowable without consideration of this interest capitalization rule). This position will be weakened by the fact that prepayment is often allowed subject to a penalty. However, if the penalty is significant the argument should still carry weight. Check with your tax advisor to determine the IRS stance on this position before proceeding. Future regulations could disagree with this position. If this position is proper then surprise your lender and request that the lender put in a tough clause restricting prepayments. Structure this clause so that it remains effective for the period during which you will be constructing another building.

2. *Refinancing.* The interest rate on the old loan on the apartment building in the above example was 12% and the interest rate on the new loan on the office building was only 10%. The new rule has forced you to capitalize the interest at a rate that is higher than the prevailing market rate. Although this is a rather inequitable result, the tax laws ignore fluctuations in interest rates. This will work to your disadvantage if interest rates decline and to your advantage if interest rates increase.

If there has been a significant decline in interest rates this new rule may make it cost effective to refinance when it may not otherwise be advantageous. For example, although interest rates have declined it may not yet be worth refinancing an older mortgage because of the legal and other closing costs involved. However, when you factor in the effects of having to capitalize this higher interest rate as part of the cost of your new building, rather than deducting it, refinancing may now prove advantageous despite the costs involved.

3. *Equity Kickers.* If a lender takes an equity kicker (an interest in the property's appreciation) in lieu of a portion of the interest which would have otherwise been charged, the capitalization restrictions can be avoided. The effects of this interest limitation, those financing restrictions discussed in Chapter 2, and the new passive loss rules discussed in Chapter 9, all act to make equity kickers a more viable financing tool from a tax perspective. If you may not get an interest deduction for a very long time it may just prove more economical to negotiate an equity kicker and a lower interest rate. The original issue discount rules must be reviewed with your tax advisor in assessing the feasibility of this approach.

4. *Partners' and Shareholders' Loans.* For partnerships and S corporations it appears that the interest capitalization rules may apply at both the entity (partnership and S corporation) and investor (partner and shareholder) levels. Thus, if a partner or shareholder borrowed money to make an investment in an entity engaging in construction, a portion of the investor's interest expense may also have to be capitalized. Future regulations will hopefully provide guidance on this so follow up with your tax advisor.

5. *Watch the New Passive Loss Rules.* The new passive loss rules limit the amount of losses which can be deducted from a passive activity—such as a rental real estate project—to the taxpayer's passive income (see Chapter 9). If excess passive losses are incurred they can't be deducted currently. Instead, they are held in abeyance (suspended) until the taxpayer sells his entire interest in the activity. When the entire interest in the activity is sold, any remaining suspended passive losses attributable to that activity are triggered and can be used to offset other income. Let's say that the apartment building and the new office building in our above example are considered separate activities for purposes of the passive loss rules. Look at what this interplay of the passive loss rules and the new interest capitalization rules can do to your interest deduction.

Let's say that you have unused losses relating to both the apartment building and the office building. You sell the apartment building the year after the office building is complete. All the previously unused passive losses associated with the apartment building are triggered. But look what happens to the interest expense you paid on the office building. The new interest capitalization rules made you add $60,000 to the tax basis of the office building. Even though you've sold the apartment building, $60,000 of the interest deductions could still be sitting in the suspended passive loss amount associated with the office building. This $60,000 may not qualify for deduction until the office building is sold.

Planning Tip. If an existing building is producing unusable passive losses and the new building being constructed will be sold shortly after it's completed, the interest allocation rule could be beneficial. The interest expense on the existing building which can't be deducted anyway (it will only increase the suspended losses) will be allocated to the new building which you may plan to sell. The interest allocated to the new building will reduce the gain on the imminent sale. This would speed up the availability of the tax benefit from the interest charges.

6. *Construction Period.* To the extent that you can limit the duration of the construction period you can limit the impact of these interest capitalization rules. This planning idea has been discussed above (also see Chapter 10).

Conclusion
The new interest capitalization rules will, in addition to all the changes discussed in Chapter 2, increase the cost of financing real estate development. Developers can, however, act to limit the impact of these rules through using some of the techniques discussed above.

ACCOUNTING FOR LONG-TERM CONSTRUCTION CONTRACTS

Tax reform has significantly changed the required methods for determining taxable income from long-term construction contracts. These new rules will have a considerable impact on the timing of profits larger construction contractors will have to report and be taxed on.

A long-term construction contract which will be subject to these new rules is defined as any contract for the construction, reconstruction, building, improvement, rehabilitation, or installation of an integral component of any real property. Real property includes buildings, roads, dams, and similar property. To be "long-term" the contract can't be completed in the same year in which it is entered into.

Since the definition of real estate construction contracts subject to these rules is so broad, Congress provided an exemption for certain smaller contracts. To be exempt from these rules the construction contract must be expected to be completed within two years from the date it commences. Also, the contractor must have had sales (gross receipts) of not more than $10 million, on average, for the three preceding years. A number of detailed rules are provided to keep taxpayers from dividing up their operations into separate companies to fall under the $10 million sales figure.

Contractors who are subject to these rules must use one of two required methods to determine taxable income from their long-term projects.

The first method is the percentage of completion method. This is similar to the percentage of completion method allowed under prior law but the rules have changed considerably. Under this method a contractor must now recognize revenues each year during the contract based on the following formula:

$$\frac{\text{Costs incurred in tax year}}{\text{Total estimated costs to be incurred}} \times \text{Contract price}$$

The profit to recognize for the year is the portion of the contract price, as determined above, less the costs incurred during the year. Accounting rules very similar to those described above for the uniform capitalization rules are required to be used in making these calculations.

Caution. Having to recognize profits based on when costs are incurred can present serious problems. For example, assume that a contractor is able to get a great buy on bricks in December. The foundation has not even been poured so the bricks won't actually be needed for some time. If it weren't for the great buy the contractor would not have bought the bricks until next year at the earliest. This advance purchase, made for valid business reasons, could trigger significant taxable income under the new formula required to be used for the percentage completion method of accounting. Contractors should now consult with their tax advisors before making any large discretionary purchases. The combination of the large purchase and tax cost could create a cash flow problem.

Contractors will be encouraged to make accurate cost estimates by a penalty provision called a "look-back rule." If there are errors in the estimates used, the tax liability for the years in question will have to be recomputed. Interest will be charged to the taxpayer for any resulting tax understatements. Similarly, interest will be paid to the taxpayer for any resulting tax overstatements.

The second allowable method for calculating income on long-term construction projects is the new "percentage-of-completion–capitalized-cost method." This method is really a hybrid of the percentage of completion method, and whatever method the taxpayer otherwise uses, such as the completed contract method (where income is generally not recognized until the contract is completed) or the cash method (see Chapter 12). Under this hybrid method 40% of the income must be taken into account using the percentage of completion method, described above. The remaining 60% of the income items can be accounted for using the taxpayer's method of accounting. Thus only 60% of the contract income can be deferred using this approach. The only way to avoid using this hybrid approach is to adopt the percentage of completion method. Finally, the look-back penalty rule will apply to the 40% of the contract which must be accounted for under the completed contract method.

Conclusion

Contractors should carefully review the impact of these new accounting rules on their tax picture. Revised record keeping procedures may be required. Also it may be necessary to structure advances and payments on future contracts differently to meet the necessary cash flow needs of any increased tax liability.

REPAIR AND MAINTENANCE EXPENDITURES

Significant tax benefits can be realized by properly planning the repair and maintenance program for a building. The objective is to maintain an ongoing, aggressive, preventive maintenance program in order to avoid unnecessarily incurring expenditures which have to be capitalized. Maintenance and repair expenditures can be deducted immediately. Capital expenditures must be depreciated over the long 27.5- or 31.5-year depreciation periods. In addition, maintenance and repair expenditures will not be subject to the strict and complex capitalization rules discussed above.

The first step is to distinguish between what is a capital expenditure and what is a deductible repair. Patching a new roof or parking lot is a deductible repair. Replacing an entire roof or parking lot is a capital expenditure which must be capitalized and written off over 31.5 years for commercial real estate (what roof lasts 31.5 years!). Everything between these two extremes, however, gets much tougher to categorize. At what point does a patch become so large that it must be treated as a capitalizable replacement? Some of the rules contained in the tax laws and various court decisions interpreting these rules will be helpful.

An expenditure will be a capital expenditure if it accomplishes any of the following:

1. Results in an asset which will be useful for more than one year. For example, if a carpenter builds a kiosk for use in a shopping center the cost of the kiosk is a capital expenditure since it results in an asset with a useful life of more than one year. Contrast this with repairs made by the carpenter to an existing display case which may qualify to be deducted immediately.

2. Materially prolongs or increases the life of the asset to which it was made. For example, replacing all of the windows in a building would make the building better withstand the elements and would thus increase its life. The cost of the windows would have to be capitalized. Contrast this with replacing one broken window. The cost of the new window would be deducted as a repair. Shoring up the foundation of a building, or inserting an expansion joint in a roof, are other examples of capital expenditures which prolong the life of a building.

3. Adapts the property to a different or new use. For example, converting an abandoned warehouse into residential condominiums is a capital expenditure.

4. Replacement or substitution of a major component. If such a replacement slows deterioration of the building and prolongs its life the expenditure must be capitalized. For example, the

installation of a new French drain and sump pump to prevent flooding of an apartment building's basement would have to be capitalized.

5. Materially increases the value of the building. For example, adding a sprinkler system would have to be capitalized since it would add to the value of the building.

A concept appearing in many of these factors is a "material" expenditure. A $100 expenditure would probably be written off immediately since, no matter how much it prolonged the life of a building, it is just not large enough relative to the value of the building to bother with. In addition, it is too small to distort your income from the building in a significant manner. The point up to which an expenditure can be deducted as a matter of policy, say $100, or $500, should be reviewed with your accountant.

With this background we can now examine steps which can be taken to help assure immediate deductibility of many expenditures.

Planning Tips. Plan for a strong ongoing and regular maintenance program. Don't let what could be annual and minor repairs develop into a major replacement requiring capitalization. Management by crisis will be a much more expensive approach when you're faced with a 31.5-year depreciation period and potentially costly capitalization rules.

Instead of undertaking a major renovation, consider the possibility of performing maintenance and repair of individual items on a rotational basis. If you have an interior designer draw up plans, and then you wallpaper, paint, carpet, replace windows, perform a host of miscellaneous repairs, and some carpentry work, the process begins to appear so significant that the costs may have to be capitalized. Contrast this to a scenario where in one year you paint and perform needed repairs. In the second year you wallpaper, replace a few windows, and perform some miscellaneous repairs. In the third year you replace a few more windows and the carpeting. And so on. This latter scenario may have a much better opportunity of being characterized as a series of deductible repair and maintenance costs. It can often pay to review your entire maintenance and repair program with your tax advisor and plan your expenditures accordingly.

Don't let the tax considerations outweigh important business considerations. If your marketing department believes that a one-time renovation followed by a grand reopening is essential, this may be far more important than the tax benefits obtainable from spreading the costs over many years.

Conclusions

Although a repair and maintenance policy may sound mundane, proper tax planning can result in significant savings. This is particularly true if major capital expenditures, which can only be written off over 31.5 years, can be avoided. Tax reform, through the longer depreciation periods, uniform capitalization rules, limitations on deducting interest expense, and other changes, has made planning in this area more complicated, but also more important to consider.

SPECIAL TAX CREDIT FOR REHABILITATING OLD AND HISTORIC BUILDINGS

Tax reform greatly restricted the benefits and availability of the special tax credit which has been available for costs incurred in renovating qualified buildings. Although the credit has been restricted, it can still be valuable in some situations, so developers should be aware of it. To understand the credit the various requirements to qualify will be reviewed, and the changes made by tax reform will be highlighted.

The rehabilitation tax credit is one which can offset, on a dollar-for-dollar basis, your tax liability. The credit is available for certain expenditures incurred in substantially rehabilitating certain old or historic buildings. The credit is really a two-tier credit, as follows:

1. Twenty percent tax credit on costs incurred in rehabilitating a building which qualifies as a certified historic structure (the building must be located in a registered historic district or be listed in the National Register of Historic Places; also, the Secretary of the Interior must approve the rehabilitation).

2. Ten percent tax credit on costs incurred in rehabilitating a building which was put into use (placed in service) before 1936.

Residential property may only qualify for the 20% certified historic structure credit. It may not qualify for the 10% credit.

This two-tier system replaces a more liberal system of credits which had been available under prior law. Not only were the credit percentages reduced, but the requirements for qualifying a rehabilitation of an old building has been greatly limited. In the past, costs to rehabilitate a building which was at least 30 years old could qualify for the credit. Now the building had to be placed in use before 1936, so it's at least 50-years old. Also, the rule is now a finite requirement—it doesn't move. Under the old rules you could wait for a building to reach the 30-year requirement. Now, the building was either put into use before 1936 or it wasn't.

To qualify for the credit the rehabilitation must be "substantial." To be substantial, the qualifying costs spent on the rehabilitation work itself, exclusive of the costs of acquiring the land and building, or enlarging the building, must exceed the greater of (1) $5,000, or (2) your investment (adjusted tax basis, which is generally cost less depreciation) in the building.

Planning Tips. Carefully monitor your expenditures. If it appears that you will be close, but not up to this requirement, consult with your tax advisor, engineer, and architect. Review all the planning suggestions and concepts discussed above concerning which repair and maintenance type expenditures should be capitalized. Also, review the planning suggestions in Chapter 10 discussing how to make real property qualify as personal property. Implement all of these planning ideas in reverse to boost your qualifying rehabilitation expenditures.

Expenditures on an addition to the building won't count toward meeting the substantial rehabilitation requirement. Carefully review all costs allocated to the addition to ascertain that they in fact relate to the addition and not to the qualifying portion of the renovation. Have your accountant consider alternative cost accounting methods of allocating costs to be certain you have taken the most advantageous position.

There is another approach to planning to meet the substantial rehabilitation test. The planning ideas discussed above focus on allocating more costs to the amount of qualifying costs needed to exceed your adjusted tax basis in the building. The other approach is to reduce your adjusted tax basis in the building. If this can be done, then a smaller amount of costs will help qualify your project for the credit. One approach to this is to donate a preservation (conservation) easement.

A preservation easement is a grant of a legal interest in the building to a qualified local historic (or other) organization. The grant conveys a right to the facade of the building so that neither you, nor any future owners, can change the facade. This restriction on the use of the building will reduce its value and hence its adjusted tax basis, which is the hurdle your rehabilitation expenditures must exceed to qualify. This can help you meet the substantial rehabilitation test. Importantly, you may also qualify for a valuable charitable contribution deduction for the value of the easement so donated. This can be a tricky technique—be sure to have your tax advisor and a real estate attorney review all aspects of the transaction.

In addition to meeting the dollar amount of the substantial rehabilitation test, the qualifying costs must be incurred within a specified time period. Generally, the rehabilitation must be completed within 24 months. Under certain circumstances this qualifying period can be extended to 60 months. If it looks like the 24-month period is insufficient, review the matter with your tax advisor and plan to qualify for the extension.

To assure that developers are really rehabilitating old or historic buildings, rather than building new buildings under the guise of a rehabilitation in order to qualify for the credit, Congress required that specified portions of the original building remain intact after the rehabilitation. Tax reform eliminated one of the methods of satisfying this test. Now to qualify a rehabilitation project the following tests must be met:

Seventy-five percent of the building's external walls must be retained as either external or internal walls

Seventy-five percent of the building's internal structural framework (beams, load bearing walls, structural supports, etc.) must be retained (this prevents a gutted building from qualifying)

Fifty percent of the building's external walls must be retained as external walls

Although a certified historic structure rehabilitation is not required to adhere to these tests, it is expected that the Secretary of the Interior may generally require compliance anyhow.

If the credit is claimed, the adjusted tax basis of the building must be reduced by the amount of the credit for purposes of calculating depreciation. Thus, if you had a building with a tax basis of $1.2 million and claimed a $400,000 rehabilitation tax credit, the tax basis of the building for depreciation would be $800,000 ($1,200,000 − $400,000). Under prior law the tax basis only had to be reduced by one-half of the tax credit (i.e., $200,000 in our example) if the building was a certified historic structure.

If the developer (owner) of the rehabilitated building agrees, the rehabilitation tax credit can be claimed by the building's tenant. However, to qualify, the tenant's unexpired lease term must at least equal the depreciation period for the property. These periods are 27.5 years for residential property and 31.5 years for nonresidential property.

Once all of these requirements have been surmounted to claim the credit, two additional hurdles must be passed to benefit from the credit earned. First, the credit will probably be earned on a passive real estate investment so that it will be subject to the new passive loss limitations (see Chapter 9). Thus the credit will generally only be available to offset income from other passive activities (other real estate investments, income earned on limited partnership interests, etc.). However, one important exception exists. Up to about $7,000 of the rehabilitation tax credit (i.e., the credit equivalent to the $25,000 loss allowance discussed in Chapter 9) can be used to offset income from any source. This allowance, however, is phased out once income reaches $200,000. (See Chapter 9 for more details.) The final hurdle to face is the general limitation on using income tax credits to offset tax liability.

The rehabilitation tax credit (and certain other tax credits which are collectively referred to as the general business credit) can only offset up to $25,000 of your tax liability and 75% of your tax liability in excess of this amount. Under prior law these credits could offset up to $25,000 of your tax liability plus 85% of the amount over $25,000.

Example. A developer earned a $53,000 rehabilitation tax credit. Assuming all the other limitations and restrictions have been dealt with, how much of her $56,000 tax liability can she offset in the current year?

The first $25,000 of the tax liability can be offset by the credit. Next, 75% of the $31,000 remaining tax liability ($56,000 −

$25,000) can be offset, or $23,250 ($31,000 × 75%). Thus a total of $48,250 of the credit can be used. The remaining credit is carried over to future years, subject to limitations in those years.

Conclusion

The Tax Reform Act of 1986 has made it more difficult to qualify for the rehabilitation tax credit. Even if a project can qualify, tax reform has significantly restricted the benefits of obtaining the rehabilitation credit. The credit will, however, be of value for those projects which can qualify.

CHAPTER SUMMARY

Tax reform has significantly reduced the tax benefits available from developing and operating real estate through a number of complicated new rules. Developers and property managers do have some planning opportunities to minimize the harsh impact of these new rules as illustrated in this chapter. If you have not already done so, review your accounting and recordkeeping systems with your accountant to make sure your systems are able to track all the information which compliance and planning with the new rules will require.

4 LEASING REAL ESTATE INVESTMENTS

GENERAL EFFECTS OF TAX REFORM

Real estate generates income and cash flow in two ways: (1) when it is leased and (2) when it is sold. This chapter reviews the impact tax reform will have on leasing. Chapter 5 will review the impact that tax reform has on the income and cash flow generated by selling real estate.

Leasing real estate may be affected in a number of ways by the tax reform changes:

1. *Rental Property Values.* The value of property should theoretically be reduced as a result of the loss of so many valuable tax benefits (e.g., depreciation, passive loss deductions, etc.). It appears, however, that many prime properties will continue to hold their value despite tax reform. Prime properties are limited in number and were often conceived with economic, rather than solely tax, objectives in mind. The rental properties most likely to suffer will be those ill-conceived properties packaged by syndicators solely for their tax benefits. Most importantly, you can no longer count on inflation to bail out these poor deals.

2. *Rents.* If the value of many properties is to decline as a result of tax reform, then it could be expected that rental rates may increase as investors attempt to recoup some lost value.

Generalizations are difficult but some trends may occur. Although landlords may try to raise rents if the value of properties declines, in reality rents, just like the property values discussed above, are probably more a function of the marketplace than of the impact of tax reform on a given landlord. If the marketplace permits rent increases, astute landlords would have already raised rents to the maximum they can obtain. If the market is very soft, rent increases may not be feasible regardless of any tax changes. One positive effect of tax reform on rental rates is that the clampdown on real estate tax benefits should reduce new construction. If the trend continues long enough, the oversupply in many markets may eventually be absorbed and rents can be increased.

3. *Percentage Rents.* In many retail leases landlords charge a base rental and a specified percentage of the tenant's sales over a certain amount (base) as an average or percentage rental. Percentage rentals are often a major component of a property's rental stream. They often serve as the landlord's major inflation hedge and his way of sharing in the property's success. Thus the ultimate value of the property being rented can be significantly affected by changes in percentage rentals. How will tax reform affect sales and hence percentage rentals? Again the economic impact of tax reform is difficult to assess, but a few generalizations may be helpful.

One objective of tax reform is to remove millions of low-income workers from the tax roles and to slash the tax liabilities of low-income workers remaining on the tax roles. Although the dollar value of the tax savings to these taxpayers will be small, it is possible that most of the savings realized by these lower-income groups will find their way directly to spending. Thus retail properties which cater to these markets could benefit. Percentage rentals on these properties should improve. Apart from these lower-income workers, the impact of tax reform on spending (apart from a rush for big ticket items at the end of 1986 to get a sales tax deduction) may be negligible. Moderate- to high-income taxpayers may save any tax cut they receive. Changes in percentage rentals from these properties are therefore hard to forecast.

The impact of tax reform on industry is likely to be very diverse. Heavy industry which has benefited significantly over the years from the use of investment tax credits and depreciation deductions is likely to fare poorly under tax reform as compared with other sectors of the economy. Service-oriented businesses (finance, consulting, etc.) are likely to fare much better. Many service businesses had very high marginal tax rates since they could not avail themselves of the many tax breaks the Internal Revenue Code offered. They will now benefit most from tax reform. The result of these changes, in very general terms, may be that retail rental properties located in regions dominated by heavy industry will fare worse than will similar properties located in regions dominated by service businesses. Percentage rentals can be expected to be effected in a similar manner.

Landlords renegotiating leases should carefully review the potential impact tax reform may have on the percentage rentals they will receive. If they anticipate noticeable declines they should try to negotiate a lower sales dollar figure at which percentage rentals will be triggered. A more favorable option would be to negotiate higher base rentals.

4. *Repeal of Sales Tax and Consumer Interest Deductions.* Tax reform has repealed the tax deductions for state and local sales taxes and consumer interest deductions (interest charged on store and other credit cards—see Chapter 8 for more details). Although there will be some flexibility to restructure consumer borrowing as home equity loans to preserve interest deductions, this approach will only be of limited utility. Theoretically, sales should decline if the cost of purchasing increases due to these tax changes, as it will. However, some economists are of the opinion that consumer spending is not that sensitive to changes in interest rates. If this continues to prove true, then sales may not be affected. Again, it's difficult to predict, but landlords should pay close attention because if changes in consumer spending patterns do occur they could be important. Different spending patterns could affect the income different properties can generate, and hence affect their values.

5. *Business Meals.* The deduction for business meals has been cut back so that only 80% of the expenditures will be deductible. In addition, to be deductible at all the expenditures must involve discussions, before, after, or during the meal, which relate directly to the patron's trade or business. These restrictions could impact the sales of certain restaurants. Landlords should watch for any impact on their percentage rentals.

6. *Lower Tax Rates.* The much lower marginal tax rates will reduce the value of planning in some situations. It doesn't mean planning for leases is not important; it just means the reward may not be the same.

7. *Repeal of Capital Gains.* After 1987 there will not be any preferential treatment for capital gains (see Chapter 5). This change

will simplify tax planning for real estate leases since many of the more complicated tax planning maneuvers for landlords and tenants had revolved around the objective of preserving capital gains. If the tax laws are later changed to bring back capital gains, then all of these complications will return. Since capital gains will still receive favorable treatment in 1987 (they'll be taxed at no more than a 28% rate even though the highest marginal tax rates are 38.5%), capital gains planning will still be valuable for 1987.

Example. Here's one example of the kind of planning which can be done in 1987 to take advantage of this special capital gains treatment. If you assign (i.e., sell) a lease, the gain will be a capital gain taxed at no more than a 28% rate. If, however, you merely sublease the property, any income will be taxed as ordinary (i.e., non-capital gain) income at up to a 38.5% rate. The key to achieving an assignment rather than a sublet is to transfer all of your interest in the lease. Have your attorney carefully negotiate and draft the transaction to support the desired tax result if it is also acceptable from a business perspective. More planning ideas for 1987 are listed below.

Tax Planning for 1987

The tax rates for 1987 will be as high as 38.5%. After 1987 the maximum rate will drop to 28%. This implies a potentially valuable one-time planning opportunity. If you can accelerate deductions into 1987 the tax benefit will be much greater. For landlords and tenants this could be an opportune time to do some overdue housekeeping. Review all current leases. If there are leases which should be cancelled try to do it in 1987. Although the payments to get yourself as a landlord out of a bad lease may not be fully deductible in the year the lease is cancelled, a portion will be. This portion will generate more valuable deductions in 1987 than in later years. If you have been putting off some general maintenance expenditures, such as painting, 1987 is the time to do it from a tax perspective. If an expense will have to be paid soon anyway you might as well do it when you can get a better tax break. Also, if you can prepay a portion of your 1988 property tax, the additional tax benefit could be valuable. If you sell (assign) a lease the proceeds will be treated as a capital gain taxed at a maximum rate of 28% in 1987. If, however, you sublet (there is a reversion of the lease to the original tenant), the income you receive in 1987 will be ordinary income taxed at rates up to 38.5%.

DEDUCTIBILITY OF BROKERAGE AND OTHER LEASE ACQUISITION COSTS

When a landlord and tenant sign a lease both parties generally incur substantial costs, for example for a brokerage commission, legal fees, and fees for an appraiser or accountant. For a landlord making concessions to entice tenants to sign in a soft rental market, the costs of getting the lease signed could be significant. The large amounts involved make the period over which these costs can be written off important. Also, many of these costs may be true out-of-pocket expenses which the tenant and landlord would hope to offset with a tax benefit. However, tax reform has dramatically reduced the tax benefits which the parties can realize.

The period over which the costs incurred in acquiring a lease must be written off should be the years which benefit from the expenditure—the lease term. This would be a relatively simple matter but for the question of what to do with renewal options in the lease. Prior law provided a mechanical test to determine whether lease renewal options had to be added to the base lease term for determining the write-off period for acquisition costs. Briefly, if the number of years in the base lease term was less than 75% of the number of years the payment would benefit, then the renewal option had to be included in the write-off period. The important point is that the facts in many lease situations were such that it was appropriate to write off the lease acquisition costs over the base lease term, without inclusion of renewal options. Tax reform has changed this: The lease term may now include all renewal options under this 75% test, as well as any period for which the parties reasonably expect the lease to be renewed.

Example. A landlord signs a 10-year lease with a restaurant to occupy the ground floor of an office building he just constructed. To entice the tenant the landlord agrees to pay the $150,000 brokerage commission and to give the tenant an additional $50,000 sign-up bonus. The tenant requests that three seven-year renewal options be included. The tenant wants to have the right to keep the location if a strong customer following develops. The tenant is even willing to agree to hefty rent increases as long as the renewal option is available. The landlord and the tenant do not formally provide for the options in the lease, but they agree that renewal is expected.

After tax reform the inclusion of these renewal options will have a significant effect on the deductions the landlord can obtain. Under prior law the landlord may have written off the $200,000 in acquisition costs ($150,000 + $50,000) over the 10-year lease term at a rate of $20,000 per year. Now the landlord can only write off these acquisition costs over 31 years (10-year base lease + three expected seven-year renewal periods), at a rate of only $6,452 per year.

Planning Tip. If lease renewals are not essential don't document them if the effect on deducting lease acquisition costs will be very costly. If the tenant wants options, determine the cost to both parties before agreeing. If you as the landlord will bear the tax burden of agreeing to the renewals, let the tenant know what it's costing you. If market conditions permit, try to negotiate concessions from the tenant to compensate you.

WRITING OFF LEASEHOLD IMPROVEMENTS

The Tax Reform Act of 1986 severely restricted the ability to plan for leasehold improvements. Under prior law a tenant could write off leasehold improvements over the shorter of the lease term or the depreciable life (accelerated cost recovery system period) for the property.

Example. A tenant signs a five-year lease for a space to operate a clothing store. The tenant spends $145,000 on leasehold improvements. In many situations the tenant could write off the cost of the improvements over his lease term of five years. Thus the tenant would deduct $29,000 in each of the five years.

Tax reform now requires that tenants depreciate leasehold improvements over the regular depreciation period for real estate. For improvements to nonresidential property this would be a 31.5-year period.

Example. Let's continue with the situation in the prior example. The tenant would now have to depreciate the $145,000 in leasehold improvements over a 31.5-year period. His deductions each year would now only be $4,603—quite a difference.

This presents a problem. If the tenant vacates the premises at the end of the five-year lease term leaving the improvements behind, he has only written off $23,015 of his investment ($4,603 per year × 5 years). The remaining $121,985 of his investment ($145,000 − $23,015) has not been deducted. The new rules will permit the tenant to deduct that amount in the year he vacates.

Let's quantify how the new rules have reduced the tax benefit to the tenant. Since the tax benefits will occur over time it is necessary to calculate their value in terms of today's dollars (i.e., present values) so that the results under each alternative can be compared. Assume a discount rate (interest rate, or cost of funds) of 12% per year and that all deductions are available to offset income taxed at the 28% rate.

Tax Benefit Under Prior Law (with Tax Reform Rates)

Annual deductions	$29,000
Tax rate	28%
Annual tax benefit	$ 8,120
Present value of tax benefit for 5 years @ 12%	$29,271

Tax Benefit after Tax Reform

The present value of the tax benefits after tax reform consists of two components: (1) the stream of annual tax benefits from the annual depreciation deductions, and (2) the present value of the tax benefit of the deduction in the final year of any remaining leasehold improvement costs.

Annual deductions	$	4,603
Tax rate		28%
Annual tax benefit	$	1,289
Present value of tax benefit for 5 years @ 12%	$	4,647 (A)
Deduction in final year	$	121,985
Tax rate		28%
Tax benefit	$	34,156
Present value of tax benefit from 5 years @ 12%		19,381 (B)
Total present value (A) + (B)		24,028

The results of this analysis show that the tax benefits after tax reform's new rule for depreciating leasehold improvements have been reduced by $5,243 ($29,271 − $24,028). Notice that in our analysis we assumed the 28% tax rate. This was done to demonstrate the impact of this one change made by tax reform. If the 50% rate available before tax reform had been used, the decline in tax benefits would have been dramatic.

What does this mean for landlords? A lot! Under prior law an astute landlord would have realized the benefits that could be obtained by the tenant writing off leasehold improvements over a short lease term (since 1981 landlords have had to depreciate leasehold improvements over the regular depreciation period for real estate, regardless of the lease term). The landlord would have then structured the improvements so that the tenant would own and write them off, and the landlord would have ordinarily given the tenant a "tenant allowance" (moneys provided by the landlord to the tenant to be applied toward the purchase of leasehold improvements), the transaction would have been restructured so that the tenant would have owned and written off the improvements. In exchange for the extra tax benefits the tenant would have obtained, the tenant would have paid the landlord additional rent, or made some other concession of benefit to the landlord.

What can be done now? The same planning idea landlords used prior to tax reform is still available, only the size of the additional benefit will be much less. An example will illustrate the application of this planning idea in the context of our earlier examples.

Example. Let's assume the same facts as in our prior examples except, as will often be the situation, the landlord will make and own the leasehold improvements. What is the present value to the landlord of owning and depreciating $145,000 in leasehold improvements?

If the landlord were to own the improvements he would have

Tax Benefit to Landlord after Tax Reform

Investment (tax basis)	$145,000
Depreciation period	31.5 yrs
Annual deduction	$ 4,603
Tax rate	28%
Annual tax benefit	$ 1,289
Present value of tax benefit for 31.5 years @ 12%	$ 10,439

to depreciate them over a 31.5-year period (40 years for the alternative minimum tax—see Chapter 11). The present value of the tax benefit the landlord will obtain is $13,589 less than the present value of the tax benefits which the tenant could obtain if the tenant owned and depreciated the improvements ($24,028 − $10,439). There clearly is still significant room for planning. With a potential $13,589 in extra tax benefits to negotiate for, the landlord and tenant should be able to find a mutually agreeable way to have the tenant own and write off the improvements so that both can share this extra benefit at the government's expense.

Planning Tip. There is another advantage to the landlord from this type of planning. The basis for the tenant deducting the remaining cost of the improvements when he vacates the premises is that the improvements are left behind. If the improvements have some value will the landlord be taxed on the reversion of the improvements to him? Although general tax principles would require this, a special rule in the Internal Revenue Code lets the landlord receive the improvements with no tax cost. For the landlord to get this tax-free reversion of leasehold improvements, their value cannot be intended to be an additional rental payment.

Net Leases and Tax Planning

A net lease is one in which the tenant agrees to pay for most of the costs associated with the rental property (such as insurance, property taxes, etc.). The landlord and his lenders may strongly prefer leases to be as net as possible. This is because the risks of cost increases will be transferred to the tenant, and the landlord and his lenders will have a more predictable net cash flow to plan with. In spite of these many business benefits associated with net leases, a number of tax problems can be caused by using net leases:

A net leased property will always be considered a passive activity for purposes of the new passive loss limitation rules (see Chapter 9).

If the leasing activity escapes the new passive loss rules the interest paid on the mortgage used to buy the property may then be subject to the limitations on the deductibility of investment interest (see Chapter 2).

If your estate consists largely of an interest in a closely held active trade or business, a portion of the estate tax on your estate may be deferred for a period of up to 14 years. This can be a tremendous benefit to your heirs, can permit the transfer of a closely held or family business intact, and may enable you to save significantly on life insurance costs (since all the insurance may not be needed to pay the estate tax). Net leased property will not qualify for this active business requirement.

Planning Tip. If business reasons dictate using a net lease, or if the lender insists on it, then use a net lease. If, however, there is any flexibility, review the considerations briefly summarized above with your tax advisor before committing to a net lease. If the business and tax factors point to avoiding a net lease, it may be possible to structure the transaction so that a lease is not treated as a net lease.

What Is a Net Lease What type of lease will be treated as a net lease? The old tax laws had a mechanical test for determining whether a lease is a net lease. Although it's not yet clear whether "net leases" in the Tax Reform Act of 1986 will be defined the same, the prior law's definition should serve as a guide. Under it, a lease is considered to be a net lease if the landlord is guaranteed a specific rate of return on his investment or is guaranteed against loss. If this is not the case a mechanical 15% test must be used. Under this test a lease is considered to be a net lease if the total of certain qualifying expenses are less than 15% of the rental income from the property. Qualifying and nonqualifying expenses for this test are:

Qualifying Expenses	Nonqualifying Expenses
Repairs	Depreciation
Management fees	Amortization
Maintenance	Rents
Advertising	Ground rents
Insurance	Reimbursed expenses

Example. A Landlord realizes the following income and expenses on the rental of an office building:

Rent		$450,600
Expenses:		
Repairs	$ 11,000	
Maintenance	19,400	
Insurance	25,000	
Reimbursed		
expenses	5,000	
Depreciation	$384,000	
Total expenses		$444,400
Net income		$ 6,200

In this example only the repairs, maintenance, and insurance expenses count toward the 15% test. Since these expenses only total $55,400, or 12.3% of rentals, the test is failed and the lease is considered to be a net lease.

Planning Tips. What can you do to meet the 15% test and avoid having a lease treated as a net lease? Take the responsibility for expenses which qualify for the 15% test. Consider paying a management fee fixed as a percentage of rentals which, in combination with other expenses you will be responsible for, will assure you of meeting the test. As an alternative, a fixed dollar management fee will limit some of the uncertainty of future cost escalations. Review the matter with your lender. If you will achieve significant tax savings by this type of planning your overall after-tax cash flow could improve. If the lender is aware of this improved cash flow, there may be somewhat more sensitivity to the planning you wish to pursue.

Planning Tip. If you can qualify for estate tax deferral, reassess your insurance needs.

Leases and Depreciation Planning
Leases present a few special considerations for depreciation planning which landlords should be aware of (for further details see Chapter 10).

You can generally begin claiming depreciation deductions on a building when it is put into use ("placed in service"). One important factor for determining when a building is placed in service is the time rent payments begin. Keep this in mind when negotiating the commencement clause in a lease. It may be advantageous to offer concessions to get a tenant in earlier. The benefits to you of being able to claim depreciation deductions sooner can exceed the cost of the concessions you have to make to get the tenant's cooperation. This same planning concept will help end the construction period and enable you to begin deducting, rather than capitalizing (i.e., adding to your tax basis) many costs (see Chapter 3).

Many leases require the landlord to pay for structural or capital repairs and improvements. The costs of other improvements and repairs is passed to the tenants. If you as landlord bear the costs of certain repairs or maintenance expenses because they were classified as structural or capital according to the lease, that doesn't mean they must be treated as structural or capital improvements for tax purposes. The definitions under the lease won't necessarily follow the tax definitions. Therefore, have your tax advisor carefully review any such expenditures for costs which may qualify to be deducted currently, or treated as nonstructural improvements which can be depreciated more rapidly.

CHAPTER SUMMARY

Tax reform has hit the tax benefits available from leasing very hard. A number of tax planning opportunities, however, remain. When negotiating a lease consult with your tax advisor before signing the lease; there may be valuable tax planning ideas which could benefit both parties. After the lease is signed, it may be too late to implement the planning ideas available.

5 SELLING REAL ESTATE INVESTMENTS

Tax reform made two major changes which will affect real estate sales. The first and most fundamental change was the repeal of the capital gains benefits. Capital gains have long been one of the most important tax benefits for real estate investors. The first part of this chapter explores these changes and their impact on real estate investment.

Another crucial change made by the tax reform legislation did not receive the media attention of the capital gains repeal: Congress dramatically changed the taxation of installment sales. An installment sale is one in which you sell real estate and the buyer pays the sales price over a number of years. The general rule had been that you reported a portion of each year's proceeds as profit subject to tax. Tax reform has made a number of changes to this rule. The second part of this chapter will review these changes.

PLANNING WITH THE NEW CAPITAL GAINS RULES

What the Capital Gains Changes Mean
Media coverage of the Tax Reform Act of 1986 has led many taxpayers to believe that capital gains will be irrelevant after 1986. Watch out! The effects of the changes are far more complicated. In order to take maximum advantage of the new rules and to avoid some of the costly tax traps created, it is necessary to understand the changes in more depth. Consider the following questions:

Can you forget the whole complicated mess of the capital gains rules after 1986?

How will the "elimination" of the capital gain rules affect your real estate investments and business after 1986?

Are there any planning ideas to save tax dollars in light of these changes?

Is the whole concept of "dealer" versus "investor" gone?

Are there any expensive tax traps to watch out for because of the capital gains changes?

The goal of the first part of this chapter is to answer these questions. In order to understand the answers and the planning tips you should consider, it is necessary to understand what "capital gains" are and how they were taxed under prior tax laws.

Are Capital Gains Gone Forever?

As the following discussion will illustrate, capital gains tax rules will continue to be important to real estate professionals, investors, and homeowners. Consider the following comment made in the report of the Conference Committee which tried to reconcile the differences between the House and Senate tax bills:

> For both individual and corporate capital gains, retain the current statutory structure for capital gains in the Code [i.e., the Internal Revenue Code—the tax laws] to facilitate reinstatement of a capital gains rate differential if there is a future tax rate increase.

Thus at the same time Congress decided to eliminate many of the complicated capital gains rules, Congress also decided to keep all the laws on the books in case they decide to resurrect the capital gains rules in the future. The possibility of all the old capital gains rules coming back should always be kept in mind when planning real estate transactions with your tax advisor.

What Are "Capital Gains and Losses"?

Capital gains and losses are the gains or losses realized on the sale (or certain other transfers or events which are treated like sales by the tax laws) of capital assets. An "asset" is simply anything of value which you own. Capital assets include stocks and bonds (for anyone except a stockbroker or dealer), your house, a piece of raw land you hold as an investment, and many other assets.

The more technical definition which the tax laws provide for capital assets is as follows. A capital asset is any property held by a taxpayer except:

1. Inventory (stock in the taxpayer's trade)—this is generally property held for sale to customers in the ordinary course of your business. Perhaps the simplest example is the goods a retail store holds for sale—such as clothing. An example relating to the real estate industry would be 40 lots in a subdivision which a developer is holding for sale. The key test is whether the developer held the property primarily for sale to customers in the ordinary course of his business. With 40 lots the answer is probably yes. In many situations the answer is not so clear. You will have to look at all the facts and circumstances surrounding the transaction, such as the taxpayer's intent, the amount of advertising done, other real estate sales, the portion of the income earned from such sales as compared with the taxpayer's other sources of income, and the time devoted to the project.

2. Depreciable property and land used in your trade or business. CAUTION—Gains on the sale of these assets can often qualify for treatment as capital gains. This will be explained in the discussion of the capital gains rules under old law that follows this section. An example would be a warehouse building a contractor owns for storing his equipment.

3. A number of other items which have no special significance to the real estate industry.

What are capital gains and losses? They are income realized or lost when a taxpayer sells capital assets. Generally, this gain or loss is calculated by subtracting your cost or investment in an asset (your "tax basis") from what you received on selling the asset (the "amount realized").

Example. An investor buys a parcel of raw land on January 1, 1985, for $50,000 in cash—no loans, no mortgages, and no other fees. This is his tax basis in the land. On March 15, 1986, the investor sells his land to a buyer for $75,000 in cash. Again, there are no loans, mortgages, or fees. The investor realized $75,000 on the sale. His gain is $25,000 (the $75,000 realized minus his $50,000 tax basis). Is the gain a capital gain? If this is the only land he owned, and he had no intention of developing it, he clearly would be considered an investor rather than a dealer so that the gain realized on its sale will be a capital gain.

In most real estate transactions, these two concepts of "tax basis" and "amount realized" are somewhat more complicated. The "tax basis" and the "amount realized" must be adjusted for a number of items. The following checklist will highlight some of the more common adjustments your tax advisor will make for you:

TAX BASIS

+   Purchase price
+   Cost of any capital improvements (lasting improvements, such as a new roof or an addition)
+   Ancillary costs to acquire the property (such as legal fees, title insurance, recording fees)
−   Any losses (such as from fire, theft, or condemnation)
−   Depreciation claimed on the property

AMOUNT REALIZED

+   Cash received on the sale
+   Fair value of any other property received (e.g., the investor could have sold his land for $70,000 in cash and a U.S. government bond worth $5,000)
+   The amount of debt which the buyer assumes on the sale

Now that you understand what capital assets are (and the broad definition above makes it clear that many assets qualify), the rules prior to the Tax Reform Act of 1986 can be reviewed. Once that is done, the new rules and planning ideas can be explained.

Capital Gains and Losses Under the Old Law
Under the old law, sales of capital assets owned or held for more than a certain period of time would qualify for a very favorable treatment. Gains recognized on the sale of these assets would qualify for a capital gains exclusion. This rule provides that 60% of the gain on the sale will not be subject to tax.

Example. An investor purchased land for $50,000. He held it for more than the requisite holding period before selling it for $75,000. The tax results are as follows:

Selling price (amount realized)	$75,000
Purchase price (tax basis)	50,000
Capital gain (long term)	$25,000
Exclusion (60% × $25,000)	−15,000
Taxable gain	$10,000
Tax rate (old law)	× 50%
Tax	$ 5,000

Without the benefit of this exclusion, the investor would have had to pay $12,500 tax ($25,000 gain × 50% tax rate), so the exclusion yielded a $7,500 savings for the taxpayer. CAUTION— This "benefit" was not always as valuable as it seemed. Certain individuals who were subject to the alternative minimum tax (AMT) may have had the amount of this exclusion taxed by the AMT (see Chapter 11).

What capital gains would qualify for this favorable treatment under the old law? Generally, the gains recognized on the sale of any capital asset owned (held) for more than six months. The gains recognized on assets held for this required time period are called "long-term capital gains." Gains recognized on the sale of capital assets not held for this minimum period are called "short-term capital gains." Thus another complication must be explained in order to understand the interplay of the prior law and the changes made by the Tax Reform Act of 1986.

Netting Short- and Long-Term Capital Gains

When a taxpayer has both long- and short-term capital gains and losses, the following rules should generally be followed:

Separate all capital gains and losses into two groups—the long- and short-term gains and losses.

Net all the long-term transactions with each other (i.e., add them up). Net all the short-term transactions with each other.

Look up the next step in the following chart:

S/T*	L/T**	RESULT
+	+	S/T taxed at ordinary rates; L/T benefits from the exclusion; S/T and L/T not mixed.
+	−	S/T taxed at ordinary rates; L/T used on a one-for-two basis to reduce ordinary income including S/T capital gains. For example, $6,000 of L/T losses can only reduce $3,000 of ordinary income. The new rules change this so that long-term capital losses can offset ordinary income on a dollar-for-dollar basis, up to the $3,000 annual limitation. For example, $6,000 of L/T losses can reduce $6,000 of ordinary income (but only $3,000 in any one year).
−	−	S/T applied to reduce ordinary income; L/T used (subject, under old law, to the one-for-two rule) to reduce ordinary income. The maximum total reduction per year for individuals is $3,000. Any unused losses are carried over for use in future years (a "carry forward").
−	+	S/T loss is first applied to reduce the L/T gain—a spoiler effect under old law since the S/T loss would otherwise be deductible against ordinary income but now acts to reduce the L/T gain available for the favorable exclusion.

*S/T = Short term (i.e., held six months or less)
**L/T = Long term (i.e., held more than six months)
"−" = Loss
"+" − Gain

One final twist needs to be mentioned. The preceding discussion of the definition of capital assets excluded depreciable assets and land used in a trade or business. Thus the building a warehouseman uses in his storage business would not qualify for favorable capital gains treatment (i.e., the 60% exclusion). A special rule may help the warehouse owner, as explained in the following section.

Certain Trade or Business Assets

Under the old law, if depreciable assets and land used in a trade or business are held for the period required for long-term capital gains (generally more than six months), they could qualify for even more favorable treatment than that available to other capital assets, as shown in the chart in the preceding section.

Net all the gains and losses realized on the sale of qualifying trade or business assets (known as "Code Section 1231 assets" after the section of the Internal Revenue Code which contains the rules affecting them). If the net amount is a loss, then that loss can be used to offset ordinary income—in full. The $3,000 limitation described above will not apply. If the net amount is a gain, it gets thrown into the above analysis—that is, treat it like any other long-term capital gain and apply the result found in the chart. With this background, the changes made by the Tax Reform Act of 1986 can now be reviewed.

New Capital Gains Rules

The new law repeals the preferential treatment afforded capital gains—that is, the 60% exclusion discussed and illustrated in the preceding section. There is also an important phase-in (transition) rule. The new law is scheduled to set the following tax rates.

New Tax Rates

1987

Taxable Income Brackets

Tax Rate	Married Filing Joint Returns	Married Filing Separate Returns	Heads of Household	Single Individuals
11%	0–$3,000	0–$1,500	0–$2,500	0–$1,800
15	$3,001–28,000	$1,501–14,000	$2,501–23,000	$1,801–16,800
28	28,001–45,000	14,001–22,500	23,001–38,000	16,801–27,000
35	45,001–90,000	22,501–45,000	38,001–80,000	27,001–54,000
38.5	Over $90,000	Over $45,000	Over $80,000	Over $54,000

1988 and Later Years

Taxable Income Brackets

Tax Rate	Married Filing Joint Returns	Married Filing Separate Returns	Heads of Household	Single Individuals
15%	0–29,750	0–$14,875	0–$23,900	0–$17,850
28	Over $29,750	Over $14,875	Over $23,900	Over $17,850

Once the new law is completely effective, all capital gains income will be taxed just like ordinary (i.e., noncapital gain) income. Thus all of an individual taxpayer's income will be grouped together and subject to the applicable tax rates. Congress, however, felt it unfair to subject capital gains to a tax rate higher than the 28% rate, as would be the case during 1987 when higher "transitional" tax rates will be in effect. Thus, for 1988 only, a special rule limits the tax rate on capital gains to 28%. If none of your income is taxed at a rate higher than 28%, then all of your income, including all of your capital gains, will be taxed together at the applicable tax rates. If your income is sufficiently high that some of your income is taxed at rates greater than 28%, then an additional calculation will be required. The effect of the calculation will be to tax all your income, excluding capital gains, according to the 1987 tax rate schedule and then tax your capital gains at a maximum 28% rate.

Planning Tip—Capital Losses. The preferential treatment afforded capital gains in the past is generally eliminated at the end of 1986. The limitations on deducting capital losses are not! For example, say an investor bought in on Houston office buildings at the worst time—his buildings have no tenants. He wants to cut his losses and sell out. CAUTION—The $3,000-per-year limitation on deducting capital losses is still effective. Don't be fooled by the press given to the idea of eliminating capital gains—the new law didn't eliminate them completely.

What can the investor do? First, he should try to coordinate the sale of his capital assets with his tax advisor to minimize the harsh effects of this limitation. Perhaps he has other assets he has been thinking about selling which have appreciated considerably. If he sells all of these gain and loss assets in the same tax year, the gains and losses can be used to offset each other. Not only can this help avoid the limitations of the $3,000 rule, but it will shelter the gain on the appreciated assets from tax. Timing is key—consult with your tax advisor *before* you sign any deal.

Planning Tip—Investor versus Dealer Status. Notice what the new law had done to the familiar concept of investor versus dealer status. Recall that under the old law, if you were considered a dealer (e.g., you subdivided real estate and sold and/or developed lots on a regular basis), any gain you realized would be taxed as ordinary income—at rates up to 50%. If, however, you could somehow maintain investor status, the gain you would recognize on the sale of your lots could be treated as a capital gain and could thus be taxed at only the maximum capital gains tax rate of 20%. With this 30% tax differential, taxpayers went to great lengths to structure their activities and transactions in order to avoid "dealer" status.

Under the new law, there is still an advantage to being classified as an "investor" through the end of 1987. Until then, long-term capital gains income can still be taxed at a preferential rate. CAUTION—After 1987, there is no benefit to being treated as either an "investor" or a "dealer" for capital gains purposes. There is, however, a severe detriment to being taxed as an investor if you've gotten into some bad deals: namely, the $3,000-per-year limitation on the deduction of capital losses. Dealers are not subject to this limitation since they don't recognize capital gains and losses—they only recognize ordinary gains and losses.

Review your real estate activities very carefully with your tax advisor. Also, consider the passive loss rules and the investment interest limitations discussed later in this book. It may be possible to benefit by taking a more active role in your real estate endeavors.

EFFECT OF THE NEW LAW ON THE REAL ESTATE INDUSTRY

The higher tax rates that will apply to capital gains income under the new law will affect the after-tax rate of return investors can expect from their real estate investments. Let's take a look at the results an investor can realize after tax.

Example—Should You Sell Now? An investor purchased raw land in 1982 for $48,000 in cash. He wants to sell the land. When should he sell it? If he had sold it anytime before the end of 1986, he would have paid a tax at a maximum capital gains rate of 20% (the rate applicable when you multiply the old maximum individual tax rate of 50% by the 40% of the capital gain which is left after the 60% exclusion). If he sells it in 1987 or later when the capital gains exclusion is gone, the maximum tax on capital gains is 28%.

Many of the articles and discussions of the new tax law advised investors to consider selling some of their appreciated assets before the end of 1986 to take advantage of the lower tax rates. Don't feel bad if you didn't. This didn't always make sense for real estate investments although it may have been advisable for stocks and similar financial investments.

Consider the following before deciding to sell any real estate investment:

1. What effect will the new tax law have on the prices of real estate in the locality where your property is? If prices are temporarily depressed because of the many restrictions the new law places on real estate, it may pay to wait. It is difficult to generalize about the impact of the new law on market prices. In areas which are drastically overbuilt (areas with the so-called see-through office buildings), the tax law change may not have a discernible effect. The outlook for the foreseeable future may be so poor that any bad tax news may not have any additional impact. On the other hand, in areas which are tight markets, where landlords and developers can pass on any cost increases to anxious tenants, the unfavorable new laws may not have any effect for a very different reason. The tremendous demand may keep prices firm. If the new laws are so unfavorable that new construction is inhibited, there may be a future increase in the value of existing properties. Many of the tax-oriented real estate syndications may not be viable without tax benefits. If many of these properties are thrown into the market, prices could decline. It's unclear at this time how much of an impact this will have on the market as a whole. Finally, good quality prime real estate may retain its value regardless of the above effects.

2. Consider closing, legal, and other transfer costs. These factors alone could have made it unwise to jump the gun and sell real estate before 1987 to take advantage of the 20% (vs. the new 28%) capital gains rate. If an investor owned financial assets which have appreciated significantly, it may clearly have been advantageous to liquidate the investment and take gains before the rates were increased. To liquidate a securities investment, the only nontax cost generally involved is commissions. For large investors, this cost can be as low as 5 cents per share. Now, contrast this with a real estate investment.

Example. An investor purchased real estate in 1982 for $48,000. The investor's raw land can be sold for $235,000 in 1986. The lot is located on a corner of what has become a major shopping area. The investor is also confident that he can sell it in future years for at least $235,000 increased by the rate of inflation. Should he have sold before the new higher capital gains rate took effect?

It certainly appears to be advantageous for the investor to have sold in 1986 and paid tax at the lower capital gains rate then avail-

SELL UNDER OLD LAW

Sales price	$235,000	(A)
Cost	48,000	
Taxable gain	$187,000	
Tax rate (capital gains)	× 20%	
Tax	$ 37,400	(B)
Proceeds net of tax: (A) − (B)	= $197,600	

SELL LATER UNDER NEW LAW

Sales price	$235,000	(C)
Cost	48,000	
Taxable gain	$187,000	
Tax rate (all income)	× 28%	
Tax	$ 52,360	(D)
Proceeds net of tax: (C) − (D)	= $182,640	

able. He would have gained $14,960 ($197,600 − $182,640). But what about brokerage commissions and legal fees? If he has to pay a 6% brokerage commission, $175 in recording fees, and a $1,500 legal fee, would it still have been advantageous to sell?

EXPENSES OF SALE

Legal fees	$1,500
Brokerage commission	
(6% × $235,000) =	14,100
Recording fees	175
Total expenses of sale	$15,775
Capital gains tax	
savings (from above)	14,960
Net cost of sale	$ 815

Although the absolute tax cost would have been less if the investor had sold before the end of 1986, he may not actually have realized any benefit. The conclusion to be drawn in many real estate transactions is that to sell based on tax considerations alone may be a big mistake. Costs, potential appreciation, reinvestment opportunities and other relevant factors should be considered. What if he wanted to sell and reinvest his proceeds in another real estate project? He may have wanted to do this to "lock in" the lower capital gains tax rate in 1986. In this scenario, it may have made even less sense to sell solely for the tax benefit—he would have been stuck paying transfer costs to sell his old investment and may have, either directly or indirectly, borne the burden of the transfer costs on the reinvestment as well (sellers can sometimes factor their selling costs into the price they ask).

Planning Tip. Don't sell real estate just to avoid any increased capital gains or other tax. Have your tax advisor make projections of the benefits and costs under all options. And carefully consider all transfer and reinvestment costs. Consider the economic and investment aspects of the transaction. Don't let the tax tail wag the business dog—don't save a few tax dollars if the decision isn't the right investment decision. NOTE—Consider each situation carefully. Don't get caught making mistakes like the investor may have in the above example.

Some examples will illustrate the impact of the new capital gains rules, and other tax reform changes, as well as the importance of considering the facts in each situation individually.

Example—Personal Residence. A retired couple has owned a house for 20 years. They bought the house for $30,000 and it is now worth $245,000. They are ready to sell the old homestead and rent a small apartment in a retirement community. The gain on the house of $215,000 ($245,000 − $30,000) exceeds the special exclusion for sale of a principal residence by taxpayers over age 55 by $90,000 ($215,000 − $125,000). The special rule lets taxpayers aged 55 and over make a once-in-a-lifetime exclusion of up to $125,000 of the gain on the sale of a principal residence. The Tax Reform Act of 1986 has left this rule intact. However, the couple will have to pay tax on the $90,000 in either case. They will be investing their proceeds (net of any tax) in very secure certificates of deposit (CDs) with the local bank. They hope to live off the interest during their golden years. What has the impact of the Tax Reform Act been on this scenario? Let's take a look at the results before and after tax reform. We'll assume they can earn 8% on their CDs and that they pay tax at the maximum rates in both cases:

BEFORE TAX REFORM

Sales proceeds	$245,000
Less tax on gain ($90,000	
× 20% maximum tax on	
capital gains)	18,000
Net proceeds invested in	
CDs	$227,000
Interest on CDs at 8%	$18,160
Tax (50% maximum tax ×	
$18,160) =	9,080
Net annual earnings	$ 9,080

AFTER TAX REFORM

Sales proceeds	$245,000
Less tax on gain ($90,000	
× 28% maximum tax on all	
income after 1987)	25,200
Net proceeds invested in	
CDs	$219,800
Interest on CDs at 8%	17,584
Tax (28% maximum tax	
× $17,584)	4,924
Net annual earnings	$ 12,660

The tax bite on the sale is higher after tax reform so that the couple has been hurt. Their principal balance is considerably lower. This detriment, however, is somewhat mitigated by the fact that the lower tax rates will provide the couple with $3,580 more net annual earnings after tax reform ($12,660 — $9,080).

Planning Tip—Estate Planning Consideration. An older taxpayer is getting on in years. He has a number of substantial real estate investment properties: a warehouse, a small neighborhood shopping mall, and interests in a couple of real estate syndications. He made his investments many years ago and they have all appreciated substantially. He is uncertain of what tax reform will do to the value of his real estate holdings. He is wondering whether to sell the investments now before the market softens. An option which the taxpayer should consider, if the economic circumstances are appropriate, is keeping the investments. If the taxpayer is planning to give the investments to his children when he dies, it might be better not to sell now. When his heirs receive the investments through his estate, they will receive what is called a "stepped-up basis."

This means that for tax purposes their investment in the property—that is, their tax basis—will be the fair market value of the property when the parent dies. Thus if the children were to sell the property immediately they would not have to pay any tax. Recall that the taxable gain on a sale is generally calculated by subtracting the tax basis from the sales proceeds (amount realized). Since on the taxpayer's death the tax basis is stepped up to the property's fair value, which should equal the sales proceeds, this calculation should result in no gain. CAUTION—Many factors, including federal taxes to be paid by the estate, inheritance taxes, the new passive loss rules, the likelihood of further declines in value, have to be considered in formulating an effective estate plan. Before implementing a plan like this, check with the attorney doing your estate planning.

Capital Gains Tax and Rate of Return

When evaluating any investment in real estate, a critical factor is your expected rate of return. Rate of return is a method of measuring how much you've earned on an investment. For example, if you invest $1,000 in a one-year CD paying 10% simple interest and you withdraw the $1,100 on maturity, your rate of return is 10% ($1,100 — $1,000/$1,000). If you invested in a similar CD which paid $500 in interest for six months, your rate of return is still 10% on an annual basis. (A 5% return for six months divided by 6/12—since you have held it only 6 out of 12 months in the year—gives you a 10% rate of return for the year.) Although economic factors—appreciation of the property and the rental stream—are critical, taxes should also be factored into any rate of return analysis. A simplified example will illustrate how the more expensive capital gains tax can negatively affect the expected return on an investment.

Example. A speculator had a hunch about the location of a new highway. He was confident that he could buy a prime piece of farmland for $200,000 and sell it in just over six months for $220,000.

	Old Law		New Law	
Sales price (amount realized)	$220,000	(A)	$220,000	(A)
Cost (tax basis)	200,000		200,000	
Taxable gain	$20,000		$20,000	
Tax rate	× 20%		× 28%	
Tax	$4,000	(B)	$5,600	(B)
Profit, net of tax = (A) − (B)	$ 16,000		$ 14,400	
Return on investment*	8.0%		7.2%	
Annualized return on investment	16.0%		14.4%	

*Return on investment is calculated by dividing the net gain after tax ($16,000 with the old law's 20% tax rate, and $14,400 with the new law's 28% tax rate) by the original cost.

As can be seen from this example, the rate of return on the investment, while still substantial, has been reduced significantly under the new tax law—by about 10%.

Will the new capital gains rules always negatively influence the rate of return on an investment? Not necessarily. A change in the assumptions used in this example will demonstrate why not.

Planning Tip—How Long You Must Own an Investment. Let's take another look at the speculator's investment. He really didn't want to hold the investment for more than six months. He wanted to sell the land as soon as the announcement of the new highway was made definite. He estimated that the major appreciation of the land would occur within one month of the announcement. How do these facts change the result? First, under the old law, if the land was not held for more than a six-month period, then the favorable 60% capital gains exclusion would not have been available. The gain would be taxed at ordinary income rates—up to 50% on the entire gain in 1986, for example. A second result will also follow. Since the speculator will only have his money invested for a one-month period (instead of the six-month period in the previous example), his rate of return on an annualized basis will increase significantly. Let's see what happens:

	Old Law		New Law	
Sales price (amount realized)	$220,000	(A)	$220,000	(A)
Cost (tax basis)	200,000		200,000	
Taxable gain	$20,000		$20,000	
Tax rate	× 50%		× 28%	
Tax	$10,000	(B)	$ 5,600	(B)
Profit, net of tax = (A) − (B)	$10,000		$14,400	
Return on investment	5.0%		7.2%	
Annualized return on investment	60.0%		86.4%	

Under this scenario, the new capital gains rules actually increase an investor's rate of return significantly. This result will be the unusual situation. However, it highlights an important fact. Be very careful in making general assumptions about how the new tax laws will affect you. The best approach will be to have your tax advisor make projections of the possible results you could face under a number of different circumstances. Then evaluate these possible results in light of the relevant business and economic factors before making a decision.

Although the gains on sales of capital assets held longer than six months (long-term capital gains) will be subject to higher taxes (28% after 1987 instead of 20% before tax reform), the gains on capital assets held less than six months will be taxed much more favorably (28% after 1987 instead of 50% before tax reform).

Planning Tip—Effect on Old Installment Sales. The new tax laws eliminate the favorable rate for sales of capital assets. CAUTION—This rule will affect the tax costs of sales you made years ago and are now receiving installment payments on. Installment payments received on old contracts for the sale of a home (if the gain wasn't rolled over into a new home) and for the sale of investment property will be taxed at the higher 28% rate beginning in 1987. A number of other changes were made to the installment sales rules. These are discussed in the latter portion of this chapter.

Conclusion—Capital Gains

Capital gains treatment has always been a primary goal of real estate investors, developers, homeowners, and so forth—a valuable goal worth planning hard to reach. Tax reform has generally eliminated the benefit of obtaining that goal. However, as the many examples, planning tips, and cautions in the preceding discussion indicate, the results may be different than expected. Also, tax planning in this area can still be important for the real estate investor.

TOUGH NEW INSTALLMENT SALES RULES

Are you planning to sell any real estate on an installment, or deferred payment, basis? Are you planning to take back debt from the buyer (purchase money debt)? Tax reform may have a rather unpleasant surprise for you. You may end up paying tax long before you expected to. As for tax simplification, the new provisions governing installment sales will eliminate any concerns you may have had about Congress putting tax advisors out of business.

These new rules can affect how you sell real estate—they may even eliminate your use of the installment method. You may have to revise some of your accounting systems. Accounting headaches will increase. You may have to prepare detailed financial statements where none were needed before. You may want to plan your borrowings differently.

To understand how these new rules affect you we'll have to review the installment sales rules which existed before tax reform. Most of these old rules are still applicable. The result of the tax reform changes in this area are to add an additional layer of complexity over the existing rules.

What Are Installment Sales?

If you were to sell real estate for cash—the entire sale price paid to you in the year of sale—you would have to recognize any gain (i.e., the proceeds less your investment or tax basis) in the year the sale took place. An alternative to this is for the buyer to make a down payment and pay the balance over a period of time (with interest on the unpaid balance). (For most real estate sales, installment treatment is automatic anytime you sell real estate and receive at least one payment after the end of the year in which you made a sale.) In these situations it would seem unfair to tax you on the entire proceeds in the year of sale. Not only would you not have received all the moneys due you, but the tax you would owe could actually exceed the down payment you receive.

The "installment sales" rules address this problem. If you make a sale and receive deferred payments you will generally have to report income only as you receive payments from the purchaser.

Example. An investor purchased real estate in 1980 for $100,000 and sells it at the end of 1988 for $450,000. The purchaser pays the investor (seller) $50,000 in cash at the closing. The balance is paid at the rate of $100,000 at the end of each year for four years with interest at prime plus 2%.

This transaction is automatically treated as an installment sale since at least one payment (actually four) will be made after the end of the tax year in which the sale occurs (i.e., after 1988). The installment sales treatment will apply to this sale unless the investor specifically elects not to have the installment sales rules apply. If you make this election you will have to recognize all the gain on the sale in the year the transaction occurs rather than as the payments are received.

When would you elect not to have the installment sales rules apply? You would make the election if you have expiring operating loss carryovers from past years (depending on the type of taxpayer you are, operating losses will expire if not used within a certain time period). Perhaps you're in a low-income bracket and would benefit from recognizing the gain in the current year. The interplay between the passive loss rules and the minimum tax may make it advantageous to take your gains now (see Chapters 9 and 11). You may have a large suspended passive loss which you could only recognize as the installment payments are received. If you elect out of the installment sales rules the entire passive loss could be recognized in the year of sale. The decision to elect not to have the installment sales rules apply can be very complicated and should generally be made with your tax advisor after projecting your tax situation under the various options available.

How Much of an Installment Payment Is Taxable?
When you receive payments, what portion of each payment is taxable? The basic rule is that the taxable portion is that which is equal to the same proportion that your gross profit on the entire transaction bears to the total price the buyer is to pay. This concept is best illustrated with a simple example.

Example. Let's expand on the example used previously. The investor sold the real estate for $450,000 and he paid $100,000 for it. Thus his taxable gain is $350,000 ($450,000 amount realized minus $100,000 investment or tax basis). The contract price is $450,000—this is the amount that the investor is to receive. What portion of each installment payment does the investor report as income?

$$\frac{\text{Gross profit}}{\text{Contract price}} = \frac{\$350,000}{\$450,000} = 77.78\%$$

Thus the investor will recognize the following amounts of income on each of the scheduled payments:

Year	Payment	Profit Percentage	Profit Recognized
1988	$ 50,000	77.78%	$ 38,888
1989	100,000	77.78	77,778
1990	100,000	77.78	77,778
1991	100,000	77.78	77,778
1992	100,000	77.78	77,778
	$450,000		$350,000

NOTE—If the purchaser were to assume a mortgage of the seller, the contract price for purposes of this calculation would be reduced by the amount of such mortgage. For example, say that in addition to the payments to be made the purchaser also assumed the $50,000 remaining mortgage outstanding on the selling investor's property. The contract price for purposes of the installment sales calculation would be:

Sales price	$450,000
Mortgage assumed	50,000
Contract price	$400,000

Now the portion of each payment which must be recognized as taxable is 87.50% ($350,000 gross profit as above divided by the new $400,000 contract price).

Interest on Unpaid Balance
A few comments need to be made about the interest charged on the unpaid balance of the installment payments. The tax laws require that a certain minimum interest rate be charged in many

transactions subject to the installment sales rules (and in many other financing situations). These rules can require that if the interest rate charged is too low, that interest can be imputed at the minimum required rate (and in certain situations at a higher rate). An example will illustrate this concept.

Example. Let's assume that a fair market interest rate at the time of the above transaction is 9%. The investor, however, only charged the purchaser interest at a 5% rate. Why would the investor charge less than the going market rate? A lower rate probably means one thing—the principal amount of the transaction (i.e., the $450,000 purchase price) is overstated. No investor would charge less than the going rate unless he got something for it—and that something is, according to the tax laws, an excessive purchase price (principal amount).

What the tax laws will then do is require that the investor and the purchaser impute interest at a minimum rate required by law, say 9% in our example. What will happen is that the investor will report a lower gain on the sale and will report higher annual interest income on the note (i.e., on the unpaid installment obligations) than what the purchaser is actually paying. Similarly, the purchaser would show a lower purchase price for the real estate than the $450,000 actually paid. Instead, he would report interest deductions greater than the amount he actually pays. The first step in analyzing this process is to calculate the actual payments the purchaser will have to make. The present value (worth in terms of today's dollars) of these payments must also be calculated:

End Year	Payment Balance*	Actual Rate	Interest Paid	Total** Actual Payment	Present Value at 9% Imputed
1988	$450,000	5%	—	$ 50,000	$ 50,000
1989	400,000	5	$20,000	120,000	110,088
1990	300,000	5	15,000	115,000	96,796
1991	300,000	5	10,000	110,000	84,942
1992	100,000	5	5,000	105,000	74,382
Totals			$50,000	$500,000	$416,208

*Payment balance is the amount of the installment notes outstanding for the year and thus the amount on which interest must be computed. Since the sale occurred on December 31, 1988, no interest is due in 1988. The payment balance is calculated by subtracting from the contract price the principal payments required by the contract—$50,000 at closing and $100,000 at the end of each of the next four years.

**Total payment is the sum of the principal payments required under the contract plus the interest payments at the 5% contract rate on the outstanding balance. The example assumes 5% simple interest with all payments made at the end of each year.

Let's take a closer look at what this chart shows to clarify the concept of the present value calculations and the imputed interest rules (the original issue discount rules). A number of simplifying assumptions were made which may differ slightly from what the law actually requires. For example, interest is calculated assuming that it is compounded once per year. All cash flows are assumed to occur on the last day of the year. The important thing is just to understand what the concept is. It's unlikely that you will ever have to calculate imputed interest. If you understand the concept you will review transactions with your accountant before closing any deal. The result will almost always be to use a sufficient interest rate in order to avoid imputed interest.

In the chart above the actual interest payments made under the note at the end of each year are calculated. These interest payments are added to the actual year-end principal payments required by the sales agreement. The net result is the total annual payment. Since the interest charged is insufficient (i.e., it is charged at only a 5% rate instead of the 9% market rate), the present value (i.e., the worth of each future payment at the date the sale took place—December 31, 1988) is less than the actual payments. Had the market interest rate actually been the 5% charged, the present value of each payment would have exactly equalled the principal amount required to be paid. These present values, however, are determined using the 9% market interest rate which is also assumed to be the minimum rate required by the tax laws.

The present value of each future payment is shown in the last column. The $50,000 down payment is not reduced since it is made at the date of the closing—December 31, 1988. No interest could therefore be due on it. The sum of all the present values of the payments is the imputed principal amount for the transaction. This is the amount that the tax laws will treat as the true sales price—$416,208. This is $33,792 less than the $450,000 sales price the investor and the purchaser agreed to in the contract. The reason for this difference is simple—the parties didn't charge enough interest. The investor agreed to give the purchaser a break on the interest rate because the purchaser agreed to pay more for the real estate than he otherwise would have.

Here's how the payment schedule looks when the true 9% market interest rate is charged on the true imputed principal amount (sales price).

End Year	Principal Balance	Imputed Interest Rate	Imputed Interest Payment	Principal Payment	Total Payment
1988	$416,208	9%	—	$ 50,000	$ 50,000
1989	$366,208	9	$32,959	87,041	120,000
1990	279,167	9	25,125	89,875	115,000
1991	189,292	9	17,036	92,964	110,000
1992	96,328	9	8,672	96,328	105,000
			$83,792	$416,208	$500,000

If the interest rate on installment obligations is less than the minimum rate required to be charged by the tax laws, then complicated imputation calculations similar to those illustrated above must be done. As was illustrated, this will have considerable effect on the amount of interest income the seller will have to report and on the interest expense the buyer may deduct. Also, since the imputed principal amount is less than the sales price the seller and buyer contemplated, each will be further affected. The seller will have a lower gain and hence will pay less tax. Although this is favorable, the additional interest the seller will have to report will eliminate any benefit. If the gain involved would have been a passive gain, it may have been available to offset passive losses the seller has from other activities. The interest income may be treated as portfolio income and may thus not be available to offset passive losses the seller has. Generally, the changes caused by the imputation of interest will cause havoc on the seller's tax planning (see the discussions of the passive loss rules in Chapter 9).

The buyer may get a bigger interest deduction. However, the tough new limitations on deducting investment interest or passive losses could prevent the buyer from getting any benefit from these interest payments. (See Chapters 2 and 9.) The offset to these higher interest deductions is that the buyer will have a lower investment (basis) in the property for purposes of depreciation (see Chapter 10). Thus his depreciation deductions will be reduced.

Pledging On and Borrowing Against Your Installment Notes
The investor in the above series of examples sold real estate for $50,000 down and took notes from the buyer for $400,000 (assuming that adequate interest was charged). The investor may have been willing to sell the real estate on the installment basis because he had no urgent need for the proceeds and was content to receive payments over four years with interest. The investor, however, may have been willing to take back the purchaser's notes because it was the only way to make the deal. In this latter situation the investor may really need cash now.

What can the investor do? It may be possible for the investor to sell the installment notes. But he may not want to do that because a sale would force him to recognize all the remaining gain for tax purposes. For example, if the investor sold the $400,000 in installment notes right after the sale for their face value of $400,000, he would have to recognize the remaining $311,112 of unreported profit. (The total profit on the sale transaction was $350,000. The investor had to report $38,888 in profit on the receipt of the $50,000 down payment (see the chart above showing the gross profit to be reported on each scheduled payment). The remaining profit would have to be reported on his sale of the installment note for its face value of $400,000.)

Is there an alternative? There was prior to tax reform. An approach used by many taxpayers to obtain cash without triggering the unreported gain was to pledge their installment notes (obligations) as collateral for loans. The investor in the above examples could have used the $400,000 notes as collateral for a

$350,000 loan from an unrelated financial institution. If the transaction were properly structured the investor could have obtained cash without triggering the gain on the installment notes since the borrowing would not have been treated as a sale of the notes.

What Did Tax Reform Do to Installment Sales?

Congress didn't like the result discussed above. As we discussed, most sales require that the sellers report any gain in the year the sale occurs. The installment method was allowed since it was felt unfair to tax a seller if the seller hadn't yet received the proceeds which would be needed to pay the tax. But if the taxpayer could readily pledge the installment notes for cash, he should have the money available to pay the tax. If loans are increased because of the availability of installment notes, then the original reason the investor was given the special benefit of the installment method is not valid because cash is available.

You would have expected Congress to say that, to the extent that you pledge installment notes as collateral for loans, you will be denied the special benefits of the installment method for the installment notes so pledged. This approach would leave the benefit of the installment method to those installment sales where you really don't generate the cash to pay the tax.

This approach is useful to keep in mind in trying to understand the objective Congress sought. Unfortunately that is all it is useful for since Congress took a far more complicated approach to achieving its objective since it recognized that it is difficult, if not impossible, to determine which installment sales transactions led to which borrowings.

The approach used by Congress attempts to deny the availability of the installment method to the extent of a pro rata share of the taxpayer's total borrowings. What portion of your total borrowings (liabilities) relate to the installment obligations you are holding? The new "proportionate disallowance rule" will determine the answer for you. The general thrust of this rule will be illustrated next since this is the key change which tax reform made to the installment sales rules. Following this general explanation, the more detailed rules, exceptions, and other changes to installment sales will be highlighted.

The Proportionate Disallowance Rule—How Much Benefit Will You Get From the Installment Method?

We explained in the prior section that to the extent that you use installment notes to support borrowings Congress will deem you to have sufficient cash that the tax deferred under the installment method should be paid. Since it's often impossible to determine which assets were pledged to support which liabilities, average figures are used. Thus the ratio of your installment debt (called "Applicable Installment Obligations" or AIO) to your total assets (technically, the face amount of all installment obligations and the adjusted basis of all other assets of the taxpayer) multiplied by your average borrowings will provide a rough approximation of how much of your borrowings are attributable to the installment sale notes you hold. This amount will be treated as a deemed payment on your installment notes (called "Applicable Installment Indebtedness" or AII).

$$\frac{\text{Installment notes}}{\text{Total assets}} \times \frac{\text{Average}}{\text{borrowings}} = \begin{array}{l}\text{Deemed} \\ \text{payment on} \\ \text{installment} \\ \text{obligations} \\ \text{(AII)}\end{array}$$

What if you didn't increase your borrowings at all since the date you sold assets on the installment method? Clearly, in this situation it would seem unfair to impute receipts on your installment notes based on borrowings which you didn't make. Unfortunately, this is not the rule. A portion of your prior borrowings will still be attributed to your recent installment sales.

The next question is: What measure is used to determine your borrowings? The general rule is that your average liabilities, determined on a quarterly basis (called average quarterly indebtedness), will be used as the measure of your borrowings for purposes of the above calculation.

Apparently the concept behind the approach chosen by Congress is that if money is truly fungible, and lenders will look to a creditor's total assets (balance sheet) and not just one specific asset, only the broad stroke averaging approach could prove administratively enforceable. A more specific approach would create endless problems of who borrowed what using what assets as collateral.

A series of simplified examples can be used to illustrate the concept and calculations involved. A number of details have intentionally been left out of the following examples in order to illustrate the new installment sales rules without forcing you to wade through confusing and unnecessary details.

Example. A partnership has the following assets and liabilities as of January 1:

BALANCE SHEET JANUARY 1

Building 1	$ 50	Mortgage	$175
Building 2	200	Equity	75
	$250		$250

The partnership sells building 1 on the afternoon of January 1 for its value of $60. The partnership thus recognizes a $10 gain and its equity increases by a like amount. On the sale the partnership receives $10 in cash and a $50 installment note. Its balance sheet now looks like this:

BALANCE SHEET JANUARY 1 (AFTER SALE)

Cash	$ 10	Mortgage	$175
Installment obligation	50		
Building 2	200	Equity	85
	$260		$260

Later the same day the partnership went to its bank and obtained a $30 loan using the installment obligation as collateral. Its balance sheet will now look like this:

BALANCE SHEET JANUARY 1 (AFTER LOAN)

Cash	$ 40	New loan	$ 30
Installment obligation	50	Mortgage	175
Building 2	200	Equity	85
	$290		$290

This last balance sheet demonstrates the abuse which Congress was addressing. Clearly the partnership should have adequate funds available after this last transaction to pay some or all of the tax due on the installment sale it made.

Let's take a look at the partnership's year-end balance sheet. Then we will be in a position to calculate the amount of the deemed payment of its installment obligation (AII). Assume that the partnership's only other transaction for the year was to use $20 of its cash to pay $15 of the principal on its mortgage on building 2 and to make a $5 distribution to its partners. Its balance sheet will look like this:

BALANCE SHEET DECEMBER 31

Cash	$ 20	New loan	$ 30
Installment obligation	50	Mortgage	160
Building 2	200	Equity	80
	$270		$270

Now let's calculate the amount of the deemed payment the partnership will be treated as receiving during the year on its $50 installment obligation (remember actual payments on the installment obligation by the purchaser of building 1 are zero). Let's assume for the situation in question that liabilities can be calculated on an annual basis. The calculation is as follows:

$$\left[\frac{\text{Installment obligation or AIO} = \$50}{\text{AIO} + \text{other assets} = \$50 + (\$20 + \$200)} \right]$$

$$\times \left[\frac{\text{Average debt} = \$175 + (\$30 + \$160)}{2} \right]$$

$$= \left[\text{Imputed payment or AII} = \$34 \right]$$

Thus, even though no payments were received on the installment obligation, and even though the installment obligation was pledged for only $30, the partnership will be taxed as if it had received a payment of $34 on the installment obligation during the year.

What portion of this deemed receipt, or AII, is taxable? Presumably the same rules applicable under prior law will be used. Thus, the gross profit percentage must be calculated. For the installment note in question this should be 83.33% ($50 profit/ $60 contract price). Thus, $28.33 of the deferred profit on the installment sale must be recognized (83.33% gross profit × $34 imputed or deemed payment, i.e., the AII).

What if building 2 was actually worth $250 and the additional $30 in debt was taken out as a second mortgage on building 2 instead of as a loan based on the pledge of the installment note? No change. Although it may seem unfair, that appears to be the rule.

Let's try one more example to show how arbitrary the new rules appear to be. It's possible that future regulations explaining these rules may change this result, but for now the following appears to be what the new rules will do. Assume that the partnership didn't take on any additional debt during the year. The only transaction, other than the sale of building 1 for $10 in cash and a $50 installment note, was the depreciation of building 2. Say that the regular depreciation on building 2 for the year was $20. Building 2 will now be shown on the partnership's balance sheet at $180. ($200 original investment or tax basis less $20 depreciation).

BALANCE SHEET (DEPRECIATION ONLY)

Cash	$ 10	Mortgage	$175
Installment obligation	50		
Building 2	180	Equity	65
	$240		$240

Based on the above data, the deemed payment of the installment obligation will be $36, calculated as follows:

$$\left[\frac{\text{Installment obligation, or AIO} = \$50}{\text{AIO} + \text{other assets} = \$240} \right]$$

$$\times \left[\frac{\text{Average borrowings} = (\$175 + \$175)}{2} \right]$$

$$= \left[\text{Deemed payment or AII of } \$36 \right]$$

The consequences of this scenario are rather surprising! The partnership had no cash transactions other than the initial sale. Merely as a result of depreciation deductions (and the previously existing mortgage on building 2) it was forced to recognize deemed payments on its installment obligation. This situation could present the partnership with a difficult dilemma. Its partners may have to report gain under the new rules even though there is insufficient cash available to pay the tax. The tax the partners will have to pay if they all owed tax at the maximum 33% marginal tax rate which will exist for certain individual income levels (after 1988) will be almost $12, or approximately 20% more than the cash the partnership has available for distribution.

With this general explanation of the new installment sales rules, the details of the actual rules can be reviewed to complete our discussion.

Highlights of the Detailed Changes to the Installment Sales Rules

The new law provides a number of additional details which are important to understanding the changes. The calculation of the deemed payment on installment debt (AII) is calculated as follows:

☐STEP 1. Determine the face amount of the AIO outstanding at the end of the year. An AIO is generally any installment obligation arising from a sale after August 16, 1986, for noninventory property (i.e., real or personal property not held for sale in the ordinary course of the seller's business). For inventory assets, the new rules will apply to installment obligations arising from sales after February 28, 1986. Real estate used in your trade or business (e.g., a warehouse if you're in the storage or moving business) or held for the production of rental income is only subject to this rule if the selling price exceeds $150,000.

☐STEP 2. Divide the AIO determined in Step 1 by the sum of all installment obligations (i.e., AIO and non-AIO installment obligations) plus the adjusted basis of all other assets. This should be the total tax basis for all your assets (the assets on a balance sheet prepared according to tax rules). In making the calculation the law permits you to calculate depreciation using the 40-year life for real estate provided for under the alternative depreciation system. The advantage of this approach can be seen by reviewing the results of the earlier example which demonstrated the effect of depreciation on the amount of deemed installment payments you must recognize. If a lower depreciation had been used in that example, then a lower deemed payment would have resulted. The general rule is that depreciation can be calculated for purposes of these computations using the periods applicable to determining the earnings and profits (the tax equivalent of retained earnings). For nonresidential real estate the period is 40 years instead of 31.5 years. (See the discussions of the alternative tax system in Chapter 10.)

☐STEP 3. Determine your average indebtedness. This should include all indebtedness, including accounts payable and accrued expenses, bank loans, mortgages, and so forth. This calculation is generally made on a quarterly basis. For taxpayers who do not have any installment obligations from the sale of inventory property (which will include many passive investors), this calculation can be made on an annual basis (as was done in all of our earlier examples).

☐STEP 3. Multiply the result obtained from Steps 1 and 2 by the average debt determined in Step 3. This result is, generally, the amount of AII—that is, the imputed or deemed payment for the year on your installment obligations.

☐STEP 5. Subtract from Step 4 any AII that is attributable to AIO arising in previous years that are outstanding at the end of the current year. The purpose of this last step is to prevent you from being taxed twice on the same item. You are not required to recognize gain attributable to AIO arising in a prior year to the extent that any actual payments on those obligations do not exceed the deemed payments (AII) you have already reported on those obligations.

Planning Tip. The only way you can assure yourself of not being taxed twice on the same payments on one installment obligation (whether actual payments or deemed payments) is to maintain separate records for each installment note you own. Your accountant must record the actual payments on each such note as well as the portion of each deemed payment allocable to each such note.

What happens if you receive payments on an installment obligation which are greater than the deemed or imputed AII payments? These amounts are treated according to the regular installment sales rules described earlier in this chapter.

Special Rules and Exceptions

A few special rules and exceptions are important to the real estate investor. First, these rules do not apply to personal use property (such as your personal residence). Certain farm property is also excluded.

Sales of certain timeshares and unimproved land will not be subject to the proportionate disallowance rule if the purchaser's obligation to repay the installment notes is not guaranteed or insured by a third person. In addition, neither the seller nor any of its affiliates may develop the land. There is, however, a cost associated with this special treatment. The seller must pay interest on the deferred tax liability.

Taxpayers who sell property on a revolving credit plan will not be permitted to account for such sales using the installment method. This change will affect retailers.

Sales of publicly traded property, such as shares in a real estate investment trust (REIT) traded on a national stock exchange, cannot be reported on the installment method.

If property subject to the passive loss limitation rules (see Chapter 9) is sold and accounted for on the installment sale method, the unused (suspended) passive losses, if allowed, will be recognized in each year in the ratio of the profit recognized in that year to the total profit to be recognized on the transaction. To trigger recognition of the entire loss in the year of sale you must elect not to have the installment sales rules apply.

Finally, a major change is the prohibition of the use of the installment method altogether for purposes of the alternative minimum tax (AMT). This rule will apply to all taxpayers who are subject to the proportionate disallowance rule discussed above—dealer sales of inventory property (e.g., sales of residential lots by a subdivider) and sales of real estate used in a trade or business or held for rental where the purchase price exceeds $150,000.

Planning Tip. If you're subject to the alternative minimum tax, as many taxpayers will be, you may receive no benefit from selling real estate on the installment method. Make sure you negotiate the sale so that you receive enough money in the year of the sale to pay any tax due. See Chapter 11 for a discussion of the alternative minimum tax.

Conclusion—Installment Sales Method

Tax reform has greatly reduced the benefit of the installment sales method of accounting for the proceeds from selling a real estate investment. Investors are advised to review proposed sales terms with their tax advisers before consummating any sale. Improper planning could result in a tax liability in excess of the cash received in the year of the sale. Also, the new passive loss rules should be considered.

CHAPTER SUMMARY

Tax reform has generally made it more expensive to sell real estate investments. This additional tax cost must be factored into any analysis of a prospective real estate investment. The result will be a lower valuation of real estate investments. The actual value of any property, as discussed throughout this book, is a result of the interplay of numerous factors such as demographic trends, economic growth, interest rates, labor costs, and tax rates.

Part Two

INVESTING IN RESIDENTIAL REAL ESTATE

6 RESIDENTIAL REAL ESTATE INVESTMENTS

GENERAL EFFECTS OF TAX REFORM

Residential real estate, other than one's principal residence, has long been a popular investment vehicle, whether a garden apartment complex, a low-income housing project, or a vacation home. Tax reform has hurt the tax benefits of residential real estate investments just as it has all real estate. However, a few special exceptions were allowed for certain residential real estate investments. Because of the interest in these investments and the many special rules applicable to them, this chapter addresses in one place the tax factors relevant to residential real estate investments, some of which are discussed in other chapters in more general terms.

One of the first questions asked about rental real estate is what is going to happen to rents. There is no simple answer since the results will vary by geographic region and are dependent on numerous factors other than taxes. A few observations, however, may be helpful.

The general proposition that rents will increase since the tax cost to landlords has increased is too simplistic. Absent rent control, most landlords are already charging the maximum the market will tolerate for their residential rental units. It is unlikely that in the short-term tax reform alone will enable landlords to raise rents to any significant degree. In areas with rent controls in place, landlords should be requesting reviews of the rents they are allowed to charge. If the rent control board considers the costs and rate of return to a landlord in setting the rents he may charge, then tax reform may justify a rent increase.

Over a longer period of time the changes made by tax reform could in fact result in rent increases. Tax reform has significantly increased the cost of construction (see Chapter 3). This increase should continue to slow the pace of construction in some markets. With fewer projects coming on the market, existing surplus units should be absorbed and rents may then increase. This trend, however, is a long-term trend, and many changes—to the tax laws, the economy, and so forth—could occur before it can take effect.

For many middle and lower income taxpayers, tax reform has reduced or eliminated the tax benefits of homeownership (see Chapter 7). This may accentuate the trend toward apartment and other types of rental living accommodations. Also, in many parts of the country inflation of home values has slowed. These effects could encourage some homeowners to opt for apartment and other rental living accommodations. This could be particularly true of many elderly homeowners who have maintained their homes for tax and investment reasons past the time they would prefer an apartment for personal comfort. On the other hand, for many higher income homeowners, the ability to deduct interest expense paid on home equity loans will represent a significant tax advantage over renting. The extent to which such a trend will benefit the residential investment market is speculative at best. But if some movement were to occur, some senior citizen communities could benefit.

NEW TAX CREDIT FOR LOW-INCOME RENTAL HOUSING

Tax reform has replaced the old tax incentives for encouraging low-income housing with an entirely new, and potentially valuable, incentive system based on a two-tier tax credit. For investors contemplating any investment in low-income housing, an understanding of this new credit incentive system is essential. CAUTION—Before making any commitments based on an anticipated low-income housing credit, carefully review the many limitations and restrictions discussed in this chapter with your tax advisor. In many instances the credit will not be available, or if available, will not be worth the bother.

Rate for New Credit

The new low-income housing credit is a two-tier credit with different percentages for different types of qualifying expenditures: (1) for new construction and rehabilitation expenditures put into use (placed in service) in 1987, the credit is available at a 9% rate; (2) for the cost of acquiring an existing building in 1987, or new or existing construction which is financed with federal subsidies (generally, financed with a loan with tax-exempt interest) the credit is available at a 4% rate. Each credit is available at the rate indicated on an annual basis for 10 years. For example, $100,000 of qualifying expenditures could generate a $9,000 (or $4,000) credit every year for 10 years, or $90,000 in total can be received. Before being overwhelmed by this credit consider that on a present value basis (i.e., in terms of current dollars) the credit will be worth much less. Also, only a portion of your actual expenditures may qualify. Finally, as noted previously, consider the numerous requirements you must meet to qualify. If the low-income housing units are occupied after the beginning of the year, these credits are prorated for the first year. This will result in a small credit in the eleventh year.

After 1987 the general structure of the credits will remain the same. However, the rates for both the 9% and 4% credits will be revised on a monthly basis by the IRS to reflect changes in market interest rates.

Requirements for Qualifying for the Credit

A number of requirements must be met to qualify for the low-income housing credit. The following discussion will summarize the main points of each of these many requirements:

1. A minimum portion of the building must be set aside for low-income families (the "set-aside" requirement). There are two alternative means of meeting this test. The owner must irrevocably choose which of the two tests will be used. The first test requires that 20% or more of the residential units in the project be occupied by individuals or families with incomes no greater than one-half that of the median income level for the area. The second test requires that 40% or more of the rental units be occupied by individuals or families with incomes no more than 60% of the median income for the area.

The income tests are redetermined on a continuing basis, both as to the tenant's income level and the income level for the area.

However, a tenant will not be disqualified solely for certain minimum changes in income. Also, if an even stricter set-aside requirement is met, greater increases in a tenant's income level will be tolerated without disqualifying a tenant.

2. The units must be suitable for, and used for, occupancy on a nontransient basis.

3. The gross rents paid by low-income families can't exceed 30% of the qualifying income level for that family. The cost of utilities (except telephone) paid for by the tenant must be included in the rental figure for this test.

4. Certain reporting requirements must be met. The taxpayer must certify to the IRS that the project has continuously complied with the various requirements.

5. The building must meet the various requirements to qualify for the low-income housing credit for 15 years (the compliance period). If the requirements are not met during the compliance period then a portion of the credit will have to be given back by increasing the taxpayer's tax liability (recaptured). If any noncompliance with the low-income housing credit rules is corrected within a reasonable period of time, the credit may not have to be recaptured. A change in ownership can trigger recapture of the credit unless certain steps are taken.

Recapture of the Credit

When the credit must be recaptured, no credit can be claimed in that year. The accelerated portion of the credit must be added back to taxable income. Interest will also be charged on these amounts. The accelerated portion of the credit is based on the structure of the credit. As noted earlier, the credit is generally claimed ratably over the first 10 years after the building is built or purchased. The compliance (test) period for which the building must meet the low-income housing requirements is 15 years. Thus the excess of the credit actually claimed, over what the credit would have been had it been claimed over a 15-year period, is the accelerated portion which must be recaptured.

Limitations on Credit on a State-by-State Basis

The low-income housing credit is limited on a state-by-state basis. The maximum credits which can be awarded in any state are based on the population of the state multiplied by $1.25. Low-income housing projects financed with tax-exempt private activity bonds are not counted toward this limit (see Figure 6.1 and Chapter 2). This is because these bonds are themselves subject to strict limitations.

A building must receive an allocation of the state's allowable credits (credit authority) for the first year in which the low-income housing credit is claimed. Low-income housing credits can't be claimed in excess of the amount of credit authority allocated to the building, even if the calculations of the credit shown in Figure 6.1 would result in a larger credit. This limitation could force a developer to become even more involved in local political matters than would otherwise be necessary. The costs and time of dealing with a government bureaucracy should be evaluated before undertaking a project qualifying for the credit.

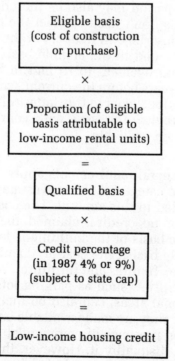

Figure 6.1 Low-income housing credit formula

Calculating the Credit

The general approach for calculating the credit is illustrated in Figure 6.1. Each of the components illustrated will be explained in the sections that follow.

Eligible Basis. Determining the eligible basis is the first step in determining the amount of expenditures which qualify for the credit. The eligible basis consists of three components:

1. The cost of eligible new construction.

2. The cost of rehabilitation expenditures. To be included, rehabilitation expenditures must at least equal an average of $2,000 per low-income housing unit. Rehabilitation expenditures incurred during a two-year period from the date the rehabilitation is begun can be included.

3. The cost of acquiring an existing building. The cost of any rehabilitation expenditures incurred before the end of the first year of the credit period may also be included. These rehabilitation expenditures don't need to meet the minimum expenditure requirement described in item 2. For the costs of an existing building to be included in the eligible basis, the building (and any substantial improvement to it) had to have been put into use more than 10 years before the current acquisition. A number of technical exceptions exist to this latter rule. If you don't meet the requirement, review the issue with your tax advisor—there may be an exception available.

A number of general requirements apply to the eligible costs in the above three categories. The investment (tax basis) of the building is included in this amount. The cost of the land is not. If the rehabilitation tax credit is claimed, the required reduction in the depreciable basis of the building is factored into the calculation of eligible basis. The cost of amenities, including personal property (i.e., fixtures and furniture), can be included. The cost of tenant facilities, such as parking lots, swimming pools, or other recreational areas, can also be included if no separate fee is charged and they are made available on a comparable basis to all tenants. The presence of commercial tenants or uses in a building will not disqualify it. However, the cost of these nonresidential facilities must be excluded from the calculation of the eligible basis. No portion of any federal grant can be included in the eligible basis.

What happens if an addition is made to a low-income housing building? A scaled-down credit, based on two-thirds of the regular amount will be allowed. These additional credits will be available annually for the remaining years in the 15-year testing period (see section entitled "Limitations on the Use of the Credit," below).

Determining the Proportion of the Eligible Basis Which Qualifies. The next step in the process is to determine the percentage of the eligible basis which can be included in the amount (qualifying basis) on which the low-income housing credit is calculated. This is done by multiplying the eligible basis, the lower of the following two ratios:

$$\frac{\text{Number of low-income units}}{\text{Total number of residential units}}$$

or

$$\frac{\text{Floor space of low-income units}}{\text{Total floor space of residential units}}$$

In calculating the two proportions, low-income units can only include those units actually occupied by low-income tenants. The figure for total units, however, includes all units, whether or not occupied.

Limitations on the Use of the Credit

If all the requirements are met, and the appropriate credit authority is obtained from the state (or appropriate government unit), a number of additional restrictions or limitations may still apply to limit the current availability of the credit. First, the credit is subject to an at-risk rule, which generally acts to limit the amount of credit which a taxpayer can claim to an amount based on the money and property for which the taxpayer is economically at risk in the investment (see Chapter 2). Generally, nonrecourse financing (debt for which the creditor can't proceed against the borrower's personal assets) is not included in the amount at risk. However, exceptions are made for financing (including seller financing)—up to 60% of the investment (tax basis) in the property—for loans obtained from certain charitable or social welfare organizations whose purpose is to foster low-income housing.

Investors must also contend with the new passive loss rules (see Chapter 9). These rules generally limit the amount of loss, or credit, generated by a passive activity (such as real estate rental) to offsetting income only from other passive activities. Thus if the taxpayer has no other passive income, then the credits would not be available until additional passive income was earned in later years. An exception is specifically provided for the low-income housing credit. This exception allows a taxpayer to use about $7,000 in low-income housing credits to offset income (passive or otherwise). This allowance, however, is phased out at income (adjusted gross income) levels from $200,000 to $250,000.

If these two hurdles are cleared, one final limitation remains. The low-income housing tax credit available can't be used to offset more than the first $25,000 of tax liability, plus 75% of any tax liability in excess of $25,000. Any credit remaining after this limitation can be carried back for up to three years and then carried forward for the next 15 tax years until it is used up.

Conclusion
The new low-income housing credit appears to be a valuable tax benefit. However, before undertaking such a project, be certain that the many limitations which exist—from the need for state credit authority to the numerous limitations applied at the individual taxpayer level—don't minimize or eliminate the planned-for benefit. Don't get caught incurring legal, accounting, and overhead costs greater than the credit available.

SPECIAL EXEMPTION FOR CERTAIN LOW-INCOME HOUSING FROM THE NEW PASSIVE LOSS RULES

To avoid unfairly penalizing those who invested in low-income housing before tax reform, a special transition rule has been provided to exempt temporarily certain investments made in low-income housing projects from the passive loss rules. As noted earlier, losses from passive investments generally can't be used to offset income from other than passive sources. To enable investors to benefit from certain losses produced by their pretax reform investments in low-income housing projects, the losses generated will not be treated as passive losses. This will provide significant flexibility in deducting these losses. This special relief will be available for a maximum of about seven years. A number of strict requirements must be met to qualify. The project will generally have to have been put into use, or subject to a binding contract, by August 16, 1986. The initial investment in the project had to be made after 1983, and the individual investor must be obligated to make at least half his total cash investment after 1986.

Planning Tip. If you invested in a low-income housing project in the past few years, bring this to the attention of the accountant preparing your tax return so that you can review the availability of this special rule.

DEPRECIATION

Residential rental property is generally depreciated on a ratable basis (straight-line method) over a 27.5-year period. Residential rental property is property for which 80% or more of the rental income is from dwelling units (see Chapter 10). If the owner is subject to the alternative minimum tax, then the residential real estate must be depreciated over a 40-year period for purposes of the minimum tax (see Chapter 11). Similarly, if the property is financed with tax-exempt bonds it must be depreciated over a 40-year period (see Chapter 2).

TAX-EXEMPT FINANCING

A number of provisions are made in the tax-exempt bond financing rules which specifically benefit low-income and other housing (see Chapter 2). For example, one of the uses for private activity tax-exempt bonds which will preserve the bond issue's tax-exempt status, is financing qualified residential rental projects. These are generally multifamily residential rental properties for moderate- and low-income families. The definition of the income categories which the project must meet is the same as that for the low-income housing credit. In addition, the mortgage revenue bond and mortgage credit certificate provisions are geared to financing targeted residential housing. Finally, qualified redevelopment bonds can be available to residential housing in designated blighted areas (see Chapter 2).

VACATION HOME

Many investors own a second residential property, or vacation home—one of the most common forms of real estate investment. As an investment, a vacation home can provide capital appreciation, cash flow, and tax benefits. The tax benefits have been substantial. They have included the ability to deduct operating and carrying costs, often creating a deductible tax loss. This tax loss was often essential since the cash flow generated was often largely dependent on the tax benefits. Finally, when the vacation home was sold, a portion of the proceeds were often taxed at favorable capital gains rates. Tax reform may affect all of these benefits.

Tax reform has significantly reduced the depreciation benefits available from real estate investments. For a vacation home put into use (placed in service) after 1986, depreciation will generally have to be calculated using the straight-line (ratable) method over a 27.5-year life (see Chapter 10).

The ability to use the tax losses from a vacation property held as an investment (i.e., not for significant personal use as a residence) has been limited or eliminated for many taxpayers by the new passive loss rules (see Chapter 9). There are, however, a few very important exceptions. Taxpayers who are actively involved in the management of their vacation homes (they approve rental terms, hire maintenance contractors, etc.) may qualify to deduct up to $25,000 in tax losses from vacation home rentals against other income. Although this $25,000 allowance is phased out when income exceeds $100,000, this exception will permit the vast majority of Americans to continue reaping tax benefits of vacation home ownership. This exception will help make vacation homes one of the best remaining "tax shelters" for most Americans. This situation will help counter to some extent the rest of the tax news for vacation homes, which is generally unfavorable.

The second benefit is that one vacation home, if certain requirements are met, will qualify for the favorable interest deduction rules available for home mortgages (see below and Chapter 7). To the extent that this special treatment isn't available, interest deductions could be severely limited or eliminated entirely. Tax reform will eliminate the deduction for personal interest expense, such as for a second home, after a five-year phaseout. Interest on a vacation home which is allocable to the period for which you use it personally (or for which you rent it to a relative at a bargain rate) will be subject to this limitation. Thus only a portion of this interest will be deductible, and this interest deduction will be eliminated entirely by 1991 (see Chapter 8).

The favorable tax benefits available on the sale of a vacation home have generally been eliminated. The capital gains benefits have generally been repealed, and tough limitations have been put on the use of the installment method of accounting (see Chapter 5). These changes will negatively impact the price of vacation home property.

Tax rates have been lowered significantly (see Chapter 8). This is both good and bad for vacation home investors. The good news is that any cash flow from a vacation home can be invested at a higher after-tax rate of return since the tax bite will be lower. The bad news is that the tax benefits of a vacation home will be worth much less. The worst news is that many vacation home investments may not show much cash flow once the tax benefits have been reduced or eliminated.

Finally, what will tax reform do to the value of vacation homes? Most likely the effects have already been felt. To the extent that many wealthy investors have lost their tax incentives, values and prices may have softened. The fact that vacation homes did receive a number of favorable benefits in the Tax Reform Act of 1986 should serve to limit this decline. For example, the property taxes on a vacation home should continue to be deductible. Special provisions were made for mortgage interest as well (see below, and Chapter 7). Importantly, don't overlook the fact that tax benefits are only one factor. Low interest rates, for example, make vacation homes much more affordable and can lead to price increases, or at least stabilize the decreases due to tax reform.

In addition to these general tax reform changes which will also affect vacation home ownership, a few changes were made specifically to affect the tax consequences of owning a vacation home. To explain these changes, an overview of the tax rules affecting vacation homes is necessary.

A number of factors must be considered in determining the tax treatment of a vacation home. If the vacation property is rented for fewer than 15 days then, primarily as a matter of IRS convenience, the rental income need not be reported for tax purposes, and the rental expenses cannot be deducted.

A critical consideration in evaluating the tax benefits available from a vacation home is the number of days of personal use. If the house is used personally by its owner for more than 14 days (or, if greater, 10% of the number of days the property is rented) then it is characterized as a personal residence. For example, an investor vacations at his cottage for 20 days in the year and rents it out at a fair price for 210 days. Although his personal use is greater than 14 days, it doesn't exceed 21 days (10% of the rental days) so the cottage is not considered a residence. This treatment as a residence has two effects. First, any interest expense incurred to carry the property, and allocable to its personal use, may qualify for the special treatment afforded home mortgage interest on a first and second home (see Chapter 7). This special treatment will permit deductions for interest on a mortgage (up to the purchase price plus improvements) on a second residence. Without this special treatment, the mortgage interest on a vacation home, which is allocable to the days the vacation home is used personally by the investor, would be treated as consumer interest, which may not be deductible (see above and Chapter 8). The mortgage interest which relates to the rental use of the home could be deductible. (CAUTION—If the vacation home fails the 14-day, 10% use, test, and is therefore not treated as a personal residence, all deductions, including interest, will be subject to the new passive loss rules.)

Example. An investor has a vacation home which he uses for two months during the year for personal vacations. Assume that this home is not a qualified second residence. He rents the vacation home at a fair rental price for six months during the year. He pays $15,500 in interest on the vacation property's mortgage for the year. His mortgage interest can be allocated to the rental use as follows:

Rental use: 6 months/12 months × $15,500 = $7,750

The $7,750 in interest expense not allocated to the rental use will be subject to the limitations on deducting personal interest expense.

Planning Tip. The IRS has advocated allocating interest to the rental use based on a ratio of the number of months rented to the total number of months used: 6 months rented/8 months total use × $15,500 = $11,625. The courts have suggested that interest and property taxes are incurred ratably throughout the year and should therefore be allocated using a denominator of the number of days in the year, rather than the number of days the property was rented (or used personally). Although the allocation advocated by the IRS could have reduced the overall tax benefits under prior law, it may actually be beneficial after tax reform because of the phaseout of the deduction for personal interest expense. Review the matter with your tax advisor to determine the best approach for you. In either case, however, tax reform will have limited the deductions for interest paid on a vacation property which doesn't qualify as a second home.

If the property in the above example were the investor's qualified second residence, then the $7,750 in interest allocable to his personal use could be deductible in full (see Chapter 7).

The second tax consequence to the number of personal days which the home is used is its effect on the deductions allowable from renting the property. If the days the property is personally used exceed 14 days (or if greater, 10% of the number of days the property is rented), then the deductions will be limited. The limitation generally works as follows: The deductions which can be claimed for the property can't exceed the income from the property reduced by the mortgage interest and property tax expenses allocable to the rental of the property.

Example. Assume the same facts as in the prior example. The investor rents the property at $2,200 per month. Property taxes are $1,400 per year. Using the same method to allocate property taxes as was used to allocate mortgage interest, $700 in property taxes would be allocable to the rental use of the home. Thus other deductions (depreciation, utilities, management fees, etc.) for the rental home would be limited to the following amount:

Rental income ($2,200/month × 6 months)	=	$13,200
Mortgage interest		7,750
Property taxes		700
Limit on other deductions		$ 4,750

Once this limit is determined, any expenses in excess of the $4,750 will not be allowed in the current tax year. Tax reform now permits any excess losses to be carried forward and used in later tax years. (In the past the unused deductions would have been lost forever.) For example, if the other deductions allocable to the rental use of the vacation property were $6,500, only $4,750 could be used. The remaining $1,750 can be used in later years.

If the investor doesn't use the vacation property as a personal residence (i.e., he doesn't use it more than 14 days or more than 10% of the rental days, if greater) then these limitations won't apply. A vacation property used fewer than 14 days or less than 10% of the rental days isn't considered a personal residence. Instead it is treated as a business or investment property (assuming it's rented at least the minimum 15 days). As a business or investment property, the passive loss rules will apply to it (see Chapter 9). If the passive loss rules apply, losses from the rental property can only be used to offset income from other passive investments (income from rental real estate projects, limited partnership interests, etc.). A very important exception to this rule allows certain active investors (i.e. those who approve rental terms, hire maintenance contractors, etc.) to deduct up to $25,000 of losses against any type of income (see Chapter 9).

Planning Tip. To the extent your investment goals and personal preferences permit, determine the optimal days of personal use and rental use with your tax advisor. Then carefully monitor your use and rental of the property to be certain you use it for only the targeted number of days. For example, if your income is less than $100,000 and you qualify for the special exception permitting you to use up to $25,000 of passive losses to offset any type of income, it may be advantageous to restrict your personal use to fewer than 14 days (or 10% of the rental days if greater). If this is done you could benefit from all the deductions on the property. If the property will not be qualified as a residence also evaluate your involvement with the management of the property to be sure that you meet the active participation test required for the $25,000 exclusion from the passive losses.

Conclusion

Tax reform has reduced the tax benefits available to owners of rental vacation homes. However, the many special rules available for vacation homes make it one of the most favored real estate investments from a tax perspective. If investors monitor the number of days they personally use the vacation home, the extent of their involvement in maintaining the property, their passive losses (or incomes), mortgage interest, and other tax characteristics, the tax benefits of vacation home ownership can be significant.

CHAPTER SUMMARY

Tax reform has had a wide ranging impact on the tax consequences of investing in residential real estate. New depreciation rules, new interest limitations, a new tax credit, and other changes all tend to make the planning process far more complicated than under prior law. It is difficult to draw general conclusions as to the effect of these varied changes on the value of residential real estate investments. The best course is to analyze each specific deal in light of the new rules with your tax advisor and to plan accordingly.

7 YOUR HOME AS AN INVESTMENT

GENERAL EFFECTS OF TAX REFORM

Tax reform has reduced the benefits of owning a home. Millions of homeowners will no longer obtain any tax benefit for their home mortgage interest and property tax deductions. Millions of other homeowners will get benefits, but these benefits will be worth far less than in the past. Finally, for some homeowners, although the tax benefits of homeownership will be less than before, homeownership will become one of the best tax-advantaged investments they can make. To understand these apparently contradictory effects of tax reform, the changes affecting home ownership must be analyzed.

Reduction in Marginal Tax Rates

Tax reform's most basic change was the dramatic reduction in the marginal tax rates individuals will pay, from 50 to 28% when the new rules are phased in (see Chapter 8). This change will considerably reduce the tax subsidy provided for so many years to homeowners. Where a deduction of $4,000 in property taxes and mortgage interest would have provided a $2,000 tax benefit before ($4,000 deduction × 50% tax rate), it will now only provide a $1,120 benefit ($4,000 deduction × 28% tax rate). The Senate Conference Committee report to the tax reform bill estimated that about 80% of all Americans will not be taxed at this 28% rate. Rather, they will be taxed at the lower 15% tax rate. Thus, for most homeowners, a $4,000 additional tax deduction for mortgage interest and property taxes will only provide a benefit of $600! This change in tax rates will significantly increase the out-of-pocket cost of homeownership. The basic presumption that homeownership is generally preferable to renting will no longer be true in many situations.

Changes in Itemized Deductions
The changes made to itemized deductions will have a similar effect. Once the new tax rules are fully effective, a standard deduction (similar to the zero bracket amount under prior law) will increase to $5,000. Thus until you exceed $5,000 in itemized deductions, which will generally only include state and local income and property taxes and mortgage interest, you won't get any additional tax benefit from homeownership. When this is combined with the reduction in tax rates, the tax benefits of homeownership become insignificant for many taxpayers. A taxpayer with a total of $9,000 in itemized deductions will only get an incremental tax benefit of $600 (($9,000 deductions − $5,000 standard deduction which would be available in any case) × 15%). See Chapter 8 for a more detailed discussion of these new rules and some planning tips.

Planning Tip. When buying a home, carefully consider the tax benefits which will actually be available. Don't count on tax benefits to meet a significant part of your anticipated expenses unless you're really sure you'll get them.

Despite these significant limitations, many higher income taxpayers will find that their home is their best real estate tax shelter. This is because of the many restrictions on the tax benefits from almost every other real estate investment. The passive loss rules, for example, may prevent investors from using losses from a real estate investment to offset their other income. The deduction for real estate taxes and home mortgage interest (subject to limitations discussed in the following section) will be one of the only real estate tax deductions available to freely offset other income. Higher income taxpayers are likely to exceed the standard deduction amount discussed above and will benefit from the itemized deductions available from home ownership. Even though the maximum federal tax rate will be 28%, when combined with state and local income taxes the marginal tax rate is significant. Thus many homeowners will be in a tax bracket exceeding 30 to 35%. Although this is less than under prior law, the tax benefit of deducting mortgage interest and property taxes will be substantial for taxpayers with large itemized deductions.

Will the reduced tax benefits from homeownership affect home sales? In some cases the reduced tax benefits may discourage a taxpayer from buying a home, or may encourage a current homeowner to sell. However, homeownership depends on much more than tax benefits. There is a tremendous social and cultural bias toward homeownership—it's the American way. Tax reform probably won't change this. Also, the most important dollar figure to most prospective homeowners isn't the dollar value of any tax benefits but the monthly mortgage payment. If the payment can be made, homeownership will be considered. If it can't be made then homeownership will not be viable. Interest rates can play a much greater role in this decision than income taxes. Finally, the ability of a homeowner to deduct interest expense paid for home equity loans used for a wide variety of purposes (discussed below) represents a significant advantage for the homeowner as compared to the apartment renter who can't deduct such interest expense.

Changes in Capital Gains and Installment Sales Rules

Tax reform also has a significant impact on the tax results of selling a home. The capital gains and installment sales rules, which had previously provided very favorable treatment for the proceeds from selling a home, have been changed significantly. However, the exceptions permitting the tax-free rollover of the gain on one personal residence into another, as well as the special provision for elderly taxpayers selling their homes, have been retained (see Chapter 5).

DEDUCTING INTEREST PAID ON A HOME MORTGAGE

Tax reform has placed important limitations on the ability to deduct interest on a home mortgage. These "limitations," however, offer tremendous advantage over renters who can only deduct the interest expense they incur on certain portfolio and passive investments. The reason for these limitations will help in understanding the new rules. Congress eliminated the deduction for consumer interest, such as car loans (see Chapter 8). To prevent taxpayers from merely using a home equity loan to pay for consumer purchases, and thereby convert nondeductible consumer interest into deductible mortgage interest, limitations were needed on the deductibility of home mortgage interest.

However, Congress didn't want to impair taxpayers' abilities to deduct actual home mortgage interest.

The solution to these two objectives was to permit the deduction of interest on a home mortgage up to the original purchase price of the home and the cost of home improvements. The original purchase price of the home is not reduced by gains on prior home sales which were rolled over on a tax-free basis into the current home (see Chapter 5). Additional amounts, but not more than the fair value of the home, can be borrowed for education and medical expenses with the interest remaining deductible. To qualify, the residence must be used to secure the debt.

Example. A homeowner purchased a home for $100,000. Two years later an additional bedroom was added at a cost of $15,000. The maximum amount of financing on which interest can be deducted is $115,000. If $120,000 was borrowed, the interest on the additional $5,000 loan ($120,000 borrowed − $115,000 permitted) would not be deductible as home mortgage interest. The interest on this additional $5,000 loan will be treated as personal (consumer) interest. This personal interest expense will only be deductible to the extent allowed by the phaseout of the deduction for consumer interest (see Chapter 8). If, however, the additional $5,000 was used to meet medical or educational costs, the interest would be deductible.

Planning Tip. Money is fungible. How can you prove to the IRS that the money borrowed on a home equity loan was used to pay for you child's education when you also purchased a new car in the same year? You could deposit all home equity loan proceeds into a separate checking account. All home improvement costs and medical and educational expenses should be paid out of that account. Avoid using the funds in that account to pay for other types of expenses which wouldn't qualify. CAUTION—Before setting up another checking account find out about any additional fees and charges you may be assessed.

These rules raise a number of problems. What if you can't determine what you paid for your home? Taxpayers rarely save tax data for more than a few years (if at all). Check with your accountant. If you sold a home recently, even if the gain was rolled over into another residence, your accountant had to have completed a tax form showing the transaction (Form 2119). This form, and the accountant's papers and notes supporting it, could contain the information you need. In some instances you can get copies of old tax returns from the IRS. Another source would be the contract for the purchase of your home. This could be in a safe deposit box, or at your attorney's office.

Taxpayers must also keep records of home improvements which they make. The best approach is to set up a file and to save copies of all receipts and cancelled checks relating to home improvements.

What expenditures are home improvements which qualify to increase the amount you can borrow? Home improvements should include all expenditures which add to the value of your home and will last for a long period of time (see the definition of "capital expenditure" in Chapter 3 for more detail). The following items may be included:

Insulation	Boiler or furnace
Hot water heater	Certain shrubbery
Alarm system	Replacement windows
Attic fan	Outdoor patio or deck
Swimming pool	Siding
New roof	Built-in appliances
Built-in cabinets	New cement walk

What Mortgage Loans Are Subject to These Rules?

All home mortgage loans after August 16, 1986, will be subject to these rules. Home mortgages which were outstanding at that date will not be affected unless they exceed the fair value of the home at that date. In addition, the mortgage interest on one additional residence, a vacation (second) home, will qualify for the home mortgage interest deduction. Generally, to qualify as a second home the other residence will have to be occupied by the taxpayer for 14 days during the year (or, if greater, 10% of the days the vacation home was rented). This minimum-use test is waived if the vacation home was idle all year (see Chapter 6). If an investor owns more than one vacation home he can designate which vacation home will qualify for this benefit.

Planning Tip. Homeowners who can take out additional home mortgages or equity loans within the above parameters should consider doing so and using the proceeds to pay off their consumer debt (car loans, etc.). The interest on the home equity loan could be deductible whereas the consumer interest may not be deductible. Watch the fees for setting up a home equity line of credit or getting a second mortgage—they could exceed any tax benefit available. If you own more than one vacation home it may be advantageous to consolidate the mortgages onto one property.

Minimum Tax Rules for Home Mortgages Differ
Many taxpayers will be subject to the new alternative minimum tax rules (see Chapter 11). The minimum tax rules for determining the deduction allowed for interest on a home mortgage differ from the rules for the regular tax system described above. Interest on a home mortgage will only be deductible for the minimum tax if the loan is used to pay for acquiring, constructing, or substantially rehabilitating the residence. Loan proceeds spent on medical and educational benefits are not allowed for purposes of the minimum tax. In addition, if a home mortgage is refinanced, only the amount up to the remaining principal balance on the original loan refinanced can qualify for purposes of the minimum tax deduction.

Example. A homeowner purchased his home for $150,000. The home is now worth $320,000. His current mortgage balance is $120,000. He refinances this mortgage with a new mortgage for $155,000. The $150,000 of the mortgage is qualified for purposes of the interest deduction for his regular tax computation. If the additional $5,000 ($155,000 refinanced loan − $150,000 original purchase price on the home) is used to pay for medical and educational expenses, the interest on it will also be deductible. For the minimum tax, however, only interest on $120,000 of the new mortgage will qualify for interest deductions, unless the additional $30,000 ($155,000 new loan − ($5,000 for medical + $120,000 original loan balance)) is used to improve the home. The $5,000 spent on medical and educational expenses will not qualify for the minimum tax.

NEW RULES FOR HOME OFFICE EXPENSES

Many homeowners maintain offices in their homes, for doing work for their regular job or for a second, often moonlighting, endeavor. The tax laws have restricted the deductions allowed for a home office since the opportunities to abuse the tax benefits are significant. Tax reform has added even more limitations. An overview of the general rules for home office deductions will highlight the changes.

To claim a deduction for a home office the office must be used exclusively (i.e., the den where the children watch television while you work won't qualify) and on a regular basis for: (1) actually meeting clients, customers, and patients (not merely through phone calls); or (2) as the principal place of business (a taxpayer can have more than one business for purposes of this test; thus an employee can moonlight and claim a home office deduction for his moonlighting business, so long as the other tests are met). Also, for an employee to claim home office deductions the home office must be maintained for the convenience of his employer. A separate structure used in connection with the taxpayer's business which is not attached to the home can also qualify.

Tax reform allows deductions (depreciation, insurance, utilities, etc.) for a home office only to the extent of the net income from the business conducted out of the home office determined without these deductions.

Example. An employee moonlighted in a separate business as a writer. He earned $5,600 in fees for the year. His expenses were: depreciation on his home office—$2,100; insurance on the home office—$123; stationery—$500; office supplies and postage—$1,830; and subscriptions and dues—$1,225. The deductions for depreciation and insurance can only be claimed up to the net income of the business determined without these items:

Fees		$5,600
Expenses other than home office		
Stationery	$ 500	
Office supplies and postage	1,830	
Subscriptions and dues	1,225	
Subtotal		3,555
Net income before home office deductions		$2,045

His deductions for depreciation and insurance are limited to $2,045. Since his home office expenses can't be used to create a tax loss to offset against other income, only $2,045 of his home office expenses can be deducted. This leaves $178 in unused deductions ($2,100 depreciation + $123 insurance) − $2,045 allowed. Tax reform permits this unused deduction to be carried over and used against income in later years.

If an employee claims deductions for home office expenses these expenses are deductible as a miscellaneous itemized deduction. This means that they will be subject to the same limitation imposed on all miscellaneous itemized deductions. That is, a deduction will only be allowed to the extent that total miscellaneous itemized deductions exceed 2% of the taxpayer's income (see Chapter 8). This restriction will entirely eliminate home office deductions for many employees.

Planning Tip. Employees who lose these home office deductions because of these limitations should bring this result to the attention of their employers. Some adjustment may be equitable.

Tax reform also closed what had become a popular loophole in the home office deduction limitations. Under prior law, if an employee couldn't meet the requirements to qualify for a home office deduction, the employer rented the home office from the employee. Depreciation and other deductions from this rental provided a tax loss. Now, however, employees and independent contractors can't claim a home office deduction if the employer leases a portion of their home.

COOPERATIVE HOUSING

A few minor changes were made to the treatment of cooperative housing corporations and their tenant/shareholders. To understand the changes, an overview of the tax treatment of cooperative housing corporations and their tenant/shareholders will be provided. The changes made by tax reform will be highlighted in the discussion.

A cooperative is a building owned by a cooperative corporation. The shareholders of the corporation, in addition to their stock interests in the corporation, obtain a right (often through a proprietary lease) to live in one of the apartments (or homes) in the building (complex). Under prior law, to qualify as a tenant/shareholder of a cooperative housing corporation, the shareholder had to be an individual who paid the full price for his stock and as a result was entitled to live in the building. Tax reform relaxed this shareholder requirement so that now corporations, trusts, estates, and partnerships may also qualify as tenant/shareholders. This change will give much needed flexibility to the ownership of cooperatives. For example, it will make it much easier for corporations to own an apartment to house their traveling executives in cities where the cooperative form of ownership is popular.

A corporation must also meet a number of requirements to qualify as a cooperative housing corporation. Generally, there must only be one class of stock. Each shareholder must be entitled to occupy an apartment or house owned by the corporation as a result of his owning stock in the corporation. Distributions which the corporation can make to shareholders must be limited. Finally, the corporation must derive at least 80% of its income from its tenant/shareholders.

If the tenant/shareholder and corporation requirements are met then the tenant/shareholders can claim deductions for their share of real estate taxes and mortgage interest paid by the corporation. This rule attempts to give homeowners who happen to own their residence in the cooperative form deductions similar to those available to homeowners who own their homes outright. The interest deductions available to tenant/shareholders in a cooperative will generally be treated as home mortgage interest deductions subject to the limitations described earlier in this chapter. Tax reform also requires the cooperative housing corporation to report the interest and tax amounts to both its shareholders and the IRS.

Tax reform provides additional flexibility to the cooperative corporation in determining the allocation of interest and taxes to each tenant/shareholder. Under prior law each shareholder was allocated a proportionate amount of the interest and property taxes of the corporation as his shares of stock bore to the total shares of stock.

Example. A tenant/shareholder (homeowner) owns 100 shares of stock in a cooperative housing corporation, which gives him the rights to a penthouse apartment. The cooperative has a total of 10 apartments and 1,000 shares of stock outstanding. The cooperative pays $400,000 in interest and $350,000 in taxes. The shareholder would be allocated 100/1,000 of each of these amounts which he could then deduct on his personal tax return. Thus he would claim $40,000 in home mortgage interest and $35,000 in property taxes.

Tax reform permits the cooperative corporation to allocate its interest and property taxes to each tenant/shareholder in a manner which reasonably reflects the costs to the corporation of that tenant/shareholder's apartment. Thus, if the penthouse apartment was assessed by the local property assessor at a value that was one-fifth the value of the total building, instead of the one-tenth value his relative share ownership indicates, this larger one-fifth ratio could be used to allocate interest and taxes.

Tax reform also acted to limit an abuse in this area. Now, if a tenant/shareholder pays interest to the corporation which should be added to the cooperative corporation's capital account, the tenant shareholder can't claim a deduction for this amount. Instead the amount paid which can't be deducted will be added to that tenant/shareholder's investment in the stock (tax basis).

A tenant/shareholder of a cooperative corporation can depreciate his apartment in a manner similar to a homeowner depreciating his house as a home office (i.e., depreciation can be claimed when the cooperative apartment or house is used in a trade or business or for the production of income). A tenant/shareholder's deductions for depreciation can't exceed his investment (the tax basis) in the apartment. Now, however, depreciation deductions in excess of the tenant/shareholder's tax basis can be carried forward and used in later years when his tax basis is increased.

CHAPTER SUMMARY

Tax reform has reduced many of the tax benefits associated with home ownership. However, the remaining tax benefits are still significant.

A number of special rules have been provided for home mortgage interest, home offices, and cooperative housing corperations. Homeowners should exercise caution in reviewing their tax situation with their tax advisor because of the complexity of some of these changes.

Part Three

Tax Planning for Real Estate Investments

8 GENERAL TAX PLANNING

Although the focus of this book is the impact of tax reform on your real estate investments, it is important to understand the general changes which tax reform made to individual taxation. These changes will affect the bottom line of any deal you're involved with. This chapter will provide an overview of the individual tax changes which should be of the most interest to real estate investors and which haven't been discussed elsewhere. The simplified illustration of the INDIVIDUAL TAX CALCULATION in Figure 8.1 *on the following page* will be helpful in understanding the RELATIONSHIP of the topics discussed.

NEW TAX RATE STRUCTURE

Tax reform dramatically changed the tax rate structure. The most significant change has been the dramatic compression of tax rates from the multitude of rates existing under prior law to, after 1987, two tax brackets—15 and 28%. The rates in effect for 1987 and 1988 are illustrated in Table 8.1. Following are the four categories of tax filers for which separate rate structures are provided; the categories are the same as under prior law:

1. *Married Filing Joint Tax Returns.* Some states have community property laws which treat income earned by a husband and wife as belonging one-half to each. This would enable couples residing in these states to divide income between them and report one-half of it on separate tax returns thus taxing income at lower rates (e.g., all at the new 15% rate, whereas had the income been reported on a single return it would have been pushed into the 28% rate bracket). The married-filing-joint tax

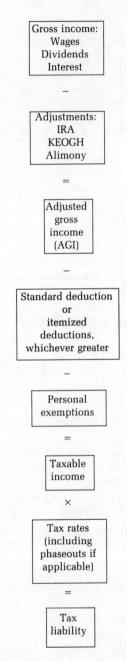

Figure 8.1 Simplified overview of individual tax calculation

Table 8.1. New Tax Rates

1987
Taxable Income Brackets

Tax Rate	Married Filing Joint Returns	Married Filing Separate Returns	Heads of Household	Single Individuals
11%	0–$3,000	0–$1,500	0–$2,500	0–$1,800
15	$3,001–28,000	$1,501–14,000	$2,501–23,000	$1,801–16,800
28	28,001–45,000	14,001–22,500	23,001–38,000	16,801–27,000
35	45,001–90,000	22,501–45,000	38,001–80,000	27,001–54,000
38.5	Over $90,000	Over $45,000	Over $80,000	Over $54,000

1988 and Later Years
Taxable Income Brackets

Tax Rate	Married Filing Joint Returns	Married Filing Separate Returns	Heads of Household	Single Individuals
15%	0–29,750	0–$14,875	0–$23,900	0–$17,850
28	Over $29,750	Over $14,875	Over $23,900	Over $17,850

is designed to alleviate this potential inequity for states without community property laws.

Surviving spouses may also use the more favorable joint return rates for a period of two tax years. A surviving spouse is any taxpayer whose spouse died in the preceding two years, who maintains a home for a dependent child and has not remarried.

2. *Married Filing Separate Tax Returns.* Married individuals who do not want to file one joint tax return can file separate returns. The rates assessed are less favorable. This filing approach has been used by couples involved in negotiating a divorce, and other special situations.

3. *Head of Household Status.* An individual who maintains a household for certain relatives or dependents (such as a child) can qualify for rates which are more favorable than those granted to single individuals. This benefit is provided because Congress believed that these individuals incur additional expenses by having to maintain a household for a child or other qualified person.

4. *Single Individuals.* For those taxpayers who don't fit into any of the above categories the single taxpayer rate structure must be used.

The rate structure is somewhat more complicated than it appears in Table 8.1 due to the phaseout of certain benefits after 1987. At certain income levels (which vary depending on the tax filing status involved) the benefits which were obtained by having income taxed at the lower 15% rate is gradually eliminated. Similarly, the benefits of the personal exemptions (see below) will also be gradually eliminated once income reaches certain levels. The result of these two phaseouts is that during some income range taxpayers will be taxed at a higher 33% marginal tax bracket as these two benefits are eliminated. During this range, however, all income, on average, will never be taxed at a rate greater than 28%. Once these phaseouts have been completed, all income, on average and at the margin (i.e., the effective tax rate on each additional dollar of income earned), will be taxed at a flat 28% rate.

One important point of these changes in the rate structure is the effect of compression of the tax rates on tax planning. Before tax reform tax rates ranged from 11 to 50%—a 39 percentage point spread. After 1987, when the new rates are effective, the spread between the lowest and highest tax rates will only be 13 percentage points (28% − 15%). In the past it had been advantageous to shift deductions to taxpayers in higher brackets and shift income to taxpayers in lower tax brackets. This whole planning approach has become far less valuable since the achievable difference in rates is far less.

Income averaging was a particularly advantageous technique for calculating income in years when a taxpayer had an unusually large increase in income. For example, if a real estate investor collected rents from properties for many years and sold a number of his properties in one year, he would have realized substantial income in that year. This could have pushed him into much higher tax brackets. The income averaging method of calculating his tax averaged this income "bump" over a number of years to reduce its impact. Since tax rates are relatively flat, and also much lower than under prior law, Congress didn't see the importance of retaining this benefit. If Congress raises rates in the future without restoring the benefit of income averaging, this could again become a problem for real estate investors.

PERSONAL EXEMPTION

Tax reform has increased the personal exemption amounts as follows:

Year	Exemption Amount
1987	$1,900
1988	$1,950
1989 and later	$2,000

These personal exemption amounts are gradually phased out once income reaches a certain level.

STANDARD DEDUCTION

The old zero bracket amount has been modified and renamed the standard deduction. For taxpayers who do not itemize their deductions, this new standard deduction is subtracted from adjusted gross income (AGI) in arriving at the taxable income on which your tax will be based (see Figure 8.1). If your itemized deductions don't exceed the new standard deduction amounts then you won't itemize. The standard deduction amounts vary by filing status and are as follows:

Filing status	1987 Amount	1988 Amount
Married filing jointly	$3,760	$5,000
Married filing separately	$1,880	$2,500
Head of household	$2,540	$4,400
Single	$2,540	$3,000

Taxpayers aged 65 and older as well as blind taxpayers will be entitled to additional standard deduction amounts which will vary depending on their marital status.

This much larger standard deduction has a significant impact on many taxpayers. The Senate Finance Committee Report anticipated that fully one-third of the taxpayers who itemized deductions before tax reform would no longer do so. This means millions of taxpayers will no longer get any benefit for home mortgage interest, property taxes, and so forth.

Planning Tip. For many taxpayers the only way to get any benefit from their out-of-pocket costs for state and local taxes, mortgage interest, business expenses, and so forth will be to "bunch" their deductions. Bunching will also be valuable to taxpayers who itemized every year in order to get the most benefit out of medical expenses and miscellaneous itemized deductions (certain investment expenses, business periodicals, etc.) because these expenses must exceed certain floor amounts to be deductible.

Example. Here's how bunching works. Starting in 1988 a married couple filing a joint tax return won't get any benefits from itemized deductions unless their deductions exceed $5,000. Let's say the couple just falls short in every year with only about $4,500 in itemized deductions. They will use the standard deduction every year. There may be a better approach. If the couple can push some of their 1987 deductions into 1988, and in 1988 accelerate some of their 1989 deductions ahead into 1988, they may qualify to itemize in 1988. They won't be adversely affected in 1987 and 1989 because they will still get the same $5,000 standard deduction in any event. Figure 8.2 illustrates how this planning technique looks.

If the couple can defer $1,000 of their deductions from 1988 into 1989 and accelerate $1,000 of 1990 deductions into 1989,

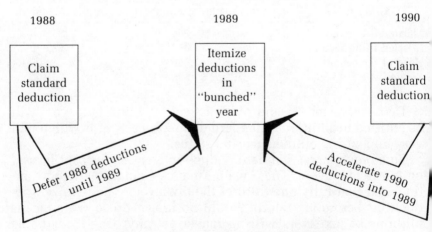

Figure 8.2 "Bunching" itemized deductions

they will have increased their 1989 itemized deductions from $4,500, for which they received no benefit, to $6,500 ($4,500 + $1,000 + $1,000), for which they will receive a benefit. Assuming the couple is taxed at the 28% rate and is not subject to the minimum tax (see Chapter 11), this will provide them with a $420 benefit (($6,500 total deductions − $5,000 standard deduction they would have been entitled to in any case) × 28%).

What kind of deductions can be deferred or accelerated? It really depends on what types of expenditures you incur and how they must be paid. For example, a common planning approach under prior law was to prepay any estimated state tax payment due in January before the end of December of the prior year in order to get the deduction on your earlier year's tax return. Under tax reform the best approach may be to defer your 1988 state tax payments to 1989. Then in 1989 you would prepay your state taxes as you probably did under prior law. The result will bunch extra state tax payments into the middle year. You may be able to plan many of your miscellaneous itemized deductions in a similar way. For example, tax return preparation fees, investment and business publications, and so forth may, within limits, be prepaid, and in some cases deferred.

For the miscellaneous itemized deductions, as will be explained in the next section, no deduction is allowed until these expenses exceed a certain percentage of your adjusted gross income. Thus bunching deductions into one year may be the only way to push your miscellaneous deductions over this hurdle amount.

ITEMIZED DEDUCTIONS GENERALLY

Tax reform made a number of changes to itemized deductions, some of which have been discussed previously in connection with the review of the new standard deduction. Tax reform repealed the deduction for state and local sales taxes. Medical expenses must now exceed 7.5% of AGI to be deductible. This change will eliminate the medical expense deduction for many of the taxpayers who were able to claim it. Miscellaneous itemized deductions (financial consulting fees, tax attorney fees, tax return preparation fees, safe deposit box rentals, union dues, employee home office deductions, job hunting expenses, investment and business publications, unreimbursed employee travel expenses, etc.) will now only be deductible to the extent that they exceed 2% of your AGI (see Figure 8.1).

Planning Tip. One planning approach is to use the bunching technique described above. If you are an employee, consider reviewing the matter with your employer. It will be advantageous to convince your employer that having lost the ability to deduct many expenses, the employer should reimburse you for them. Employers who are concerned that employees continue reading certain publications, and so forth, may be willing to bear some additional costs.

If you run a small business on the side, your expenses incurred in connection with that business are deductible in full (on Schedule C of Form 1040). Carefully review all the expenses incurred in connection with your side business, and all the amounts which you have been deducting as miscellaneous itemized deductions, with your tax advisor. It may be possible that some of the expenses you had been treating as itemized deductions should more properly be treated as deductions relating to your side business. Expenses which you can reclassify like this will continue to be deductible in full without regard to the new 2% floor rule. The sections that follow will address some of the other changes affecting itemized deductions.

Business Meals and Entertainment Expenses. New restrictions have been placed on the ability to deduct business meals and entertainment expenses. Only 80% of the amount which would otherwise be deductible (i.e., after application of various other restrictions) can be deducted. Even meals incurred as an employee on an out-of-town business trip are subject to this cutback. Meals are also now subject to the same business purpose test which applied to entertainment expenses under prior law. Therefore, a bona fide business discussion must occur during, directly before, or directly after the meal. The discussion must relate directly to the conduct of your business. Tickets to entertainment events (sports, etc.) can only be deducted up to 80% of their face value. Thus premiums paid to obtain choice tickets will not be deductible.

Casualty Losses Must Be Claimed for Insurance To Be Deductible

In the past, taxpayers sometimes didn't submit an insurance claim for certain casualty losses in order to forgo an increase in their insurance premiums. Since a portion of the loss was often deductible for tax purposes, the cost of avoiding an increase in insurance rates was reduced. Tax reform prohibits the deduction of any casualty loss on personal use property (i.e., property not used in a trade or business) unless a timely insurance claim was filed for the damage. Although this rule was probably directed at reducing tax deductions for unreported automobile insurance claims, it can be important to homeowners and owners of vacation homes as well.

New Limitations on Interest Deductions

New limitations will greatly restrict the ability of taxpayers to deduct interest expense as an itemized deduction. Starting in 1987 the deduction for consumer-type interest will be phased out. The percentage of interest disallowed in each year is as follows:

Tax Year	Interest Disallowed
1987	35%
1988	60
1989	80
1990	90
After 1990	100

Interest subject to this tough new rule is consumer interest such as interest on an automobile loan and on credit card balances where the payments were for personal expenses. The following types of interest expense are not subject to this limitation. They may, however, be subject to other limitations described in the chapters indicated:

Investment interest (Chapters 2 and 11)

Home mortgage interest (Chapters 7 and 11)

Interest in connection with a passive activity (Chapter 9)

Trade or business interest (Chapter 9)

Planning Tip. To avoid the restrictions on consumer interest deductions, consider paying off consumer interest loans and taking out a home equity loan. The interest on a home equity loan may be deductible even if the loan proceeds are used to purchase consumer goods, such as a car. (For a discussion of the rules and limitations applicable to home mortgage interest deductions see Chapters 7 and 11.) Also, since consumer-type interest is not deductible for purposes of the minimum tax (i.e., there is no phase-in period as there is for the regular tax), plan carefully to avoid the minimum tax during the phase-out period of the regular tax consumer interest if you have significant amounts of consumer interest which cannot be converted into deductible home mortgage interest (see Chapter 11).

FAMILY TAX PLANNING OPPORTUNITIES CURTAILED

Tax reform has significantly curtailed the planning opportunities many taxpayers had pursued as a family unit. One common strategy was to transfer assets to children. The children would be taxed (if at all) on the income at their low tax rates (as low as 11%). This would compare very favorably with the result the parent would often have achieved by retaining the income and being taxed at the parent's much higher (up to 50%) tax rate.

Tax reform has limited the benefits of this type of planning significantly. First, as discussed earlier, the tax rate schedule has been compressed. Now the marginal savings by shifting income may only be the 13% difference between the new 15 and 28% rate brackets. Also, if significant income is involved, the child will quickly be pushed into the same maximum 28% tax bracket the parent is subject to.

The second charge is potentially more costly. For a child under the age of 14 all unearned income (interest, dividends, etc.) in excess of $1,000 will be taxed at the parent's highest marginal tax rate.

Example. A grandmother is living on social security and municipal bond income and pays no tax. The grandmother gives her grandson, your child, $10,000 as a birthday present. The grandchild can be taxed at the parents' highest tax rate on the earnings on the $10,000. It doesn't matter that the grandparent who gave the gift pays no tax. This rule can be particularly costly in 1987 when the highest tax rate is 38.5%.

Planning Tip. A number of steps can be taken in response to these changes. First, the child can invest in growth stocks which pay no dividends. When the child reaches age 14 the stocks can be sold and income-producing investments can be made. (Once the child reaches age 14 the above rule won't apply.) United States government Series EE bonds may be a good investment since the interest doesn't have to be reported currently. Consider giving the child stock in a family controlled company. If no dividends are paid no tax will be due. When the child reaches age 14 the stock can be repurchased at what will probably be a much higher rate due to the growth in the company during that time period. Any gain will then be taxed to the child at his or her rate at that time.

Tax reform also eliminated another very popular family tax planning device—one often used by real estate investors— namely, Clifford trusts. A Clifford trust involved the transfer, usually by a parent, of assets to a trust for the benefit of another person, often a child. The trust would exist for more than 10 years (usually 10 years and 1 month — to meet tax law requirements). During this time period the income earned on the trust would be paid and taxed to the child, presumably at the child's lower tax rate. At the end of this period the trust would terminate and the assets would revert to the parent. This approach had been used frequently with real estate.

Example. A doctor invested in a building where his medical practice would be located. When his depreciation deductions ran out he transferred the building to a Clifford trust and then rented it from the trust for use in his medical practice. If properly structured the doctor could have obtained deductions for rent paid to the trust and the rent collected would have been taxed at the child's low tax rate.

Tax reform has eliminated the use of Clifford trusts. For trusts set up after March 1, 1986, all their income will be taxed to the parent setting up the trust (i.e., the "grantor").

With all these restrictions, does it still pay to pay attention to family tax planning? Definitely.

Planning Tip. The gift and estate tax make family planning important to consider for many taxpayers even if there is only minimal income tax benefit. The tax assessed on estates and gifts has not been lowered by tax reform—it is still a very high 50%. Thus even if there is no income tax benefit to transferring assets to a child, there may be a substantial long-term savings by avoiding the gift and estate tax. Also, for purposes of the gift tax, a $10,000 per-year gift can be made, for example, a transfer from a parent to a child, with no gift tax consequences. If both parents join in making such a gift then $20,000 can be transferred each year with no gift tax consequences. If you could face a substantial estate tax, it may be very advisable to take advantage of this annual tax-free transfer of up to $20,000. Thus, with or without tax reform, gift and estate tax planning should receive careful attention and should be reviewed periodically with your estate planner and insurance agent.

Planning Tip—Don't Forget State Taxes. State and local taxes could present some tricky problems in light of tax reform. Many tax planners plan only (or primarily) for federal taxes, assuming that the state tax matters will be simultaneously planned for. This approach could be very costly after tax reform. The results will depend on how your state's tax system is tied into the federal tax laws and how quickly your state will modify its system to reflect federal tax reform. For example, some states assess a tax that is basically a percentage of your federal tax liability. If you pay tax in one of these states, your state tax bill, unless the state government acts, will probably decline (or increase) in approximately the same manner as your federal tax bill. Other states use a modified version of the federal tax base (i.e., income less certain deductions) and then assess a tax on this amount. Since most taxpayers will see their tax base increase after tax reform (due to passive loss limitations, IRA restrictions, longer depreciation periods, etc.) their state tax bill could increase dramatically unless the state modifies its tax rate. Finally, depending on the fiscal situation of each state, the responses could differ dramatically. Although many states have announced their intention to conform their tax systems to reflect tax reform, other states may not act so quickly. If a state has budget problems, it may be tempted to delay changing its tax system, or if it does change the tax system, it may not completely offset the tax reform changes. Some states follow federal tax laws and some don't.

Will the state lower rates? When? How much? Carefully review these matters with your tax advisor—don't get caught with an unexpectedly large state tax bill.

CHAPTER SUMMARY

This chapter has provided a cursory review of general tax planning after tax reform. It should be clear, however, that tax planning for the real estate investor is still a complicated, but potentially valuable, activity to engage in. Given the many complexities and interrelationships with tax rules covered in other chapters (such as the passive loss rules, etc.), planning should be done with a broad scope and on a regular basis with your tax advisor.

9 PASSIVE LOSS LIMITATION RULES MAY LIMIT YOUR WRITE-OFFS

INTRODUCTION

The passive loss limitation rules are perhaps the most complicated and controversial of the many changes enacted as part of the Tax Reform Act of 1986. Because of this complexity this chapter is organized differently than the other chapters in this book. There will be some intentional repetition of key concepts at different points to make it easier to read each section without having to refer to other parts of this chapter. This introductory section is designed to give you a working understanding of the passive loss rules.

If your income is less than $150,000, look at the section later in this chapter dealing with real estate losses which can bypass these passive loss rules (see "Bridge 2—Losses from certain real estate activities treated as from active business"). If you invest in low-income housing or rehabilitating old or historic buildings and your income is less than $250,000, also look at the section discussing a special exception for these activities (see "Bridge 3—Certain credits on real estate investments can offset active income"). The rest of the chapter will expand on these concepts noting planning ideas and uncertainties which you should follow up with your tax advisor about. A few general statements can be made about the complicated new passive loss rules:

1. New regulations, court cases, revenue rulings, and professional commentaries will be necessary to fully understand and properly plan for these complex new rules. Although many

changes made by the Tax Reform Act of 1986 rely on existing tax concepts (e.g., depreciation periods have changed but the methods of calculating the new depreciation deductions are not new), the new passive loss rules include many new terms and concepts to which no existing body of law will necessarily be applicable. What does this mean? It means you should exercise a great deal of caution in planning any transaction subject to these rules. When reviewing possible results of various investment or development activities with your tax advisor, consider a number of hypothetical scenarios using different possible interpretations of the law. Throughout the discussions that follow a number of the possible interpretations of the new rules will be pointed out. Some may provide valuable money-saving tax tips. However, some may not prove to be the correct interpretations of the law once regulations and rulings are issued and cases are decided—so carefully review all planning with your advisor.

2. These new rules are critical to the real estate industry. Many investors and developers have made commitments based on the presumption that losses generated from their activities would provide a tax benefit. These assumptions may no longer be valid. As a result, the status of all existing investments and contracts should be reviewed with your tax advisor.

3. New commitments should be made only after the careful consideration of the impact of the new passive loss limitation rules. This is particularly true since the phase-in of these new limitations won't apply to investments made after the Tax Reform Act of 1986 becomes law. This means that all losses from passive activities will be subject to limitations (see below). The structure and nature of new real estate investments will change significantly in response to these new rules. We'll explore some of the possible changes in the discussions that follow.

4. The entire approach to tax planning—particularly for investors who had heavily sheltered other income with losses generated by passive real estate investments—will change. Planning will be much broader in scope. In the past a real estate tax shelter investment may have been planned in relative isolation of other tax matters (i.e., buying a tax shelter simply because tax losses are needed). Future planning will encompass much more. The investor's relationship and involvement with the investment will have to be considered. Other types of income available

to offset any losses will have to be carefully examined in light of the new passive loss limitation rules (as well as the other harsh investment rules discussed in this book). In the past the nature of a taxpayer's other income was not as critical.

5. The real estate industry will survive. In 1981 the maximum marginal tax rate was reduced from 70 to 50%—a full 20% reduction. The effect of this reduction was similar to the effect that the new passive loss rules will have, namely, the value of tax benefits on which investors and developers made commitments, and on which the real estate tax shelter industry was reliant, was reduced significantly. In spite of this, the industry adapted, survived, and prospered so much that Congress again saw the need to act. There is no reason to expect anything different now.

This chapter will attempt to provide some guidance in the important issues now facing the entire real estate industry. Many questions will also be raised which each taxpayer should review with his own tax advisor.

Since tax credits earned on passive activities are generally treated in a manner similar to losses from passive activities they are not discussed extensively. The concepts are the same and the implementation of the various nuances of the passive loss limitation tax credit rules can be left to your accountant.

Before attempting a detailed analysis of the passive loss rules, an overview of the provisions will be provided.

OVERVIEW—PASSIVE LOSS LIMITATION RULES

In reviewing the new passive loss limitation rules it will be helpful to look at the three broad categories of income. This is presented merely to illustrate the general concepts involved and should not be considered a complete portrayal of the new rules.

Bridge 1. Certain portfolio income earned by a passive activity (e.g., interest on a business' working capital balances) will have to be treated as portfolio income.

Bridge 2. Certain real estate activities in which the investor actively participates (not materially participates), can be used to offset any kind of income depending on the taxpayer's income level (i.e., will be treated as losses from an active business). There is a $25,000 limitation on the amount which can qualify

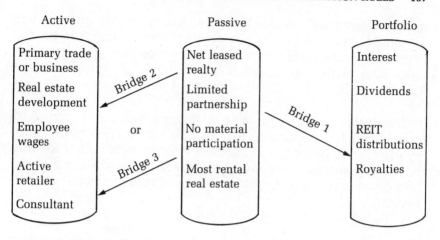

Figure 9.1 Three types of income for passive loss rules

for this special treatment. This $25,000 allowance is phased out at income levels from $100,000 to $150,000.

Bridge 3. The special tax credits (about $7,000 worth) available for low income housing and for rehabilitating certain old or historic buildings can be used to offset active business and portfolio income up to an equivalent of $25,000. It is not, however, necessary to participate actively to claim this benefit. This $25,000 allowance is phased out at income levels from $200,000 to $250,000. You can use only up to $25,000 under bridge 2 and 3, not $25,000 under each.

NOTE—The concepts illustrated will be discussed in detail in the pages that follow. This illustration will help provide a structure for these discussions.

As the three boxes in Figure 9.1 show, each income category contains different types of income. In addition, there are a limited number of crossover points or "bridges" between the various categories of income. These crossover points and income types will be discussed in detail in the following sections.

What the new rules attempt, in the broadest of terms, is to prevent (or at least to limit severely) the ability of taxpayers to use losses in the passive income category to offset income and gains in any other income category. A very simple example will illustrate. The nuances of personal exceptions and zero bracket amounts (or standard deductions as they are now called) haven't been dealt with in great detail in order to help highlight the key point—the impact of the passive loss limitations.

Example. An investor with a strong aversion to paying income taxes has purchased real estate shelters every year from a syndicator, in order to use the losses to shelter his other income. His other sources of income are salary from his job as a reporter and dividends and interest on a large inheritance which he has invested.

	Income
Salary	$135,000
Dividends	23,000
Interest	12,000
Real estate tax shelter losses	(167,000)
Taxable income before exemptions, and so forth	$ 3,000

After factoring in his personal exemption and the effects of the zero bracket amount (similar to the standard deduction), the investor would in fact owe no tax. What will the new passive loss limitation rules do to him?

In the simplest terms, the investor will have to treat his income as having fallen into three categories as follows:

	Active Income	Passive Income	Portfolio Income
Salary	$135,000		
Dividends			$23,000
Interest			12,000
Real estate tax Shelter losses		$(167,000)	
Totals	$135,000	$(167,000)	$35,000

He will generally not be allowed to use the losses from the passive category of income to offset the income and gains from the other categories. Thus, when these provisions are fully effective he will no longer be able to avoid paying taxes. (Some possible ways to plan around these rules, as well as the important exceptions provided by the new laws—the bridges—will be reviewed in the material that follows.) His positive income from salary and portfolio earnings will be taxed. Thus, ignoring exemptions and other refinements, he will have income of $170,000 ($135,000 active income and $35,000 portfolio income). He will owe a tax in 1988 of $47,600 ($170,000 × 28%), ignoring standard deductions and personal exemptions. This result is exactly what Congress sought to achieve in making the changes to investment taxation in the Tax Reform Act of 1986.

With this overview of the new passive loss limitation rules, let's attempt to brave some of the details, exceptions, transition rules, and other complexities.

What Happens To Losses You Can't Use?

What happens to the losses that the investor couldn't use? They are not lost forever. Rather, they are carried forward to future years (called "suspended losses") and used in one of two ways:

1. If the investor has income or gains in the passive income category in future years, and has an unused losses carried forward (losses incurred in prior years) he can apply those losses against the current income to obtain a tax savings. For example, his real estate tax shelters may have elected to use accelerated depreciation deductions (see Chapter 10). Accelerated depreciation deductions in early years are necessarily followed by smaller depreciation deductions in later years. When the depreciation deductions decline his real estate tax shelters may lose their shelter (i.e., "burnout"), which means they will generate taxable income. Under old law the deductions in early years would have been used to offset income from other sources. Under the new law they will be used to offset the income earned in later years by the same investment (or other passive investments).

Planning Tip. Before rushing out to buy real estate deals which are supposed to generate passive income to be offset by your otherwise unusable passive losses, review the status of your existing tax shelter investments with your tax advisor. If your existing shelters will burnout in the near future (they will begin generating taxable income instead of losses) reassess this strategy. Also, a broader approach will generally be needed. Rather than merely buying a real estate syndication which will generate passive income you may have to restructure your entire investment strategy. If you have significant passive losses it may be advisable to reinvest all of your assets producing investment income in assets producing passive income (such as limited partnership, master limited partnerships, or rental real estate).

2. To the extent that the investor has not been able to use up his undeducted loss carryforwards from prior years before he sells his investment, he can use these losses to offset the gain he would otherwise have to recognize on the sale, and offset any other type of income. The types of sales or other transfers, which are sufficient to trigger these previously unused losses will be described below.

Planning Tip. Taking advantage of the unused loss carry forwards to offset future losses or the gains on future sales is important. But consider the time value of money (a dollar today is worth more than a dollar in a year from today). If an investor holds his tax shelter investments for eight years before selling them, the value of using the previously unused losses to offset the gains is not going to be worth much in terms of today's dollars—an eight-year wait is a long time. Thus, when planning income and tax shelter (if "tax shelter" is even appropriate any longer) investments, consider ways to use losses as they are generated or as soon as possible after that. Don't actively plan to use losses on the sale of an investment many years into the future—this should only be the last resort if all other planning efforts fail.

Example. An investor is in a maximum 28% tax bracket for all years in question. An appropriate interest rate (discount factor) to use in calculating the impact of the time value of money (present value) on his tax planning is 12%. The investor faces two investment scenarios: (1) he can invest in a deal which will generate $20,000 in annual tax losses for eight years, which can be used fully by her in each of those years; or (2) he can invest in a deal which will generate the same total deductions as a $160,000 "suspended loss" eight years in the future. What is the value to him of each investment's tax benefits in terms of today's dollars?

Investment 1. The first investment will throw off $20,000 in losses in each year. At his 28% tax bracket (the highest rate when the new law becomes fully effective) he will realize a $5,600 tax savings each year for a total savings of $44,800 ($5,600 × 8 years). The value of a $5,600 tax savings received at the end of each year for eight years (i.e., the present value of a $5,600 payment, an annuity, for eight years at a 12% discount rate) is $27,819.

Investment 2. The second investment will provide a single tax benefit in the eighth year. This could be the result where the tax losses in early years remain unused and are applied to reduce the tax on the eventual sale of the investment. The tax savings in the eighth year will also be $44,800 ($160,000 tax benefit multiplied by his tax rate of 28%). The value of this tax benefit in terms of today's dollars is, however, only $18,095.

Thus, the real value to our investor of properly planning to take immediate advantage of his passive investment losses under the new laws is $9,724 ($27,819 − $18,095).

Unfortunately for many taxpayers the far less favorable alternative illustrated in the investment 2 scenario could be common. Congress specifically intended this result. It believed that given the difficulties of measuring actual economic loss for nonparticipating ventures (e.g., passive real estate syndications), it was appropriate to postpone determining whether the venture generated an overall gain or loss until the nonparticipating investor disposed of his entire investment (interest) in the venture. What it takes to dispose of your entire interest in a venture is itself a tricky matter which will be discussed in the following section.

WHEN CAN YOU USE YOUR DEFERRED LOSSES?

As noted, any passive losses which can't be used to offset current passive income (or other income, via one of the three "bridges") are suspended. These suspended losses can be used to offset passive income in future years. Losses that still remain can then be used to reduce any gain you realize when you dispose of your investment.

Example. An investor owns a limited partnership interest in a real estate tax shelter. The investment was made in 1986 when 19-year depreciation write-offs were still available. As a result of these favorable depreciation deductions the investor realizes losses each year of $25,000. Since this is the investors only passive investment the losses are suspended and remain unused since there is no other passive income to offset them against. By 1991 the investor has accumulated unused (suspended) losses of $125,000 ($25,000 per year for the five years 1987–1991).

At the end of 1991 the investor sells his limited partnership interest for a $200,000 profit. This profit is reduced by the $125,000 in losses not yet used. Thus the gain which will be taxed is only $75,000.

Since there is obviously a strong incentive for taxpayers to use their losses, Congress put in a few restrictions to prevent investors from taking advantage of their losses before they actually dispose of their investment or their entire interest in an activity.

Generally, to trigger your suspended losses you must dispose of your entire interest in an activity in a taxable transaction. A sale to an unrelated party and certain abandonments of your investment are sufficient. A sale to a related party, or a sham transaction undertaken solely to trigger your suspended losses, won't work.

NOTE—Tax credits earned on investments in passive activities are not triggered on the disposition of your entire interest in an activity. Instead, they are generally held in abeyance until you have passive income which they can offset. Special rules permit these credits to be used as basis adjustments. A discussion of these rules, however, is beyond the scope of this text.

Thus merely changing the form in which you own your investment won't be enough.

Examples. The investor in our example decides to transfer his limited partnership interest to a new corporation he formed (in tax jargon he did a Code Section 351 tax-free transfer to a controlled corporation). He hopes to then use the $125,000 in losses since he has "disposed" of his investment. After all, he no longer owns it, his corporation does. This type of transfer will not be sufficient to trigger the accumulated tax losses. To take advantage of the losses you must dispose of your entire interest in the investment. Since the investor in our example controls the corporation which now owns the limited partnership investment, he will not be treated as having disposed of his entire interest in it.

The same rule will, to some extent, apply if you transfer your investment or business real estate to another person in a tax-free swap (see Chapter 10) for his investment or business real estate (a Code Section 1031 "like-kind exchange").

What if you give your property away? Still no luck. Our investor won't be able to claim the benefit of his accumulated losses if he gives the property to his children. What will happen is the $125,000 in losses will be added to the children's investment ("tax basis") in the investment. Thus when the children sell the investment their gain will be reduced by the amount of accumulated losses their father had. This benefit may be far in the future.

What happens if the activity is no longer "passive" to you? Say you take an active role in the operations. Then all the accumulated losses can be used to offset the future active income you realize.

Another example is a developer invested in a retail store located in one of his office buildings. He provided the seed money to get the tenant started and took an option to increase his interest if he decided to become more involved at a later date. The investor took no other part in the store's operations. Thus the investor did not meet the material participation standard. Therefore, it was a passive activity for him. A few years later, as the retailer's novel concept began to take off, the developer exercised his option to increase his ownership percentage. He also took an active role in expanding to other locations with this new retail concept. The losses he realized during the start-up stage of the business can now be used to offset the profits he will realize as the business expands. He doesn't have to wait to sell his investment—it was sufficient that he started to participate materially.

A critical item in determining whether you have disposed of your entire interest in an activity in order to trigger your suspended losses is the definition of an activity.

For example if you have invested in a general partnership that owns two garden apartment buildings and the partnership sells one of its two buildings, does this constitute a disposition of your entire interest in the activity of renting the apartment building that was sold? If it does, then any suspended passive losses you have will be triggered and can be used to offset the gain realized on the sale of the building. If it isn't considered to be a disposition of your entire interest in the activity of renting that building, then your suspended losses won't be triggered.

The answer to this question isn't simple. If the two buildings were next to each other, shared a parking lot, and were managed by the same people, the sale of one-half the complex probably wouldn't trigger suspended losses associated with the building sold. If, however, one apartment was a low-income project in New York City managed by a New York agent and the second apartment was a luxury complex in one of Los Angeles' posher neighborhoods and was managed by a resident agent, the sale of one property would probably be sufficient to trigger the suspended losses associated with it. Most situations won't be nearly so clear-cut. If you own a single cooperative apartment, for example, and do not have other interests in the apartment building (or project), the sale of the single apartment should qualify as the sale of your entire interest in an activity. If, on the other hand, you own a 50% interest in an entire apartment building, the sale of a portion of the building won't qualify as the sale of your entire interest in an activity. Future IRS Regulations will be essential for guidance. See the discussions below concerning the definition of activity.

NOTE—Given the tough stance the passive loss rules take toward limited partnership investments, future regulations could apply a tough standard too. Also, in a limited partnership it may be more difficult to argue that different projects constitute different activities if the limited partners rely solely on one management team to run all of the partnership's operations. This risk should be evaluated very carefully in analyzing a possible investment in a master limited partnership which owns a number of properties. One final issue must be reviewed with respect to the use of these suspended losses. The above examples generally assumed a single activity thus it was easy to determine the loss relating to that activity. If a number of activities are involved the suspended losses must be allocated proportionally between each activity based on the losses of that activity as compared to the total suspended losses.

Suppose an investor invests in three real estate syndications, which produce the following passive income or loss:

Syndication 1	$(100,000)
Syndication 2	24,000
Syndication 3	(27,500)
Net passive loss	$(103,500)

The investor's suspended loss allocated to syndication 1 is calculated as follows:

$$\frac{\text{Loss from the activity}}{\text{Total passive losses}} \times \text{Net passive loss} = \text{Allocable loss}$$

$$\frac{\$100,000}{\$100,000 + \$27,500} \times \$103,500 = \$81,176$$

For syndication 2 the allocable loss is:

$$\frac{\$27,500}{\text{Total passive loss allocated}} \times \$103,500 = \$22,324$$

$$\$103,500$$

No loss is allocated to syndication 2 since passive income was realized from that activity. Now consider what happens if syndication 1 was really a master limited partnership which owned 45 projects across the country, each of which is deemed to be a separate activity. The bookkeeping becomes absurdly burdensome. This complicated tracking of the losses allocable to each activity, however, is necessary to determine the suspended loss which will be triggered if an investment activity is sold.

WHO IS SUBJECT TO THE PASSIVE LOSS LIMITATION RULES?

The passive loss limitation rules apply to individual taxpayers, estates, trusts and to certain corporations. The objective of making these limitations applicable to so many types of taxpayers is to prevent individuals from avoiding the limitations by structuring their activities or investments in a different form (e.g., holding a real estate tax shelter in a corporation).

Example. A reporter decides to try to avoid the new passive loss limitation rules by setting up a corporation of which he is the sole employee. The corporation rents his services to his former employer and other newspapers for a fee (a "loan-out" corporation). The corporation pays his salary for performing the work it has arranged for him. He has his corporation invest in tax shelter investments to use the losses generated to offset its income (i.e., the fees it collects from newspapers for renting them his services). It won't work. The loss limitation rules will be applied to his personal service corporation.

Two classes of corporations are subject to the passive loss rules. Certain closely held (i.e., owned by a small group of people) C corporations within the passive loss limitation rules.* Which C corporations are subject to these rules? Those with five or fewer individuals who own, directly or indirectly, more than 50% of the corporation's stock during the last half of the year are the primary target. These corporations will, however, be considered to materially participate in an activity (and thus not be subject to the passive loss rules) only where they meet a special material participation test described below.

The rules which apply to these closely held corporations are as follows. Losses from passive activities (such as real estate syndication investments) cannot be used to offset portfolio (i.e., dividend and interest) income. These corporations will, however, be allowed to use losses from passive investments to offset income and gains from active business income. This latter rule may leave some planning flexibility. For example, in certain instances it may be advantageous to hold real estate in corporate form. CAUTION—see the discussions in Chapter 1 on corporations before proceeding.

Corporations to which the owner–employees render substantial services (so called "personal service corporations") will be subject to the general passive loss limitations. That is, they don't qualify for the special benefit closely held corporations receive. A personal service corporation is a corporation the principal activity of which is the performance of personal services. These

---

*C corporations are "regular" corporations, that is, corporations which are subject to the corporate level tax. Contrast it with an S corporation (formerly "Subchapter S corporation" or "tax option" corporation) which is generally not subject to the corporate-level tax; instead S corporations make a special election to have their shareholders taxed on their earnings (See Chapter 1).

personal services must be substantially performed by employee–owners who, directly or indirectly, own stock in the corporation. These employee–owners must own, in the aggregate, more than 10% of the stock in the corporation.

LOSS LIMITATION CATEGORIES

The most important matter for the taxpayers subject to the passive loss limitation rules is the definition of the different income types and what incomes and gains are to be included in each category. The three broad categories of income which must be considered in applying the new passive loss limitations, illustrated in a preceding section of this chapter, are:

Income generated from passive activities

Income generated from active business activities

Portfolio income (i.e., dividends, interest, royalties, etc.)

Let's take a closer look at each of these categories:

Income Earned from Passive and Nonpassive Activities

A business or investment (often referred to as an activity) will generate passive income if the taxpayer earning the income does not materially participate in the activity. "Materially participate" is one of the new keywords for the passive loss limitation rules (we'll see a few more before we're done). With certain exceptions described below, the nature of the business is not always important—what is important is that you materially participate.

For example, you could own an interest in an obviously active business but spend your time on the golf course—this won't count. You have to be actively involved in the business yourself. If you materially participate in the business then the activity will generate nonpassive (i.e., active) income (or losses as the case may be). Thus the first two of the three income categories can be dealt with together.

Congress' reason for chosing this "material participation" standard will help in understanding it. Congress felt that a taxpayer who is actively involved with a business on a regular basis is much more likely to have made (and continue to keep) his investment for economic reasons, rather than for tax reasons. On the other hand, a taxpayer who is not actively involved with an activity on a regular basis (i.e., a passive investor) is likely to be more concerned about the tax-reduction features of the investment than the economic features. Since a major objective of tax reform is to cut back the number of tax-motivated transactions, this approach seems useful.

What does it take to "materially participate"? You must be involved in the activity on a (1) regular, (2) continuous, and (3) substantial basis. In addition, this material participation must occur throughout the year. In fact, whether you meet the standard is tested each year. Thus it will generally not suffice to work for a small portion of the year, or for one year but not in other years, in order to render a business an active endeavor when, in reality, your participation is negligible.

Because the material participation standard is a new concept its definition is not clear. Future regulations, revenue rulings, and court cases will be necessary to help clarify its meaning. Some understanding, however, can be obtained by reviewing a checklist of the examples, rules and guidelines which appear in the Congressional Committee Report which describe this new standard. When assessing your involvement in an activity to determine whether you are materially participating, consider all the facts and circumstances. Also, remember that no one criterion is conclusive. The following rough guidelines will be helpful:

1. Interests in all real estate rental activities will generally be treated as passive regardless of whether you materially participate! Note that real estate rental activities will "generally" be treated as passive activities—it doesn't say "always." Real estate brokers, developers, consultants, property mangagement companies, and many other important players in the industry will qualify as materially participating in some of their businesses. These rules are particularly critical to investors, developers and others—they must all determine what categories their income and losses (including real estate related income and losses) fall into in order to determine to what extent they can currently use their losses.

2. Working as an employee providing personal services (e.g., a construction worker, a sales clerk, a full-time real estate broker, a lawyer) will be material participation.

3. Owning an interest as a limited partner will generally not be treated as material participation. The partnership agreement (the legal document, or contract, which governs much of the relationship between the partners in a partnership) will usually limit the potential involvement of limited partners. Most importantly, under the state laws which govern partnerships, limited partners are not allowed to actively participate in the management and operation of the partnership. If they do, they will lose their limited liability. (Limited liability means that if the partnership defaults on a loan, for example, the limited partners will generally only be liable up to the amount of their investments ("capital contributions"). If the limited partner actively participates in the management of the partnership he could lose this valuable limitation.) Regulations will be issued defining situations when limited partnership interests will be treated as active endeavors—that is, the limited partner will be treated as materially participating. One purpose of these regulations (exceptions to the general rule) is to prevent tax-avoidance schemes.

Example. A consultant decides that it will be to his advantage to treat his earnings as a shopping center promotions consultant as passive income. He will then be able to apply the passive losses from his shopping center tax shelters against his consulting fees. Remember, passive losses can only offset passive income. Since his shopping center syndication losses are clearly passive, his only means of currently benefiting from them is to earn sufficient passive income to offset them. This could save him significant tax. He knows that income earned as a limited partner is passive income. Thus if he could convert his consulting fees into passive limited partnership income he could then offset the two.

Our consultant and a friend join forces. The friend agrees to serve as a general partner and the consultant serves as a limited partner in their new shopping center promotion partnership. His shopping center clients now pay their fees to the partnership. He takes some income out of the partnership as a salary ("guaranteed payments"). Most of his earnings, however, are taken as "passive" partnership distributions on his limited partnership interest. He will then try to offset his shopping center promotion income with his tax shelter losses. However, the regulations which the IRS will issue will prohibit such schemes from succeeding, since income for personal services will not be treated as income from a passive activity.

4. If you serve as a general partner in a partnership your activities should be examined to determine whether you meet the material participation standard. If you also own a limited partnership interest, the income from that interest will be treated as passive income that does not meet the test.

5. Your services to, and other involvement with, the activity should relate to the operations of the activity and should make a significant contribution to them. Merely approving a financing target or making general recommendations regarding, for example, the selection of employees or managers, or appointing others to perform all of the significant active operational functions, may not be sufficient.

6. If the business is your principal business it is likely that you materially participate. For example, assume you work 35 hours a week as a real estate broker actively selling homes, and spend only a few hours a week managing another business. Most likely, you will be regarded as materially participating in your brokerage business but not in the side business.

Planning Tip. There may be a way to use this concept to your advantage. Remember the consultant in our earlier example. He wanted to convert active consulting fee income into passive income in order to offset it by his passive tax shelter losses. If he were involved in a number of different activities, each of which occupied no more than say 10 hours a week, he might be able to treat them as passive since he may not materially participate in any of them. CAUTION—This is a new concept on which the law is not fully clear, so you should carefully review any planning in this area with your tax advisor before proceeding. If the IRS considered all his activities as comprising a single related endeavor, then he would realize active income and his new plan would also not succeed.

7. If you are regularly at the place or places where the principal operations of the business activity are conducted, the material participation test will be easier to meet. It is, however, possible to materially participate in an activity without being present at the principal place of business. To do this you should

be regularly, continuously, and substantially involved in providing services integral to the activity. Examples include finding new customers and negotiating terms with potential customers.

8. When evaluating your involvement, management functions will generally not be treated any differently than nonmanagement functions, for example, physical labor.

9. Mere formal and nominal participation in an activity will not help meet the material participation standard. The genuine exercise of independent discretion will. For example, checking off boxes on reports sent to you by a promoter will not suffice.

10. Knowledge and experience in the industry will be important in demonstrating that you materially participate in an activity through participating in management.

11. The size of your ownership interest in the business in which you are trying to prove material participation is not necessarily important.

12. Merely providing services to a business as an independent contractor (rather than as an employee) will not help meet the test. On the other hand, using employees or independent contractors to perform daily functions will not necessarily prevent you from being treated as if you materially participate in the activity.

Special tests are provided to determine whether a closely held C corporation or a personal service corporation materially participates in an activity. Both of these types of corporations will be considered to materially participate in an activity if they meet the following test: One or more shareholders owning more than one-half the value of the corporation must materially participate in the corporation's activity. A second alternative material participation standard is available only for closely held C corporations.

A closely held C corporation will also be treated as materially participating in an activity if it meets each of the following requirements (generally during the past full year):

1. It has at least one full-time employee who rendered substantially all his services in the active management of the business.

2. It had three or more full time, nonowner employees, substantially all of whose services were directly related to the corporations business.

3. The deductions attributable to the business for such items as utilities, management fees, rents, compensation (but not including interest, taxes and certain other items) exceed 15% of the gross income from the business.

These rules are important. If a closely held or personal service corporation meets the appropriate tests it will be a material participant in the activity and the income or loss from that activity won't be subject to the passive loss limitations.

Now that you've waded through the morass of the material participation standard, you have hopefully, with the assistance of your tax consultant, been able to determine whether income you earn (or the loss you incur) from various activities is "active income" or "passive income." With this determination you've completed two of the three key building blocks of the passive loss limitation rules. The third income category, portfolio income, must now be considered. Following an analysis of portfolio income we can review the few crossovers ("bridges") among the three categories.

Portfolio Income
The third major income category in the new passive loss limitation rules is portfolio income. This category will generally include:

Interest

Dividends

Royalties

Gains or losses on the sale of investment property which does not qualify as a passive activity

Gains or losses on the sale of property that normally produces interest, dividend, or royalty income

Dividends on C corporation stock, REITS, and regulated investment companies (RICs) (see Chapter 1).

The following items are not treated as generating portfolio income:

General and limited partnership interests

S corporation stock

Property leases

Gains or losses from the sale of these items

BRIDGES AMONG THE THREE INCOME CATEGORIES

With this understanding of portfolio income we have completed our discussion of the three income categories. Now we will examine some important exceptions to the rules governing these categories. The first are the "crossovers" or "bridges" (see Figure 9.1.). These bridges provide rules which move (i.e., recharacterize) certain income from one of the three major income categories to another:

Bridge 1. Certain income earned in a passive activity will be moved to the portfolio income category.

Bridge 2. Losses on certain passive real estate activities will be moved to the active income category.

Bridge 3. Credits for low income housing and rehabilitating old or historic buildings will be moved to the active income category.

Once the three "bridges" are reviewed the framework will be in place to examine the detailed rules applicable to real estate and then the mechanics of the loss limitation rules.

Bridge 1—Certain "Passive Income" Must Be Treated as "Portfolio Income"

Although income and gains from general and limited partnership interests, S corporation stock, and so forth are not treated as portfolio income, there is an exception. If the income earned on, or the gain from the sale of, these items is due to portfolio assets, then that portion of the income or gain will be treated as portfolio income rather than as income from a passive activity. Thus portfolio income from a passive activity is separately accounted for as portfolio income, not as passive income.

Examples. A passive investor is a 50% partner in a partnership which had $10,000 in losses on a passive real estate investment and $8,400 in dividends on a stock mutual fund it has invested in. The investor will be treated as if he realized $5,000 in passive gains (50% partnership interest × $10,000) and $4,200 in portfolio income (50% partnership interest × $8,400) for purposes of applying the new passive loss limitation rules. The income and loss will not be allowed to offset each other.

NOTE—Congress believed that passive activities will produce losses far more often than active businesses and that portfolio investments will generally produce income and gains. The abuse Congress sought to prevent is the use by a passive activity (e.g., a real estate tax shelter) of portfolio income (e.g., interest on a CD) to offset passive losses. This is the purpose of the requirement to treat certain income earned in a passive activity as separate portfolio income. This rule does not appear to apply to active businesses, such as a brokerage firm, since Congress did not see the same potential for abuse.

There is a very limited exception to this portfolio income reclassification rule. Portfolio-type income (e.g., interest) will not be treated as portfolio income if it is earned in the ordinary course of the business activities.

An example is if a retailer owns a 10% interest in a partnership operating a retail store. The store earns interest on its charge sales and installment sales. In addition, its controller deposits the daily cash receipts in a noninterest-bearing account where they sit until disbursed at month's end to meet payroll and other bills. The interest earnings should not be subject to the rule requiring that portfolio income be taken into account separately (as was the case for the passive investor, in the previous example).

Planning Tip. This exception above is very limited. Moneys invested temporarily to meet working capital needs of the business *must* be accounted for separately—just as in the example with the passive investor. Congress believed that such interest (or other portfolio-type earnings) on working capital balances are "not a part of the trade or business itself." Thus, if controller of the retail store deposited the daily cash receipts in an interest-bearing checking account, the interest on that account may have to be accounted for separately from the interest earned on installment sales. This interest will then have to be reported as a separate item to the partners. The partners will in turn have to treat this interest as portfolio income for purposes of applying the passive loss limitation rules on their personal tax returns.

The other interest income earned by the retail store, along with its primary income from sales, will be treated separately.

If this seems confusing and difficult and burdensome to implement in your business, it is.

Example. An investor owns a 40% interest in a limited partnership which operates a shopping center. The shopping center has been a great investment and the partnership has been accumulating funds for a renovation project. Congress says the interest on this fund is "not a part of the trade or business [of the shopping center operations] itself"! Therefore, the interest must be reported separately as passive income. It cannot be used to offset the tax losses realized on the rental operations.

The objective of this rule concerning earnings on working capital and other balances is to prevent taxpayers from arranging their investments so that tax shelter losses will be offset at the entity level (e.g., the limited partnership operating the retail store or shopping center in our examples), and thus avoiding the limitations at the individual investor level. The result, however, seems excessive.

Bridge 2—Losses from Certain Real Estate Activities Treated as from Active Business

Now the three key types of income for the passive loss limitation rules, and the exception to these rules, have been explained. Next, the rules and exceptions affecting the treatment of rental real estate activities can be reviewed.

As mentioned in our discussion concerning the "material participation" standard (i.e., how much you must do for an activity to be considered an active rather than passive activity), an interest in real estate rental activities will not be considered an active business, no matter how much you participate. What this means is that losses from real estate investments will only be available to offset income from other passive investments (e.g., from limited partnership interests). Real estate losses won't be available to offset wage or active business income. However, there is a major exception to this rule. This exception—bridge 2 —enables certain investors to treat certain passive real estate rental losses (which remain after being netted against any passive real estate gains) as losses from an active business. This means these losses *can* be used to offset income from wages or active businesses in which you materially participate.

Congress provided this exception to enable "moderate-income" taxpayers who hold real estate to provide financial security (i.e., a significant nontax purpose), and for which the taxpayer has significant responsibility, to deduct losses against other income and receive the tax benefits.

To qualify for this real estate loss exception (of up to $25,000) you must meet both an income and a participation test. You must have adjusted gross income (all of your income less certain adjustments but excluding IRA contributions, passive losses and certain other items) of less than $150,000. The full $25,000 allowance (see Figure 9.1) is permitted for taxpayers with adjusted gross income up to $100,000. For adjusted gross income above this amount the $25,000 allowance is phased out at the rate of 50 cents for each additional dollar of income.

Example. A real estate broker has adjusted gross income for purposes of the passive loss limitations of $120,000. He also has $32,000 in losses (in excess of his other passive income) that would qualify for this special $25,000 allowance. How much can he use? First, the loss in excess of $25,000 is clearly in excess of the allowance. Thus $7,000 ($32,000 − $25,000) can immediately be treated as a loss carryover (suspended loss) to future years. Next, a portion of his allowance will have to be reduced because his income exceeds the $100,000 mark. The $20,000 excess ($120,000 income less $100,000 phase-out point) will reduce his allowance at a rate of 50 cents for each dollar, or $10,000. Thus he can use only $15,000 of his real estate losses to offset income from his wages as a real estate broker. His total suspended loss carryforward to future years is $17,000 ($7,000 + $10,000).

The other requirement to qualify for this allowance is that the investor must "actively participate." This standard is less than the material participation standard discussed above. It is not necessary for you to be regularly, continuously, and substantially involved to meet this active participation test. To actively participate and get the benefit of up to $25,000 in tax losses, you must meet the following requirements:

1. You must own at least 10% of the value of the activity (i.e., there cannot be more than 10 investors) during all times during the year in which you are an owner.

2. You must make management decisions or arrange for others to provide services (such as repairs) in a significant and bona fide sense. For example, you could approve new tenants, decide on rental terms, or approve repairs of large (capital) improvements. You don't even have to do these directly—you can hire a rental agent and repairman.

3. The management decisions you make must not be contrived to meet this active participation test. For example, if a promoter sets up a deal specifically to qualify you for this test it may not work. For example, if the promoter of the investment really takes care of all the management decisions and sends you reports for you to merely check off boxes in order to make "decisions" this will not be enough.

Planning Tip. If you hire a management company to run the property you will not necessarily be disqualified from meeting the active participation test. However, have your lawyer carefully review the management agreement. The agreement should clearly indicate that the investor is involved in the decision-making process. The contract must support the position that all decisions will not be made by the management company. The management contract should say that no repair greater than a certain amount (say $250) can be made without your approval. The management company should provide you with periodic reports and statements. Investors are also advised to keep a log (diary) of all telephone calls, visits, and other actions taken concerning the property.

Bridge 3—Certain Credits on Passive Investments Can Offset Active Income

A similar rule allows the benefit of the special tax credits for low-income housing (see Chapter 6) and rehabilitating old or historic buildings (see Chapter 3) to be used to a limited extent to offset income from wages or other active businesses. This final "bridge" is similar to the second one in that it acts to recharacterize certain real estate tax benefits as "active" amounts. Also, the limitations and phaseout of this allowance are structured like the second bridge previously discussed. However, note that only one $25,000 allowance is permitted—that is, you can use bridge 2 and/or bridge 3, but not in excess of $25,000. Credits are limited in a manner that makes their value equivalent to deductions. For example, if you're in a 28% tax bracket $7,000 of low-income housing or rehabilitation tax credits would provide you with the same tax benefit as a $25,000 passive loss deduction [$25,000 × 28% = $7,000].

These credits (but not the losses from the low-income housing or rehabilitation activities) can be used to offset up to $25,000 in active income. This $25,000 allowance is also phased out at a 50-cents-per-dollar rate, just as in bridge 2. The phaseout, however, begins at $200,000 of adjusted gross income. Thus, by the $250,000 income level this allowance is unavailable. There is one important difference between this allowance and the one discussed in conjunction with bridge 2. Investors are not required to actively participate to claim this tax benefit. Thus you can invest in a real estate limited partnership, as a limited partner, and still get to use up to about $7,000 in low-income housing or rehabilitation tax credit.

With the framework of the three types of income and the major exceptions or "bridges" between them, we can now look at the additional rules applicable to real estate generally. Remember, the general rule is that losses from all real estate rental activities can only be used to offset income from passive investments.

Planning Tip. If your income is under $200,000 you can invest in a passive real estate limited partnership and use these tax credit benefits in a manner very similar to prior law.

WHAT BUSINESSES ARE TREATED AS REAL ESTATE RENTAL ACTIVITIES

The Tax Reform Act of 1986 places severe limitations on real estate. This creates a great incentive to define your activity as something other than real estate in order to avoid these limitations. To prevent these "end runs" around the new laws, Congress addressed the definition of "real estate activity" in two parts. The first addresses the definition of rental activity, which will be discussed in this section. The second part of the definition addresses the more general question of what an activity is. This will be discussed in the next section.

In determining whether your business must be treated as a rental activity subject to the passive loss limitation rules, consider the following:

A real estate rental activity receives payments which consist principally of payments for the use of tangible property, rather than for the performance of substantial services.

Some activities will not be treated as rental activities even though payments are received for the use of tangible property because significant services are rendered in connection with the payments (such as a hotel).

If the expenses of daily operations are significant in relation to the rents produced from the property, or in relation to the depreciation and carrying costs of the property, then the activity may not be treated as a rental activity.

To determine whether "services" are being rendered consider whether the services are primarily for the convenience of the occupant. The services must also be of a different nature than those services customarily rendered in connection with the rental of rooms or other space for occupancy only. For example, maid service would be such a service. Trash removal utilities, and providing laundry rooms (washers and dryers) to apartment tenants, would not, since it's customary for landlords to provide them. Maintaining the common areas and recreational facilities for a mobile home park may count as qualifying services.

Planning Tip. These examples and descriptions of qualifying services were extracted from the Committee Reports for the Tax Reform Act of 1986, and from cases, rulings, and regulations which they referred to. These sources, however, don't seem to address some important developments in the real estate marketplace. CAUTION—the following example will probably be defined as rental real estate activities in future regulations. This appears to be the result intended by Congress. What about the growth of "smart office buildings"—those which provide a full range of telecommunication, computer, and other advanced electronic facilities and support? Are these material services? Should these "services" be distinguished from rental activities?

What about the shopping center industry? The leasing and operation of a shopping center (perhaps other than a small strip or convenience center) requires much more than merely providing trash removal and utilities. To operate a successful shopping center, active, often onsite, management is necessary. It is not uncommon to develop a special theme and marketing program for the specific center. Such a theme and marketing program, based on extensive demographic analysis and the expertise of qualified personnel, are all drawn on to determine the tenant mix (selection of different tenants for the project as well as the location of each tenant within the mall) which will optimize the revenue from the project. In addition, security services are also commonly provided. Some shopping center landlords monitor tenant sales and actively consult with tenants concerning the market and new trends. At what point are substantial services being provided?

Certain apartment buildings are designed exclusively for elderly tenants. Clearly they don't constitute the active businesses which nursing homes do. Nevertheless they often provide many services. Weekly maid service (as contrasted with daily maid service in a hotel), meal service (often through a full-time cafeteria), a registered nurse on duty, and regular entertainment activities may be provided (movies, bingo, etc.). Do these services meet the "material service" test?

In today's office market (and even other real estate market segments), landlords are being forced to make a whole array of concessions to tenants in order to induce them to sign leases. Many of these concessions take the form of services and amenities which historically landlords never would have dreamed of providing. At what point do these additional services and amenities become significant for purposes of the above test?

Planning Tips. The law is very new. It is not clear how these standards must be applied. Further, it is not clear how Congress considered these nuances of the industry. When making any decision, consult carefully with your tax advisor. And remember—consider all the various penalty provisions before acting (see Chapter 12). Discuss all the various concessions and services you do, or could, provide. Use the examples above as guidelines. In the discussions that follow we'll see how to use these considerations to plan around the harsh new passive loss rules to the extent possible.

The period for which the property is rented can also be a factor. if the term is long relative to the useful life of the property and if there is a low turnover of tenants, it is more likely that the activity is a rental property.

The Committee Report gives a number of examples. Renting an automobile under a short-term lease with the lessor providing a number of services such as maintenance, oil changes, cleaning, and renting hotel rooms to transients would not be rental activities. These activities can be compared with leasing a boat under a bare charter (i.e., no services) and renting apartments (even on a month-to-month basis). Unfortunately, these examples don't clearly define the standards set forth. If the depreciable life of real estate is 40 years for purposes of the minimum tax (see Chapter 11), then surely a month-long lease is a very short rental period relative to the 40-year "life" of the property. As for the extent of services provided, the Committee Report is silent in its examples. Further, the Committee Report's mixing of the standards for lease term and the services rendered by the landlord into a single set of examples makes it difficult to draw conclusions.

If the standards are so confusing and inconsistent, taxpayers, with the careful advice of their tax advisors, could, in appropriate circumstances, consider characterizing their activities as something other than pure rental activities. CAUTION—This is probably not what Congress intended so proceed carefully.

Apartment Rentals. If you rent apartment buildings and the lease terms are very short relative to the life of the property, carefully consider the services you can, or could, render. Trash removal and utilities won't help you avoid characterization as a rental activity. Do you provide a 24-hour doorman, valet service, package room, bagel and newspaper delivery on Sunday morning, security or guard service, an on-site health club, a library, and so forth? Carefully consider all possible activities. Perhaps the provision of all the above services under apartment leases which are five years or less will suffice. If future regulations indicate otherwise, consider whether health club and other services may be more properly treated as a separate business.

Shopping Centers. Clearly a long-term lease to an anchor tenant for 30 years would be difficult to treat as insignificant in comparison with the useful life of the building. However, short-term leases with temporary tenants may be possible to consider insignificant. How about the kiosks that only sell gifts and foodstuffs during the Christmas season? Also consider the nature and extent of the services you provide—for example, security and guard services, advertising and promotions, on-site management, monitoring lease compliance, tenant selection, day care facilities, lost and found, special events, and consultation for tenants concerning marketing, store hours, cleanliness, repair and maintenance policies. What experienced shopping center owner would not, either personally or through a qualified employee, take the time to walk regularly through his mall and advise local tenants on ways to improve operations?

Renting Property. Renting property under net leases where the tenants bear the responsibility for most expenses, or where the landlord is guaranteed a specified rate of return or is guaranteed against loss, will generally be treated as a rental activity. (See Chapter 2.)

The toughest part of this rule is the net-lease requirement. Many landlords are used to renting their properties only on a net-lease basis. The planning ideas in Chapter 2 discussing the investment interest limitation rules can be to help understand this aspect of the passive loss rules as well. Whether it is possible to restructure your lease terms in order to meet certain objective standards the tax laws require in order to avoid net-lease classification is uncertain. Although interest expense subject to the passive loss rules will not be subject to the investment interest limitations, the planning ideas discussed in Chapter 2 can be helpful in understanding both of these limitations.

Scope of Rental Activity

Why is defining the scope of any activity so important? If a number of ventures are really the same activity, then showing that you materially participate in any one of the ventures will be sufficient to treat the income or loss from all of the ventures as active. If each venture were treated as a separate activity then you would have to show that you materially participated in each one of them in order to treat them as active. Also, as was discussed earlier in this chapter, you can't get the benefit of accumulated unused losses until you dispose of your entire interest in an activity. If you could divide a business or investment into many small components it would be easy to sell a small piece and get your losses while still maintaining an interest in the business. Obviously the definition will have to be somewhere between these two extremes.

Other complications arise when you do more than just rent real estate. Many businesses involve the conduct of both a rental activity and other activities not involving the rental of tangible property. For example, the construction or development of real estate will not be considered a passive activity. A retailer, for example, may own the building in which it operates. The retail activities will probably qualify as an active business. The rental of other parts of the building in which the retailer also occupies space will probably be a passive rental activity.

Planning Tip. If the retailer were a corporation, other than a personal service corporation, any losses realized from its rental of the building could be used to offset the profits from its retail operations. This is an example of one situation where it may still be advantageous to own real estate in the C corporate form. CAUTION—see the discussions in Chapter 1 before following through on this type of planning.

The purpose of these rules is to prevent the use of passive rental losses to offset the income realized from your simultaneously running an active business—retailing, development, or construction, for example.

Example. A developer buys raw land and builds apartments. The developer is regularly and substantially involved in all phases of the construction process. He then rents the apartments out to tenants on one-, two-, or five-year leases. As the landlord he provides no services other than utilities and trash pick-up. Large tax losses are generated by the depreciation and other deductions from the apartments.

The development and construction activities are an active business. Therefore the profits earned on these activities can't be offset by the losses generated on the developer's passive rental of apartments. Losses incurred on development activities, to the extent not limited by other rules (such as the limitations on deducting certain business start-up costs, or the new capitalization rules discussed in Chapter 3) can be used to offset active income. Once the developer puts the property into use any losses resulting could not be used to offset active income. These losses will be subject to the passive loss rules. How are costs and expenses supposed to be allocated between the same developer's development and rental "activities"? There don't seem to be many answers yet. The discussions in Chapter 3 may provide some guidance. But check with your tax advisor. Hopefully future regulations will clarify these matters.

Planning Tips. Meanwhile, plan carefully. Review all cost allocations with your accountant. It may never have mattered for tax purposes which checking account you took your salary from before—the construction businesses account or the apartment (operating) account. It may be very important now. Remember that the losses from your apartment rental activity can't offset income from your construction business. If the construction business is showing a profit and the rental business a loss, make certain that all expenses which should properly be paid by your construction company are paid by it and not by your apartment rental business.

How do you decide what ventures are separate activities and which are parts of the same activity? Consider:

The economic interrelationship of the various undertakings.

The business purpose which could be served by carrying on the various undertakings separately or together.

The degree of organizational interrelationship between the various undertakings.

Separate real estate rental projects built and managed in separate locations can constitute separate activities.

Different stages in the production and sale of a particular product that are not carried on in an integrated fashion are separate activities.

Normal commercial practices are very important.

The fact that the same individual will have ultimate management responsibility for various activities, or that a common source of financing or goodwill benefits all the activities is not determinative to treating the various endeavors as one activity.

An artificial characterization of various undertakings as either one or several activities will not be accepted.

The fact that the undertakings are conducted in one or several entities (partnerships, corporations, etc.) will not be determinative.

If an investor buys land primarily to hold it for investment (appreciation), any activity conducted on the land (such as farming) will only be considered part of the same activity if the income generated from the farming or other activity exceeds the expenses allocable to it. In other words, to be part of the same activity as holding the land, the farming must reduce the costs of carrying the land.

Translating these rules into workable standards is tough. Additional guidance is needed. A few suggestions, however, can be made. Because of the uncertainty, consult your tax advisor before making any decisions.

If you own and lease an office building, will the passive losses generated from the rentals be offset by the income earned on the services you provide? The answer may depend on how you organize and conduct the service activities. It's possible in most rental situations to contract with an independent company to provide almost any service you could provide. Since independent companies can provide services, you may be able to structure your operations in order to have the services treated as part of a single activity including the rental operations, or as a separate activity. Alternatively, they may be properly treated as part of the rental activity.

The first step is to determine which approach is to your advantage. If it is advantageous to have rental and service activities treated separately consider, with your tax advisor, taking as many of the following steps as possible:

Set up a separate company, division, and so forth to provide the services.

Get bids from independent contractors. Save all the bid information. This will help show that the service can in fact be rendered independently. Also, it can help show that you intended to run the service business as a separate operation; if your prices are reasonably in line with those offered by an independent company, it means it is economically feasible for you to conduct the service operation as an independent venture.

Submit bids and advertise to get jobs with other landlords; if you're really running a separate business you would probably pursue other customers.

Set up a distinct chain of command to operate the separate service business. Support this with changes to job descriptions and organizational charts. Have your attorney check that all legal documents support what you are doing. For example, if there is a statement about the nature of your businesses—a certificate of incorporation, shareholder agreement, or partnership agreement—it should be broad enough to encompass these new activities. Finally, in determining how many rental real estate activities you have, each building will be treated as a separate rental activity unless the separate units are operated and managed as a single centralized project.

EFFECTIVE DATES OF THE NEW PASSIVE LOSS RULES

The final matter to consider is when these rules go into effect. Generally, they will become effective for all losses starting in 1987. Check with your accountant for exceptions.

However, for investments made before the Tax Reform Act of 1986 was enacted on October 22, 1986, these rules are phased in over a five-year period so that only the following percentages of your losses are disallowed in each year:

Year	Loss Disallowed
1987	35%
1988	60
1989	80
1990	90
1991 and later	100

CAUTION—See the discussion in Chapter 11 concerning the alternative minimum tax (AMT). There is no phase in of the passive loss rules for the AMT. If you're subject to the AMT you may not get any immediate benefit from your passive losses. Also, if you have passive losses on investments made before tax reform, and passive gains made on investments after tax reform, the gains on these latter investments must be netted against your passive losses before the phase-in rules can be used. This required procedure will further limit your ability to use losses.

Planning Tip. You can still plan to take advantage of losses on pretax reform investments to the extent that they are not disallowed during the phase-in period. CAUTION—if you have these types of investments have your tax advisor review the impact of the (1) AMT; (2) the investment interest limitation; (3) the elimination of capital gains; (4) the limitations on deducting capital losses (see Chapter 6); (5) the lower tax rates, (6) the new limitations on the amount of tax credits which can be used to offset your tax liability; and (7) any other relevant tax and nontax factors. You want to be very careful to avoid investments primarily for their tax benefits.

CHAPTER SUMMARY

These complicated new passive loss rules will significantly affect many real estate activities and investments. As a general rule economically sound real estate will continue to be a good and sought-after investment. Marginal properties, whose ownership could have been supported by tax benefits in the past, will no longer be desirable. Whatever situation you face, the new passive loss rules should be carefully incorporated into all tax planning.

10 DEPRECIATION WRITE-OFFS—SQUEEZING OUT TAX BENEFITS UNDER THE NEW RULES

INTRODUCTION

Depreciation has always been one of the most important tax benefits for real estate investors, perhaps *the* most important one. The Tax Reform Act of 1986 has dramatically reduced the value of this benefit in a number of fundamental ways. The number of years over which a real estate investment can be written off has been significantly lengthened. The tax benefit that's left from your real estate depreciation deductions is then reduced even more by the much lower tax rates. The tougher alternative minimum tax may also have a very detrimental effect (see Chapter 11).

Is there anything the real estate investor, developer, tenant, and promoter can do to mollify the harsh effect of these new rules? Yes!

This attack on the real estate industry's most cherished tax benefit means one thing—you must now plan much more carefully. The primary objective of this chapter is to give you an arsenal of planning ideas to use.

CAUTION—Many of the planning ideas discussed here are very technical. Proper implementation will often depend on interpreting fine shades of meaning in a number of court cases and then applying these interpretations to the unique facts facing you. Some of the planning ideas are aggressive and controversial.

The discussions are designed to get you thinking about many of the money-saving planning ideas available—but don't try implementing them without securing expert tax advice.

Before jumping into the planning tips let's take a brief look at depreciation itself—what it is, why it's so important, and what the basic rules are.

WHAT IS DEPRECIATION?

Depreciation is the systematic deduction of the cost (tax basis) of an asset over its life.

Example. Assume you build an office building for $1.25 million in 1988. You will realize benefit from this expenditure for many years. (Even though much of this amount will be financed, it will often be treated the same way for purposes of depreciation.) Presumably you will rent the building at whatever rate the market will bear (or the rent control laws will permit) for a number of years. At some point, however, the building will become physically or economically obsolete. Over this period of time (the "useful life" of the building) you will hopefully realize a profit by having rented the office building for more than the building cost you to build and maintain.

If tax were due when you finally razed the building at the end of its useful life, you would simply subtract the cost of building and maintaining the building from all the rental payments you received. (This, by the way, is part of the concept behind the new rules for carrying forward unused passive losses discussed in Chapter 9.) Taxes, however, are assessed on a yearly basis. Therefore a mechanism is necessary to determine how much "profit" you have "earned" in each tax year.

This mechanism is depreciation. All that depreciation does is allocate the cost you paid to construct your office building to each of the tax years in the building's useful life.

The task of determining the number of years the office building (or any other asset for that matter) will be useful is difficult and subject to varying opinions. Even if the useful life could be reasonably estimated you would have to determine how to allocate the $1.25 million cost to each year of the building's useful life. Congress sought to simplify this process (we'll soon see why they didn't) by establishing statutory useful lives of assets which taxpayers must use. Congress also established procedures to allocate each asset's cost to each period in its useful life. These procedures are called "depreciation methods."

The system of statutory useful lives and depreciation methods is known as the accelerated cost recovery system (ACRS). We'll just call it "depreciation" or "write-offs" because that's all it really is.

WHY IS DEPRECIATION IMPORTANT TO REAL ESTATE INVESTORS?

Apart from the important purpose depreciation serves in determining taxable income, depreciation has been the essence of why real estate has been a "tax shelter." Since depreciation is an expense (deduction) for tax purposes, it enables investors to reduce their tax bill. Since depreciation is not an out-of-pocket cost it enables you to reduce your tax bill without reducing the cash you can take out of your investment. A simple example will illustrate this fundamental concept.

Example. An investor builds a six-unit apartment building for $450,000. To finance the project he takes out a 10-year interest-only balloon mortgage for $400,000. The remaining $50,000 investment is financed from personal savings. The interest rate for the 10-year term is the prime rate plus 4%. Let's assume that the investor pays simple interest at 14%, compounded annually.

His taxable income is as follows:[a]

Rental income	$72,000
Less estimated vacancy	2,000
Net rental income	$70,000
Maintenance and repairs	2,000
Depreciation ($450,000/27.5)	16,000
Mortgage interest ($400,000 × 14%)	56,000
Taxable income (loss)	$(4,000)

[a] All numbers approximated.

Assuming you were actively involved in managing the apartment building (and met the other requirements discussed in Chapter 9 concerning the special allowance to use rental real estate losses against other income), you would also get a tax benefit of $1,120 (28% maximum tax rate × $4,000 loss).

One of the most important economic benefits you will get from this investment (in addition to any appreciation in the value of the building) is the cash flow. But the property lost $4,000! The depreciation expense, however, was not an out-of-pocket expense. The cost of the building was not paid for in this year. Rather, the $450,000 was met by a $50,000 cash investment made in the year you acquired the building. The rest is met by the mortgage. So actually your cash flow is the taxable income or loss computed for tax purposes *plus* the depreciation deduction which you didn't pay for—$12,000 ($4,000 tax loss + $16,000 depreciation).

If the passive loss rules don't prevent you from using this tax loss to offset the tax you would otherwise owe on other income, then include the $1,120 tax benefit as well for a total cash flow of $13,120. This represents a 26% cash return on your $50,000 investment ($13,120/$50,000).

CALCULATING DEPRECIATION—OLD RULES, NEW RULES

To understand how to calculate depreciation you must first understand the two basic types of assets, each of which is depreciated using different rules. The first type of property is known as "real property." This includes buildings, improvements to buildings, and most structures and improvements permanently attached to land. The second type of property is known as "personal property." This includes assets such as cars, file cabinets, furniture, and so forth. Valuable tax savings opportunities can be found in carefully drawing the distinctions between these two types of property—we'll see these in the planning discussions that follow.

Depreciating Buildings—Prior Law
Under the rules before the Tax Reform Act of 1986 most real property was depreciated over a 19-year period. These write-offs were calculated ratably (the "straight-line" method) or on a more rapid ("accelerated") method. The straight-line method was often chosen, even though depreciation deductions were lower in earlier years, to avoid rules which could require that an amount of

any sale proceeds equal to the accelerated depreciation taken on the property, up to the amount of gain realized on the sale, be treated as ordinary income (taxed at rates up to 50%) rather than as capital gains (taxed at rates of up to only 20%). This rule is called "recapture."

Prior law also required you to assume that you were entitled to one half-month's depreciation deduction in the month you purchased (or completed construction of) the building (called a "midmonth convention"). The value of depreciation benefits under these rules, as compared with their value under the new rules, will be shown below.

Depreciating Fixtures and Equipment—Prior Law

Most personal property was written off under prior law over a five-year period often at a much faster rate than the straight-line rate usually used for buildings. Only one half-year of depreciation deduction is allowed in the year the asset is purchased or built (a "half-year convention").

Depreciating Buildings—New Law

The Tax Reform Act of 1986 has changed these rules dramatically. Now real property (buildings and improvements) must be written off over much longer periods. Also, the accelerated methods available under prior law are no longer available. Thus only the slower straight-line method can be used. The midmonth convention under prior law is still used. The new law extended the application of the midmonth convention to include all real property (some property avoided this rule under prior law).

Unlike prior law, different depreciation periods are prescribed for residential and nonresidential property. Residential property is defined as a building with 80% or more of its rental income from dwelling units. If this test is met in one year but not the next the classification of the building as residential could change from the first year to the next year. A dwelling unit is a house or apartment used to provide living accommodations. It doesn't include a hotel, motel, or inn which rents more than half of its units on a transient (temporary) basis. If you live in one of the apartments then an imputed fair rental value of your apartment will be considered as rental income from a residential unit. Residential real estate is written off over a 27.5-year period. Non-residential real estate (we'll call it "commercial real estate") is written off over a 31.5-year period.

Examples. An investor owns a small building which has medical offices on the part of the first floor facing the street. The back portion of the first floor is parking space under the building. On the second and third floors are five two-bedroom apartments. The fourth floor is a penthouse apartment where the investor lives. The rent from the medical office is $60,000 per year. The rental apartments bring in $20,000 each for a total of $200,000. The total rental from the building is thus $260,000 ($60,000 medical office + $200,000 apartments). The rent from dwelling units is only 77% of the total ($200,000 apartment rental/$260,000 total rent). The test of 80% or more rental income from dwelling units is failed. The investor will have to depreciate the building over the 31.5-year period applicable to commercial real estate. However, the value of the investor's fourth-floor penthouse apartment can be added. If the fair value of his apartment is $40,000 or more, then the 80% test will be met ($240,000 apartment rental and imputed fair rental on the penthouse/$300,000 total rental plus imputed fair rental on the penthouse). He can write off the building over the 27.5-period applicable to residential real estate. In addition, like prior law, the new rules permit only one half-month's depreciation deduction in the month the property is put into use.

Another example is when an investor purchases (or completes construction on) a warehouse on January 1. He should be entitled to a one half-month's worth of depreciation deductions for January. He will also get 11 full months of depreciation for the remaining 11 full months he holds the property during the year.

If his investment (tax basis) in the building was $1 million, he would get approximately $30,423 in depreciation deductions ($1,000,000/31.5-year depreciation period = $31,746 depreciation per year × (11.5 months allowed/12 months in the year)).

If the investor purchased the building on January 31, he would have the same result.

Planning Tips. If you are constructing a building, carefully watch the date you can begin claiming depreciation. Generally, depreciation can be claimed when the building is used for its intended purpose—usually rental (placed in service). If you're close to the end of the month, try to complete the building and put it in use (or close the purchase on the building) before the start of the new month—it will mean an extra half-month's worth of depreciation deductions for the month you complete it and a full month of deductions in the next month. For some planning ideas on how to speed up the date on which you can begin depreciating a building, see the discussion concerning the new capitalization rules in Chapter 3.

Another planning tip is when negotiating the purchase or sale of a building give consideration to what the sale date will do to your deductions. NOTE—The new laws create an interesting twist to this standard tax planning point. In the past both the buyer and the seller would want to argue about the closing date in part because of the depreciation benefits which would end or begin on that date. What one party stood to gain the other stood to lose. Now, however, the buyer or the seller may be subject to the passive loss limitation rules—so one or the other may not get any benefit from additional depreciation deductions (see Chapter 9). Thus only one party may stand to gain from the depreciation deductions. If business and financing considerations permit, consider the impact of this new twist to both parties during the sale negotiations.

Example. How badly has the new tax law reduced the value of your depreciation benefits? Let's compare the results the investor got in the prior example to what he would have received under the old law. To simplify the example we'll make a few assumptions. We'll calculate depreciation on the straight-line method assuming equal deductions in each year. Assume all tax benefits are received at year-end. Finally, one complication must be dealt with: The tax benefits will be received over a long period of time so that we must discount them to determine their worth in terms of today's dollars. This discounting process incorporates the time value (interest cost) of money into our analysis. Assume a 12% interest (discount) rate is appropriate.

OLD LAW

Depreciation [$1,000,000 cost/19 years]	$ 52,632
Tax rate	× 50%
Annual tax benefit	$ 26,316
Present value of tax benefit of $26,316 per year for 19 years at 12%	$193,838

NEW LAW

Depreciation [$1,000,000 cost/31.5 years]	$ 31,746
Tax rate	× 28%
Annual tax benefit	$ 8,889
Present value of tax benefit of $8,889 per year for 31.5 years at 12%	$ 71,989

The difference in tax benefits is tremendous! On the same building the value of your depreciation tax benefits dropped from $193,838 to $71,989—a decline of $121,849! Notice that the tough new depreciation rule is only part of the cause. The reduced tax rate is responsible for $65,288 of the reduced benefit.

Planning Tip. Is tax planning for depreciation deductions still worth while? In many cases the benefits of planning will be significant. But in many situations it won't be. For example, if the passive loss or other limitations will prevent you from taking advantage of the results of your planning efforts, then don't bother. Some of the tax planning you did in the past may no longer be worth the cost. With much lower tax rates the value of any tax savings is substantially reduced. If you're in the lower 15% rate bracket, each $100 in tax savings is only worth $15. This is exactly what Congress intended. CAUTION—When considering tax planning ideas with your tax advisor make sure the potential for savings can reasonably exceed the fee you will have to pay for the advice.

Certain land improvements are now depreciated over a 15-year period using the 150% declining balance method with a switch to the straight-line method at the time which maximizes deductions. Depreciable land improvements can include, for example, sidewalks, roads, bridges, fences, landscaping and shrubbery. It does not include buildings and their structural components. The declining balance method is illustrated in the following discussions on personal property. Sewer pipes are depreciated over a 20-year period.

Depreciating Fixtures and Equipment—New Law

Personal property (cars, equipment, furniture, etc.) which real estate investors will encounter will generally be written off over a five or seven-year period on an accelerated basis. For example, most cars, light trucks, and utility vehicles will be depreciated over five years. Most office furniture, fixtures, and equipment (desks, files, safes, and certain communication equipment) will be depreciated over seven years. This accelerated basis is calculated at twice the rate of the ratable (straight-line) method. A half-year convention applies to personal property. The following example illustrates how this works for five-year property.

Example. Let's say you purchased a utility vehicle for $10,000. This vehicle is written off over five years. If you wrote off the vehicle using the straight-line method you would deduct $2,000 per year in depreciation ($10,000 cost/5 years). This can be translated to a 20% depreciation rate ($2,000 write-off/$10,000 cost). The new law provides for an accelerated depreciation rate that is twice this rate (called the "200% declining balance method"). Thus a 40% rate is used. In the first year, in accordance with the half-year convention, a 20% rate is used (one-half the regular 40% rate). Depreciation is calculated as follows:

Year	Cost-Depreciation	Depreciation Rate	Depreciation
1	$10,000	40% × 1/2	$ 2,000
2	8,000	40	3,200
3	4,800	40	1,920
4	2,880	40	1,150
5	1,730	—	1,150
6	580	—	580
			$10,000

ª The law permits a switch to the straight-line (ratable) method when this method would provide larger deductions. In the fifth year the accelerated (200% declining balance) method would provide a depreciation deduction of $690 (40% × 1,730). Switching to the straight-line method, however, provides a deduction of $1,150 ($1,730 of costs not yet written off divided by the 1.5 years remaining in the depreciation period). The half-year convention results in pushing depreciation into the sixth year.

The calculations for seven-year property are made in a similar manner

Special Write-Off of Personal Property

The new law provides that up to $10,000 of personal property can be written off in the year it is purchased for use in your trade or business (mere passive investment won't suffice). This special allowance is phased out, on a dollar-for-dollar basis, when qualified investments exceed $200,000.

Example. An investor renovates his medical/apartment building. He spends $35,000 on carpentry work, carpeting, certain equipment and so forth. Of the $35,000 spent, $10,000 is properly treated as five-year-personal property. The investor could elect to expense the $10,000 personal property acquisition under this special rule instead of writing it off over the five-year period illustrated above.

What's the tax benefit to the investor of this immediate deduction? Assuming he is at the maximum 28% tax rate, the new law provides that, beginning in 1988, his benefit would be $2,800 ($10,000 × 28%).

CAUTION—Before jumping the gun consult your accountant—will the new passive loss or other limitations in the new law prevent you from realizing the value of this immediate write-off?

What is the value of the tax benefit of this immediate write-off as compared with the investor depreciating the property over the regular five-year period? (A 12% interest (discount) rate has been assumed.)

Depreciation		Tax Rate		Tax Benefit		PV Factor		PV
$ 2,000	×	28%	=	$ 560	×	.8929	=	$ 500
3,200	×	28	=	896	×	.7972	=	714
1,920	×	28	=	538	×	.7118	=	383
1,150	×	28	=	322	×	.6355	=	205
1,150	×	28	=	322	×	.5674	=	183
580				162				82
$10,000				$2,800				$2,067

ª Depreciation figures are taken from the chart in the previous example. A PV factor is the fraction resulting from the mathematical formula which converts a future cash flow into its value in terms of today's dollars. PV is present value.

Although the total tax benefit of writing off the property is $2,800 ($10,000 cost × 28% tax rate), its value in terms of to-day's dollars is only $2,067. The $733 reduction ($2,800 − $2,067) can be thought of as the interest you could have earned over the same period on these tax benefits if you had received them all at once.

Next, what's the present value of the tax benefit of immediately writing off the $10,000 in qualifying property?

$10,000 cost × 28% tax rate × .8929 PV factor (since the tax benefit is assumed to be received at year-end) = $2,500

Thus, the value of this additional benefit is $433.

What does this mean? Any invester who can claim this extra benefit without much hassle should claim it. For larger investors the value of the benefit is likely to be very small relative to the income or loss from their property. If it can be claimed easily it should be claimed. If any expense or hassle is involved it may not be worthwhile; it's simply not a sufficient dollar amount. For personal property which must be written off over seven years (most fixtures and furniture) the value of this tax benefit will be even greater.

Planning Tip. If you're buying assets so that the $200,000 phaseout may be reached, consider delaying some of your purchases to the early part of the following year if business considerations permit. This could enable you to write off the costs immediately, rather than over a six-year period as illustrated in the earlier example. Note also that some personal property is written off over periods other than five (six) years. If you have a choice between properties, expense those which would have to be depreciated over longer periods first. These refinements, however, are probably not critical for most real estate investors. This special write-off provision is limited to the taxable income from the trade or business. Thus it can't be used to create a loss.

If the property you deducted under this special provision is switched (converted) to a personal use (e.g., you give a type-writer which you deducted to your son to take to college), a portion of the earlier deduction may have to be added back to your taxable income (recaptured).

NEW ALTERNATIVE DEPRECIATION SYSTEM

It was mentioned earlier that although a primary purpose of the ACRS depreciation rules was to simplify calculating deprecia-tion the system wasn't very simplifying. The new alternative depreciation system is but one example of the complexities that exist.

For purposes of determining the AMT an additional deprecia-tion deduction is required. Depreciation must be computed us-ing a much less favorable rate. The difference between the depreciation calculated using the general rates described thus far (e.g., 27.5 years for residential real estate) and the rates re-quired under the new alternative depreciation system, is treated as a tax preference item (TPI). Tax preference items enter into the AMT calculation. All this is explained and illustrated in Chapter 11.

Congress has also required this less favorable depreciation de-duction for property used predominantly outside the United States (i.e., foreign real estate being depreciated by a U.S. taxpayer), for property leased to certain tax-exempt entities, for property fi-nanced with certain tax-exempt bonds (see Chapter 2), for com-puting earning and profits (the tax equivalent of retained earnings in financial statements), and so forth. Also, you can irrevocably elect to write off your real property improvements using these less favorable deductions. For real estate a 40-year period using the straight-line method is employed. For land improvements such as roads and fences a 20-year period is used. Sewers are written off over 50 years. If this treatment is used for personal property (furniture, fixtures, etc.) the property will be written off over a longer period than under the regular rules discussed earlier (over the "asset depreciation range (ADR) midpoint life").

For furniture and fixtures (which are not structural components of buildings) the alternative depreciation system depreciation period is 10 years. For typewriters, copiers, and the like it is six years. For assets which weren't assigned asset depreciation range ("ADR") midpoint lives, the alternative depreciation system requires that a 12-year depreciation period be used.

Planning Tip. Why would you want to elect to write off your real estate investments over a 40-year period if you could use the 27.5 or 31.5-year period? If you can't get any benefit from the extra deductions, and claiming them could create additional AMT problems, the longer depreciation period may actually be worth electing. (See Chapter 11 and review the elections with your accountant.)

With this background on depreciation and the effects of the Tax Reform Act of 1986 we can now look at a number of tax planning ideas which you can use to try to mitigate the harsh effects of the new depreciation rules. CAUTION—As has been repeated so often, don't try to implement any of these planning ideas without first securing competent professional tax advice.

Planning Tip—Start Your Depreciation Write-Offs as Soon as Possible. Your depreciation write-offs will be lower under the new law, so get the most you can out of them. Begin depreciating your buildings as soon as possible.

When can you begin depreciating a building? As soon as it is in a condition or state of readiness and availability for its assigned function. Let's say you are building a warehouse designed to the specifications of a tenant. The building is designed to accommodate the specific machinery and handling equipment your tenant will use. The building is completed in March. Inclement weather has held up the delivery of the special handling equipment until May. Thus the building will not be usable until some time after May when the equipment can be installed. When can you begin depreciating the building? There could be a good argument to begin writing off the building in March when it was in a condition to accommodate the special equipment, even though the building could not be used by the tenant until much later.

Watch the depreciation start date on leased property. Many investors don't begin writing off their buildings until the lease for the building commences. Often this is correct since the tenant may be obligated to begin paying rent when the landlord's work on the premises is completed—and the building is not ready for use until this time. But sometimes depreciation can be claimed sooner. If the building is ready to be occupied by a tenant, check with your tax advisor. It may be possible to begin depreciating the building even though a tenant is not available for a long time. The key is that the building must be ready and available for use as a rental and that you are seeking to rent it.

It is important to watch the date at which depreciation is to begin for another reason. If a building is ready in December but you overlook this fact and begin depreciating the building in January of the following year, you will have lost a month's worth of depreciation forever! Once depreciation is missed it is gone—it can't be recaptured by claiming more depreciation in later years.

Additional planning opportunities may be available when you're building a multifloor or multiunit project. Consider rushing the completion of construction on identifiable floors, units, or other segments of the project. This may enable you to begin depreciating those segments even though the rest of the project is not yet complete. By concentrating your resources you can often improve the depreciation write-offs on a project significantly. When a floor or wing is complete get a certificate of occupancy to support your position. Better yet—get a rent-paying tenant in that area.

This type of planning was very important in light of the changes made by the Tax Reform Act of 1986. Here's why: The passive loss limitation rules (which could reduce or eliminate the benefit of your depreciation and other write-offs) is being phased in over a number of years for buildings placed in service before the effective date of the act: 35% of your passive losses can be disallowed in 1987. In 1988 this amount increases to a 60% disallowance. The phaseout continues until 1991 when all your passive losses could be disallowed.

When you combine these two factors there was a tremendous incentive to claim depreciation on a property as soon as possible. In the past the major incentive for trying to get your depreciation write-offs as soon as possible was the time value of money—the write-offs were worth more the sooner you got them. Under the new law having placed a building in service before the effective date of the act may mean the difference between using deductions now or many years in the future (when the passive loss carryovers are eventually triggered—see Chapter 9) and it also may mean the difference in getting deductions worth 38.5 cents on the dollar versus deductions worth only 28 cents on the dollar.

Example. An investor put a $2 million office building into service on February 1, 1986. The depreciation deduction will be $92,105 ($2,000,000 cost/19 years × (10.5 months in use/12 months in the year)). If the investor is subject to the passive loss limitations then only $36,842 in losses (assuming that the depreciation deductions increase the losses directly for purposes of our example) will be available to offset his other income (60% of the loss is disallowed in 1988 so that only 40% of the $92,105 loss can be used). Since the maximum tax bracket in 1988 is 28%, the usable loss will provide a tax benefit of $10,316 ($36,842 in loss × 28%). Thus the average tax benefit the investor will get for each of the 12 months he has the building in use in 1988 will be $860 ($10,316 tax benefit/12 months the building was in use).

Let's say the investor was able to get the building into use on November 1, 1987. What will his tax benefits be? He will be able to claim depreciation write-offs of $7,937 ($2,000,000 cost/31.5 years × (1.5 months in use/12 months in the year)). The loss we are assuming his depreciation benefit will generate will also be subject to the passive loss limitation rules. But since the building was placed in use after the effective date of tax reform all of an investor's passive losses are disallowed. Thus he will not be able to benefit from 65% of the $7,937 loss. This loss will not provide him with any tax benefit. The average tax benefit the investor will get for each of the two months he has the building in use in 1987 will be zero. This example illustrates the importance of placing real estate in service as soon as possible and the impact of the passive loss rule phase-in on the value of depreciation deductions.

There are many ways to accelerate the date a building is placed in service. Consult with your experts—architect, engineer, general contractor, tax advisor, and so forth. Each project will have its own special factors that will help or hinder your efforts; be creative and analyze all the circumstances of each deal for opportunities. The following are a few examples.

1. Consider the flow and scheduling of work on a construction or renovation project. Many projects are planned so that job 1 is started and completed before job 2 begins. When job 2 is completed then job 3 is started. This approach may be acceptable if you're not in a hurry. But if the business and tax benefits are sufficient, it may be worth incurring the additional efforts and costs to reorganize the job flow. It may be possible to reschedule the job sequence so that jobs 1, 4, and 17 are done at the same time. List all the major jobs that must be complete. Then make a chart showing the jobs in their order of absolute priority, that is, which jobs must be done before certain other jobs can be done. (This approach is an operations research technique known as PERT—Program Evaluation and Review Technique, or CPM—Critical Path Method.) For example, the foundation obviously must be poured before the brick work can be done. But landscaping, parking lot improvements, fencing, and access roads located away from the immediate building site may be done in almost any sequence. Once this grid of required priorities is established, you and your engineer, architect, and general contractor can determine the optimal sequence for the construction process which will simultaneously complete as many tasks as possible. As in any construction process, you will have to monitor the work flow continually to adjust for the many changes and delays that may occur. Union and other work rule restrictions will also have to be taken into account. Another advantage of this type of analysis is that it can help you identify bottlenecks in the construction process—in advance, when you can best plan for them.

2. Examine the location of the mechanical equipment in the building. Many building designs automatically call for the mechanical equipment to be located on the roof or upper floors. In some instances it may be possible to redesign the building so that much of the mechanical equipment is located in the basement. This approach can significantly accelerate the construction process since lower floors may be completed and put into use much sooner than if they had to await completion of the upper floors containing the mechanical equipment.

3. Review your building design and material choices with your architect. It may be possible to substitute certain prefabricated components. Even if additional expense is incurred, it may still

be beneficial if the additional rent and tax benefits you can earn by getting the building into use sooner are substantial.

4. If you are developing a building and the tenants are going to be responsible for the leasehold improvements, it often can be more efficient to require the tenants to use your general contractor rather then their own: If the tenants are going to use their own contractor, it may not be possible to start construction of the leasehold improvements until your contractor is completely finished. There could be union conflicts or other problems if the tenants use a different contractor. Also, if your general contractor already has an office, supervisor, workers, materials, and so forth on site, it will probably be much more efficient to have the work done by him. If you decide to require the tenant to use your contractor, have your lawyer put appropriate language to this effect in the lease agreement. Also, be certain to require the tenant to have acceptable plans and specifications completed by a given date. There won't be any benefit to this planning idea if the tenant is able to delay the entire project by not having adequate plans in on time (see Chapter 4).

5. Set up construction and project milestone dates. For example, all architectural plans must be complete by August 1, the test drilling and general site grading must be complete by September 15, and so forth. Monitor the progress of the work. If something is not completed by its due date, follow up immediately. If this approach is not used it is possible for the entire project to be delayed for a significant period of time before anyone responsible takes action. Consider negotiating penalties or incentives for all participants to complete their tasks by the appropriate milestone dates. For example, if a tenant does not have complete and acceptable plans and specifications to you by the pertinent date in the lease, your contribution (allowance) toward his improvements will be reduced. Perhaps a bonus could be offered to the general contractor for completing work on or before a milestone date, and a penalty required if work is completed more than some reasonable time after the milestone date (unless due to factors beyond the contractor's control such as weather, strikes, etc.).

6. A related planning point has to do with the new rules for construction period expenses. As explained more fully in Chapter 3, tax reform requires that many costs incurred during the construction of a building be added to your investment in the

building rather than deducted (i.e., they must be capitalized). Many of these costs were written off ("amortized") over a 10-year period under prior law. Others were deducted immediately. The new rules will require that many of these costs be capitalized as part of the cost of the building and be depreciated, as part of the building, over 27.5 years for residential property, 31.5 years for nonresidential property, or 40 years for property subject to the alternative depreciation system (e.g., for purposes of the alternative minimum tax). To the extent that you can plan to limit the amount of expenses which must be capitalized under this rule, you will be able to minimize the costs which must be written off over the tough new depreciation periods. A key planning idea in this regard is to get your building into use as soon as possible so that the construction period will be considered over. Once the construction period ends the new rules requiring capitalization of many costs will no longer apply (see Chapter 3).

Planning Tip—Depreciating Land. Every real estate investor knows that you can't depreciate land. That's true most of the time. But sometimes certain land improvement costs can qualify for depreciation over the new 15-year-depreciation period. The key to qualify is that the improvement must be depreciable. Although this may be obvious for some improvements such as fences there can be a number of less obvious land improvement costs which can qualify to be depreciated. Careful planning can net you a much better depreciation deduction from your investment. First, a little background.

The concept underlying depreciation is that the expenditure you make for an asset, such as a building, will provide you a benefit for a long period of time. Therefore, it doesn't make much sense to let you write off the cost of the asset or building in the year you pay for it. The building, however, will not last forever. At some future time the building will be worn out by use and the effects of the elements. The costs you spent in acquiring the building should be written off over this period of usefulness. Now take a look at land. Land, just like the building, will provide you with value for a long period of time. Therefore, just like the building, the amount you pay to acquire land shouldn't be deductible in the year you pay it. The costs associated with acquiring land are therefore added to your basis or investment in the land (i.e., they are capitalized). What about the period of usefulness? Unlike buildings, land will theoretically be usable forever. It is not affected by use or the elements (in most cases). When your building is worn out and useless you can tear it down and start again with a new building on the same land.

Thus land is not considered to be a wasting asset for tax purposes and therefore can generally not be depreciated. However, some costs associated with land improvements can, in certain instances, qualify for depreciation write-offs. The key is to identify and segregate these depreciable land improvement costs from other land costs.

Some land improvement costs are never depreciable. The costs associated with general clearing and grading of land are considered integrally related to the land itself and can never be deducted. These costs must be added to your investment in the land. The only tax benefit they will provide is a reduction in the amount of any gain you may have to report when you ultimately sell the land.

What land improvement costs qualify for depreciation? The costs of improvements so closely associated with the development of a building that the improvements will have to be abandoned contemporaneously with the abandonment of the building qualify for depreciation. The theory is simple: These land costs are so integrally related to the building that they will become valueless when the building itself becomes worthless or is abandoned.

Examples of qualifying land improvement costs include the construction of a moat surrounding a building or of berms designed to visually blend the building into the surrounding land (since they can only have a use with the specific building they were designed for). The costs of digging foundations should qualify. The costs of backfilling and grading to lay sewer pipe, constructing access and utility roads, related improvement costs in certain industrial parks, and excavation and grading closely associated with, and uniquely related to, the facility being constructed may qualify.

Example. A developer is constructing a multiuse office, shopping, and residential project. The site on which the project will be constructed is covered with dense brush and other wild shrubbery. A few small sloping hills also dot the plot. The site must be cleared and graded in order for the project to be completed. The costs associated with this clearing and grading can't be depreciated; the developer must add these costs to the investment (tax basis) in the land. The residential units in the planned complex should have an entranceway distinct from the commercial facilities. It is determined that this can best be accomplished by providing a below-grade driveway and lobby area. The developer feels that this approach will provide the maximum privacy for the residential facilities. The opposite approach, of making the commercial entrance ways below-grade, was not even considered. The retailers and other commercial users greatly value the visibility the project offers them from a nearby highway. The department store anchoring the shopping mall wants to have direct access to its lower-level selling floor and package pickup area. This is accomplished by significant earth moving and grading to contour the land to the department store's building design. The costs incurred in preparing the land for both the residential units and the department store should be depreciable.

Planning Tip—Maximizing the Amount of Property Which Can Be Depreciated When You Acquire Real Estate. This is a standard planning idea that has been used for many years. The very long 31.5-year depreciation period the new law mandates for real property makes this planning idea even more important.

When you purchase land and a building, or the assets of a business which include land and a building, the purchase price must be allocated among the land, building, and other assets. This allocation process is critical to determining the tax benefits you will later be able to obtain. The portion of the purchase price which must be allocated to the land will not qualify for depreciation deductions. This will be one of the least favorable allocations you can make. The portion of the purchase price which can be allocated to the building will qualify for depreciation deductions over a 27.5- or 31.5-year period for residential and nonresidential property, respectively. This is significantly more advantageous than the allocations made to land. It is not, however, the best allocation which you can make.

Many times when acquiring land and a building, and almost always when dealing with the acquisition of a business, other assets will exist to which you can allocate portions of the purchase price and get even more favorable tax benefits. For example, if you are acquiring a warehouse or apartment complex, there may be tools, equipment, furniture, and other fixtures which you are acquiring. To the extent that a portion of the purchase price can be allocated to these assets you may get a significant tax advantage. This is because many of these non-real estate assets can be written off over much more rapid depreciation periods and using accelerated depreciation (often at a rate twice as rapid as the rate allowed for real estate). An example will illustrate.

Example. An investor is planning to buy a building from a developer. The sales price is $855,000. The parties agree that $145,000 of this should be attributable to the land and $710,000 to the building. Before signing the sales contract the investor consults his tax advisor. A review of the premises shows that $90,000 of the cost allocable to the building is actually for the purchase of carpeting, removable shelving and paneling, certain light fixtures, planters, lobby furniture, and electronic and data processing hookups. The tax advisor determines that these properties can properly be treated as personal property depreciable over a five- or seven-year period under the new law. The investor renegotiates the contract to specify that $90,000 of the cost is allocable to these items and only $620,000 to the building itself. What is the tax benefit?

The value of properly characterizing this property is the additional value of the more rapid depreciation deductions as compared with the slower depreciation deductions which would be allowed had the costs been treated as allocable to real property. Since these benefits will be received over long periods of time, a present value analysis is necessary in order to consider the time value of money. The approach will be to calculate the present value of the tax benefits under each option and to compare the results.

Value of Tax Benefits without Planning. Without the advice his tax advisor provided, the investor would have treated the $90,000 as part of the cost of the building. As such, the $90,000 would have been depreciated over the 31.5-year period required by the Tax Reform Act of 1986. Let's assume that the appropriate discount rate (cost of funds, interest rate) that should be used in the analysis is 12%. The value in terms of today's dollars (present value) of all future tax benefits the investor could realize from this is determined as follows:

Depreciable investment (tax basis)	$90,000
Depreciation period	31.5
Depreciation per year	$ 2,857
Maximum tax rate (after 1987)	× 28%
Tax benefit per year	$ 800

The present value of an $800 tax benefit to be received for 31.5 years when the discount rate is 12% is $6,479. (This is the present value of an annuity of $800 for 31.5 years at 12%.)

Value of Tax Benefits with Tax Planning. To simplify the example, assume that the entire $90,000 is properly treated as five-year property. A large portion may actually have to be treated as seven-year property.

The value of the tax benefits if the $90,000 is treated as five-year personal property is the sum of the present values of the tax benefits earned in each of the six years for which depreciation is claimed. This is computed as follows:

	Year 1	Year 2	Year 3	Year 4	Year 5	Year 6
Adjusted basis	$90,000	$72,000	$43,200	$25,920	$15,552	$45,184
Dep'n %	20%	40%	40%	40%	St. Line[b]	St. Line[b]
Depreciation	18,000	28,800	17,280	10,368	10,368	5,184
Tax rate	28%	28%	28%	28%	28%	28%
Tax benefit	5,040	8,064	4,838	2,903	2,903	1,452
Present value factor[c]	.8929	.7972	.7118	.6355	.5674	.5066
Present value	4,500	6,429	3,444	1,845	1,647	735
Total present value	$18,600					

[a] Dep'n % = The depreciation rate for five-year property under the new law.
[b] St. Line = Straight-line depreciation. At a point in time where it will maximize deductions, the new law permits a switch to the straight-line (ratable) method.
[c] PV factor = The mathematical fraction necessary to convert a future cash flow into terms of today's dollars assuming a 12% interest rate.

Value of Tax Planning on Purchase of Building. The value of the tax planning advice the investor received is easily computed. The excess of the present value of the tax benefits of depreciating the $90,000 reclassified assets as five-year-class property over the present value of the tax benefits of leaving the $90,000 classified as realty is the benefit of planning:

Present value with planning	$18,600
Present value without planning	6,479
Value of tax planning	$12,121

Planning Tips. Up to $10,000 of the $90,000 allocated to personal property in the above example could qualify for immediate deduction under the elective expensing provisions discussed earlier.

Another planning tip is when doing this type of planning be certain that your tax advisor considers the impact of the new passive loss rules. If you will not be able to obtain the projected tax benefit, the value of the planning may be reduced or even eliminated.

The previous example makes it clear that there can be a tremendous advantage to allocating as much cost as possible to the assets which can be depreciated the most rapidly. But how can you do this? There are a number of ways to allocate the purchase price of a number of assets. Consider each of the various methods and then review the matter with your accountant to see which of the acceptable approaches is the most advantageous.

1. *Sales Agreement.* The first and most obvious place to look concerning the allocation of the purchase price is to the contract you and the seller signed. If the contract provided for an allocation and that allocation is the result of reasonable arm's-length negotiations (i.e., the result of good-faith negotiations between adverse parties), it should be used. So long as the contract allocations were not contrivances to achieve a tax benefit for one of the parties the IRS is likely to accept them. If the purchaser and seller are related it may be difficult to justify the allocations. One solution is to obtain independent bids from third parties as to each of the assets in questions. An independent appraiser could also be used.

Obviously you should carefully consider the tax consequences of the sales contract's provisions during any negotiation. It is thus very important to consult with your tax advisor during negotiations. It will probably be too late for most tax planning ideas in this area once you have signed the contract.

Under prior law the seller's and buyer's interest were often adverse. For example, the buyer would want the maximum allocation in the sales contract to the building so that he could maximize later depreciation deductions. The seller, on the other hand, would have wanted the maximum allocation to the land. Why? The price paid for the land in excess of his investment (tax basis) would probably have been taxed as a capital gain—at a maximum tax rate of 20%. However, to the extent that the sales price which was allocated to the building exceeded his investment (tax basis) in the building (which would have been reduced by prior depreciation deductions), he could have been taxed at ordinary income—at tax rates up to 50% (i.e., as a result of depreciation recapture).

Look what tax reform has done to this bargaining process. There will generally no longer be any difference between "depreciation recapture" and capital gains. If the maximum tax rate for all types of income is 28% (after 1987), then the seller will no longer have any incentive to fight with the buyer to allocate sales costs to the land. The buyer, however, will still benefit tremendously from the allocation of the purchase price to the building. Two results will follow: the tone of negotiations will change, and the IRS will look with an even more suspicious eye at contract allocations that appear to be unusual.

2. *Appraisal.* Sometimes the most objective method of allocating the purchase price to the various assets is to obtain an independent appraisal. An appraiser can use numerous techniques and independent professional judgment to estimate the fair value of each of the assets purchased. The actual purchase price can then be allocated to each asset based on its relative value.

Example. An investor purchased a building and land from a seller for $434,000. The sales contract was silent as to the allocation of the purchase price between the building and the land. The investor hired an appraiser who determined that the value of the building was $367,000 and the value of the land was $198,000, for a total value of $565,000. The investor could then allocate the purchase price between the two as follows:

Building =

$$\frac{\text{value of building } \$367,000}{\substack{\text{value of building + land} \\ (\$367,000 + \$198,000)}} \times \$434,000 \text{ price} = \$281,908$$

Land =

$$\frac{\text{value of land \$198,000}}{\text{value of building} + \text{land}} \times \$434,000 \text{ price} = \$152,092$$
$$(\$367,000 + \$198,000)$$

$$\underline{\$434,000}$$

CAUTION—A number of problems can arise when dealing with an appraisal. An appraiser can be expensive. And the IRS is not obligated to accept an appraiser's conclusion if it believes the appraisal is not fair.

3. *Capitalization of Rental Value.* This is a common technique used in the real estate industry. If a building or land can be rented for a certain rental value determined from market rates for similar properties, these rentals can be "capitalized" by a rate ("cap" rate) to obtain an estimated value of the property. If the building is currently leased, that rental rate may provide a starting point. Cap rates are rough approximations determined by market values of similar types of properties.

Examples. The investor buying a property knows that similar buildings sell at cap rates of about 9.5%. The building is currently rented at $30,000 per year. But the investor has already negotiated a renewal rent to begin shortly at an annual rate of $42,500. He feels this rate is appropriate for the property. The value of the property could be estimated as follows:

$$\text{Property value} = \frac{\text{fair rental value \$42,500}}{\text{cap rate 9.5\%}} = \$447,368$$

This approach is useful if a number of real estate properties are acquired for a single sales price.

In some instances it may be possible to use the capitalization approach to value the building being purchased. In these situations the difference between the capitalized rental value of the building and the total purchase price may be allocable to land.

4. *Tax Assessor's Values.* It is sometimes helpful to look at the local property tax bill and to allocate the total purchase price paid by the relative values in the tax assessor's bill.

For example, when an investor buys a property containing a small apartment house and the underlying land. The purchase price is $2.5 million. The sales contract is silent as to any allocation. The tax assessor's roll shows the building valued at $1,540,000 and the land valued at $535,000. The ratio of these two values can be used to allocate the purchase price in the same manner illustrated earlier for the allocation of the appraiser's estimates. Using this approach the investor would value his land at $644,578 and the building at $1,855,422.

Since there are no hard-and-fast rules it may be possible in appropriate circumstances to use the method which will prove most favorable to you. Be careful, since penalties can be assessed for improperly valuing assets. Thus it's best to make the decision in consultation with your tax advisor.

In allocating the purchase price for assets, you must be aware of a change which tax reform has made. In allocating the purchase price for certain acquisitions of a going concern (a business), the "residual method" may have to be employed. This allocation method, in general terms, requires that the purchase price first be allocated to cash and cash-type items. The remaining portion of the purchase price is then allocated to marketable securities. Next, the remaining portion is allocated to all other assets up to the amount of their fair market values. The remaining portion is allocated to goodwill. Since goodwill can't be deducted for tax purposes, the allocation to goodwill will be detrimental.

Planning Tip. Stay alert for tools, fixtures, equipment, planters, and other items which can be written off quickly.

Planning Tip—Using a Tax-Free Like-Kind Exchange To Increase Your Depreciation Deductions. Again, a time-honored tax planning device may continue to prove advantageous after tax reform. First, a bit of background on what a like-kind exchange is.

A like-kind exchange is one in which an investor or owner exchanges real estate with another taxpayer for that taxpayer's real estate which is of a like kind. The key is that the transaction must be a reciprocal transfer of properties and not a sale and repurchase of a new property. The real estate traded and received must be used in the trade or business of the investor, or held by him for investment. If the transaction is properly structured the investor will not be taxed on the transfer. The theory behind this favorable tax treatment is that the investor has not liquidated his investment. He continues to hold similar property and has not realized any cash with which to pay any tax which would be due. If nonlike-kind property (called "boot") is received in the exchange, this principle will be violated and gain may have to be recognized. Nonlike-kind property could include cash, furniture, or relief of mortgages (i.e., the recipient of your property assumes your mortgage and you do not assume a mortgage of his of a similar amount).

What is "like-kind" property? It is liberally defined to include a broad array of real estate. Investment property (e.g., raw land held for appreciation potential) can be exchanged for property used in a trade or business. Similarly, real estate used in a trade or business (e.g., a warehouse or a parking lot) can be exchanged for property held for investment. Thus the properties exchanged must be of a like or similar nature or character but not of a similar grade or quality. Thus a 20-year lease for a warehouse could not be exchanged for a fee ownership in another warehouse under the like-kind exchange rules. However, raw land held for investment could be exchanged for a shopping center held for investment since the grade of the properties is not a factor.

CAUTION—When planning to do a like-kind exchange, be careful that the transaction is completed within the required time periods or you could find yourself subject to an unexpected tax. The property you intend to receive in exchange for your property must be identified within about 45 days of transferring your property. Also, the exchange must generally be completed within 180 days after the transfer of the property exchanged, or the extended due date of your tax return if later.

When you exchange appreciated real estate for other real estate and the like-kind exchange requirements are met, you won't have to recognize any gain for tax purposes. But you won't get away for free. Eventually you will have to pay the tax you owe. The concept behind a tax-deferred exchange is that your investment has not been liquidated. So when you do liquidate your investment the tax you deferred on the earlier transfer will be due. The mechanism to accomplish this deferral and eventual payment of tax is the "carryover basis." What this means is that your investment (tax basis) in the property exchanged carries over and becomes your "investment" (tax basis) in the property you receive. The appreciation remains untaxed only until you liquidate your investment. At that time the difference between what you sell for and your low carryover basis will be taxed.

Examples. An investor buys land in New Hampshire for $100,000 in 1984. The investor had made a shrewd investment—by 1987 his land was worth $250,000. He decides to move to Oregon and prefers to keep his investment land near him. He has two options: (1) sell the appreciated land for $250,000 and pay his 28% capital gains tax on the $150,000 appreciation ($42,000 in tax) or (2) exchange his land in a tax-free like-kind exchange for a small garden apartment building located in Oregon. The apartment building is worth $250,000 and has no mortgages on it. He opts for the apartment building since he wants to put off paying tax as long as possible. The transaction is arranged to qualify as a tax-free like-kind exchange. The investor avoids any current tax. His $100,000 investment (tax basis) in the land carries over and becomes his tax basis in the apartment building. Thus if he sold the apartment building the next day for its $250,000 value he would have to report $150,000 in taxable gain—the exact gain he deferred on the exchange of the land. If he holds the apartment building for one year and sells it in 1988 for its then fair value of $350,000, his taxable gain is $250,000 ($350,000 amount realized less $100,000 tax basis). Notice that this gain is comprised of two components—the $150,000 gain deferred on the original exchange and $100,000 in additional appreciation on the apartment property.

With this background we can now ask the important question: How can a tax-free like-kind exchange be used to boost your depreciation deductions? The planning concept is to obtain in the trade real estate which has a more favorable land-to-building ratio so that more of your investment (tax basis) will qualify for depreciation.

Another example is if the investor in the previous example decides not to sell his garden apartment building in 1988. Instead he holds it until 1989 when it is worth $500,000. He now has a lot of confidence in his real estate acumen and decides to exchange the garden apartment building for a real estate investment which will provide greater deductions to shelter the cash flow. He spots an office building which he feels would be a good candidate. The office building has a value of $500,000—the same as his garden apartment. He negotiates a tax-free exchange. Notice what he has accomplished. The garden apartment had a lot of land relative to the building—garden apartment tenants like to have trees and grass. Thus only 70% of the value of the garden apartments was allocable to the building; therefore only 70% of his original $100,000 would have qualified for depreciation. The office building he has just received in the exchange is far less land-intensive. As a highrise office building with minimal land (since the parking deck was built under the building), fully 95% of the value of the property is allocable to the building. Now $95,000 of his $100,000 tax basis in his investment (which actually would have been reduced by depreciation claimed on the garden apartments) can be depreciated. On a larger scale this type of planning can significantly boost depreciation write-offs. The increase the investor realized when exchanging her original real estate investment—idle land—for the garden apartment would have been even more significant.

Planning Tip. Tax reform has increased the advantages of a like-kind exchange in a few ways. Under prior law the gain on the sale of real estate was often taxed at the 20% capital gains rate. After tax reform the gain will be taxed at 28%. This higher tax rate will encourage the use of a tax deferred exchange. Also, the much lower depreciation deductions available after tax reform remove what had been an incentive to use a taxable sale, rather than a tax-free exchange, because of the larger depreciation deductions then available.

In two other respects tax reform disfavors the use of a like-kind exchange. Any suspended losses the taxpayer has on his existing property won't be triggered on a like-kind exchange. Generally, the suspended passive losses will only be triggered on a taxable sale. Carefully evaluate this factor before consummating a like-kind exchange. A sale even with the higher 28% tax rate may thus be preferable (see Chapter 9). A corporation subject to the alternative minimum tax could pay tax on a like-kind exchange as a result of the book income preference described in Chapter 1.

Planning Tip—Lease the Land for Your Real Estate Investment Instead of Buying It, To Boost Deductions. A ground lease is simply the long-term leasing of land as contrasted with the purchase of land. It is a technique which has been in use at least since biblical times to gain the use of land. Tax reform and the current economic environment provide some important reasons to consider this traditional real estate financing too carefully.

Inflation had provided a major incentive to own tangible assets, particularly land. Tangible assets, as compared with financial assets like bonds and CDs, have historically proved to be great inflation hedges. Many unrealistic real estate syndications and deals not only became viable but lucrative because of this important factor—inflation sufficiently increased the value of the deal to make everything work out. If inflation has really subsided for the near future, then one of the most important values of land ownership has been reduced in importance. This may make a ground lease more palatable.

Tax reform has drastically reduced the value of depreciation tax benefits as described earlier. Incorporating a ground lease into a real estate transaction instead of purchasing the land may be a means of increasing the deductions the investment can provide. This is because your investment to acquire land cannot be depreciated. The rental payments under a ground lease, if properly structured, can be deductible. To the extent that tax reform encourages the use of more equity and less debt in real estate deals, the financial (leverage) benefit of a ground lease will be of greater importance.

Let's take a look at the effects a ground lease can have on a real estate investment.

Example. A builder is going to construct a small warehouse at a cost of $1 million. The land for the project should cost about $500,000 in the area he wants and with the rail/highway access he feels essential. He will be able to secure a mortgage at 14% with a 25-year amortization period. The lender is willing to lend him up to 75% of the project's total cost. The builder anticipates the following results:

Tax results:

Rents, net		$250,000
Expenses:		
Operating	$ 48,500	
Depreciation[a]	31,750	
Mortgage[b]	162,500	242,750
Income		$ 7,250
Cash flow:		
Income (above)		$ 7,250
Tax cost @ 28%		(2,030)
Add noncash expense:		
Depreciation		31,750
Cash flow		$36,970

Cash return on investment:

$$\frac{\text{Cash flow}}{\text{Investment}^c} = \frac{\$36,970}{\$375,000} = 9.86\%$$

[a] Depreciation is calculated by dividing the $1 million cost of the building by 31.5 years (rounded).

[b] A $1,125,000 mortgage is obtained. This is for 75% of the total cost (75% × ($1,000,000 building + $500,000 land)). With a 25-year amortization period monthly payments of $13,542 are due. The annual payments approximate $162,500. Assume that all the payments on the mortgage are deductible interest in order to simplify the calculations.

[c] The builder must invest $375,000. This is 25% of the total cost since the lender will only advance up to 75% of the costs (25% × ($1,000,000 building + $500,000 land)).

Now let's see what happens if the builder leases the land instead, using a ground lease:

Tax results:[a]

Rentals, net		$250,000
Expenses:		
Operating	$48,500	
Depreciation	31,750	
Mortgage[b]	108,300	
Ground rent	60,000	248,500
Income		$1,450
Cash flow:		
Income (above)	$ 1,450	
Tax cost @ 28%	(406)	
Add noncash expense:		
Depreciation	31,750	
Cash flow	$32,794	

Cash return on investment:

$$\frac{\text{Cash flow}}{\text{Investment}^c} = \frac{\$32,794}{\$250,000} = 13.12\%$$

[a] Assume the same facts as in the prior calculation unless indicated otherwise.

[b] The mortgage has been reduced since the builder is no longer financing the land purchase. Now the mortgage is only $750,000 ($1 million building cost × 75% lending ratio). On a 25-year, 14% mortgage the annual payments are about $108,300.

[c] The builder only has to invest 25% of the cost of the building, or $250,000, since the land is not being purchased.

Although the cash flow under the ground lease option has been reduced, the cash return on investment has increased. This is due to the fact that the ground rentals are an additional cash expense the builder must bear. However, the ground lease has enabled him to convert what would have been a nondeductible expenditure into a deductible expense (i.e., the rent payments under the ground lease). Importantly, the ground lease has enabled him to invest less. Thus, the lower cash return still translates into a higher overall return on his investment.

There are many advantages and disadvantages to using a ground lease. Consider the following:

The land you want to buy may not be available. The owner may simply not want to sell.

Legal constraints may prevent the owner from selling even if he wanted to.

The landowner's estate planning needs may be better served by the liquidity the ground lease offers.

If the landowner will subordinate the fee (ownership interest), the ground lessee/builder will be able to obtain much greater leasehold financing.

Leasing the land rather than selling it may enable the parties to avoid expensive transfer costs and brokerage fees.

Planning Tip—Ground Leases and the Passive Loss Rules. The ground lease could, depending on what future Treasury regulations say, possibly prove to be an excellent tax planning device to use in light of the passive loss rules enacted as part of tax reform (see Chapter 9 for a discussion of the passive loss rules). Generally, the losses realized on passive activities (rental of real estate, investments made as a limited partner, and activities in which you're not materially participating) cannot be used to offset income from active endeavors (wages as an employee, etc.) or portfolio income (interest, dividends, etc.). If you have excess losses from passive activities which you cannot use currently, the ground lease may offer a viable solution.

Example. An entrepreneur has started a successful wholesale operation. He also has passive losses from tax shelters he invested in before tax reform introduced the passive loss rules. He wants to do something to take advantage of these passive losses, but he cannot use them to offset income from this wholesale business since it's active business income under the new rules. The entrepreneur decides to buy land which he leases to the business. He anticipates using the ground rental income as passive income to offset his otherwise unusable passive losses.

This approach may be a great planning idea but it should be taken carefully. Congress realized that investors may try to use ground leases in just this way. Congress also felt that this could be too easy a way around the new passive loss rules. Therefore, Congress has specifically directed the Treasury Department to issue regulations providing rules defining income which should not be treated as passive income. One of the three areas Congress specifically suggested be looked at is ground leases. Thus it is too soon to determine how viable a planning tool ground leases will be. When these regulations are eventually issued you should review with your tax advisor what planning opportunities remain for ground leases.

Planning Tip—Removing Architectural Barriers to the Elderly and the Handicapped.

A valuable tax benefit that was due to expire was made permanent by the Tax Reform Act of 1986. Although often overlooked, this special tax benefit for removing architectural barriers to the handicapped and elderly can provide a valuable tax benefit and encourage you to do a social good which could please your customers or tenants.

Many expenditures made to modify a building, such as installing ramps, certain handrails, special bathroom facilities, and so forth, must be treated as real property improvements. This means that they must be written off over the 27.5- or 31.5-year period mandated for residential or commercial property, respectively—not much of a tax benefit, as illustrated in our earlier discussions. There may be an alternative—the special treatment afforded expenditures (up to $35,000) to remove architectural barriers. You may be able to deduct qualifying costs immediately. A simple example illustrates the value of this special benefit.

Example. A developer acquired an older building which is not accessible to the handicapped or elderly. In order to encourage the patronage of these customers he installs ramps at the main entrance (which previously only had steep stairs). He installs curb cuts, handicapped parking stalls, special bathroom equipment, and handrails. The cost of these improvements is $35,000. If these expenditures had to be treated as real property improvements he would obtain the following annual tax benefits:

Expenditures	$35,000
Depreciation period	31.5
Annual depreciation	$ 1,111
Tax rate	28%
Annual tax benefit	$ 311

The present value (i.e., the worth in terms of today's dollars) of this $311 tax benefit for 31.5 years, assuming a 12% discount (interest) rate, is $2,519.

If the developer had realized that these expenditures had qualified (or had he been able to redesign them so that they would qualify) he could have used the special treatment available for architectural barrier removal costs. If this were done he would obtain an immediate deduction for the $35,000 costs. The present value (assuming the costs are spent at the beginning of the year and the tax benefit is realized at the end of the year) is $8,750 (the present value of the $35,000 deduction × 28% tax rate). Thus he would have obtained an additional tax benefit of $6,231 ($8,750 − $2,519).

Planning Tips. If the developer in the previous example made the qualifying improvements in 1987, the additional benefit would be even greater. This is because the entire $35,000 deduction in 1987 could offset his tax at the high 38.5% maximum tax rate in effect for 1987, whereas all the deductions (except the first) he would obtain by depreciating the expenditure would only provide a tax benefit at a 28% rate. At the 38.5% tax rate in 1987 he would realize a $12,031 tax benefit (the present value of the $35,000 deduction × 38.5%). This is approximately $9,512 ($12,031 − $2,519) more than the benefit of depreciating the expenditure for 31.5 years. This means that the government has paid for about 34% of the cost of his improvements—not a bad "discount" ($12,031/$35,000).

Many expenditures may qualify for this special treatment:

Grading the ground to attain a level with a normal entrance to a building.

Sidewalks reconstructed with minimum widths and maximum gradients.

Ramps installed with nonslip surfaces and handrails.

Floor coverings with nonslip surfaces which make floors safely accessible.

Parking spaces located near entrances and large enough to permit handicapped people to enter and exit safely.

Stairs with adequate handrails and risers which do not exceed specified amounts.

Entrances on a level served by an elevator or ramps and of certain minimum widths to accommodate wheelchairs.

Doorways of sufficient widths for wheelchairs.

Water fountains hung no more than a specified height from the floor so that wheelchair-bound patrons can use them.

Public telephones located no more than a maximum distance from the floor and with equipment to facilitate use by the hearing impaired.

Bathrooms where toilet stalls have certain minimum dimensions to permit access by the wheelchair-bound and where the fixtures are located within certain maximum distances from the floor.

Elevators installed for the handicapped, and certain components of elevators such as control panels which are designed for handicapped use and are located within certain distances from the floor.

Identification signs to enable the handicapped to locate any special facilities (such as those listed above).

Let's take a brief look at the requirements which expenditures must meet to qualify. The general requirement is that the expenditures must be made to remove access barriers to the handicapped and elderly. Since these terms are broadly defined, most expenditures you think will qualify will probably qualify. Handicapped persons are those with physical or mental disabilities that either functionally limit their employment or substantially limit one of their major life activities (e.g., walking). Elderly are defined as persons aged 65 or older. The expenditures must be incurred with respect to your trade or business. You must have your accountant make the necessary election on your tax return and maintain the necessary records to substantiate your deduction. The expenditures must also be made on an existing building (i.e., the costs for these expenditures associated with new construction or as part of a comprehensive renovation won't qualify).

A number of planning tips should be kept in mind when making expenditures that might qualify for architectural barrier removal expenses. If you might spend more than the maximum $35,000 in any year, consider spreading the expenditures over two or more years so that you can take maximum advantage of the special benefit. Review plans to repair your buildings very carefully. Sometimes expenditures you're planning to make anyway can be slightly modified to qualify. Not only will you receive a much greater tax benefit, you will greatly assist a large portion of the population to have easier access to your building.

Planning Tip—Maximize Depreciation by Identifying Property Which Can Be Written Off Over Five or Seven Years.

This is another conventional planning tip which in modified form can provide tremendous benefit under tax reform. In many instances the additional benefit of using this planning idea after tax reform will be greater than the additional benefit obtained when using it before tax reform—despite the much lower tax rates now existing.

The concept of this planning idea is similar to that of maximizing the amount of property which can be depreciated when you acquire real estate. The more property which can be treated as personal property (furniture, equipment, planters, certain plumbing hookups, etc.) rather than as real property (buildings and their structural components), the better your depreciation write-offs will be. Personal property can often be written off over either a five- or seven-year period using accelerated depreciation methods (i.e., calculations which push more of the depreciation deductions into earlier years). This contrasts very favorably with real property, which must be written off over 27.5 or 31.5 years. For an illustration of the additional tax benefits which can be achieved from this idea see the example in the earlier section concerning maximizing the amount of property to be depreciated.

Let's take a closer look at what types of property can qualify as personal property—this is the key to this planning idea. CAUTION—The following discussion has been greatly simplified in order to illustrate the types of planning you may be able to do. The decisions to be made, however, are very technical ones which should only be made with a tax advisor knowledgeable in this area. (The larger national accounting firms and certain architectural and engineering firms often have departments which conduct this type of analysis.) In general, for property to qualify as personal property (and thus be depreciable over a five- or perhaps seven-year period rather than the 27.5- or 31.5-year period applicable to real property), it must meet the following two tests:

1. It must be movable (e.g., a bookcase anchored with screws) rather than inherently permanent (e.g., built-in furniture which can't be removed without destroying it or damaging the property to which it is attached)

2. It must be more in the nature of an accessory to the conduct of your business (e.g., special plumbing hookups and additional exhaust fans in a restaurant) rather than a structural component of the building (e.g., a roof) which relates directly to the building's ability to serve as a building (it wouldn't be much of a building without the roof).

The following is a checklist of questions to ask yourself in attempting to determine whether property can be considered movable:

1. Is the property permanently attached to the building or can it readily be detached and moved? Removable hooks, adhesives, and screws will be more indicative of movability than would cement and permanent adhesives.

2. How difficult is it to move the property in question? Will it take a significant amount of time? Are special permits, personnel, or equipment necessary to move it or can your regular maintenance people move it?

3. How much damage will be done to the property being moved and to the building it is being moved from (e.g., built-in furniture)?

4. Has the particular property or similar property been moved in the past?

When constructing a building or renovating an existing building, keep this planning idea in mind at the design and planning stage. In some situations it may be possible to redesign certain property in order to make it qualify. For example, if the plans called for expensive imported tile cemented to the lobby floor of the building, consider whether a nonpermanent cement could be used and whether that would be sufficient to enable the property to qualify as personal property. Carpeting may be another viable option if it fits in with the design scheme for the lobby. Rather than permanently gluing or nailing expensive paneling to the subwall, consider fastening it with screws which can readily be removed. The additional labor costs to install with screws should be compared with the additional tax benefits you may obtain. Based on the earlier examples it could be a very favorable payoff.

Following are examples of some properties which have qualified in different types of real estate projects. Remember that the facts and circumstances of every project can differ, so more or less property may qualify in any particular project.

Department Store. Decorative lighting fixtures, display racks, carpeting, movable partitions, escalators, removable paneling, certain planters, curtains, hookups for computers in the credit collection department and so forth.

Supermarket and Restaurants. Counters, display racks, waste compactors, signs, certain exhaust fans, certain plumbing and electrical hookups, kitchen equipment, refrigeration equipment (including pumps, condensers, and similar equipment), trash bins, and so forth.

Office Building. Furniture, equipment, removable files and bookshelves, removable paneling, carpeting, decorative light fixtures, certain hookups, electrical connections and possibly a special raised floor to accommodate computer equipment, and so forth. If you're dealing with a "smart" office building be alert for certain portions of security systems, special telephone, telecommunications and computer equipment and their support systems which may qualify. Your building may have a large portion of costs which qualify for this more favorable tax treatment. NOTE—It's a tough question in many cases since these components could be so integrated into the building that the IRS could argue that they do not qualify. The best approach is to begin reviewing the matter with your tax advisor during the planning stage.

CHAPTER SUMMARY

The Tax Reform Act of 1986 has hurt real estate's most cherished tax deduction—depreciation. As has been illustrated throughout this chapter, you can't change the periods over which Congress has required you to depreciate real estate, but you can carefully plan with your tax advisor to minimize the harsh impact of these new rules.

11 ALTERNATIVE MINIMUM TAX—TOUGHER TAX BITE TO WATCH

Most real estate investors have heard of the minimum tax, more technically the alternative minimum tax (AMT). Many of you, however, have probably never concerned yourselves with it to a great extent since you didn't have to pay it. The Tax Reform Act of 1986 will change that. What had usually been a trap for only the wealthiest and most heavily sheltered taxpayers to worry about will now be a costly problem for a large portion of taxpayers, including many real estate investors. The minimum tax could become so common that it will effectively become a second tax system, with its own deductions and its own determination of gains and losses, to be reckoned with as an essential component of every tax planning strategy.

WHAT IS THE AMT?

Our tax system has always been used as a means of promoting social and policy goals which Congress felt appropriate. For example, for many years Congress felt it appropriate to encourage long-term investment in production facilities and the economic infrastructure to help improve America's competitive edge. A major tax incentive used to encourage this type of investment was capital gains (see Chapter 5). By favorably taxing the gains realized on investments in capital assets, Congress sought to promote the investment it believed the country needed. The favorable tax benefits afforded capital gains were provided by permitting taxpayers to exclude 60% of any gain realized from taxation.

There were, however, limitations to Congress's generosity. While capital formation was a worthy goal, so was tax equity. Thus, to maintain some equity in the tax system, Congress decided that everyone (at least in theory) should pay some minimum amount of tax. It's as if Congress directed taxpayers to take advantage of the special breaks left in the Internal Revenue Code, but not to take too much advantage. The answer to this situation was a minimum tax.

The Concept and Structure of the Minimum Tax

Understanding this simple concept will help you understand the structure and workings of the minimum tax. Congress wanted taxpayers to take only a certain amount of advantage of the special tax breaks in the Internal Revenue Code. What the minimum tax does is require taxpayers to either add back to their income the benefits of these special tax breaks (known as tax preference items, or TPIs, since they receive preferential treatment), or to recalculate the items entirely (called "adjustments"). To simplify our discussions we will refer to both tax preference items and adjustments as TPIs. This now "whole" income figure (i.e., an income amount calculated without the full benefit of preferential tax treatments) can then be taxed at a rate sufficient to assure that every taxpayer pays the minimum amount of tax Congress deemed appropriate.

The minimum tax will thus serve to limit the benefits available from the special tax breaks which exist. The tax rate on this "whole" income figure (the alternative minimum taxable income, or AMTI) was (and still is) set at a rate less than the regular tax rate. Also, to ease the administrative burden and assist moderate-income taxpayers, Congress provided a liberal exemption amount below which many taxpayers would not have to pay the minimum tax.

Illustration of Alternative Minimum Tax

Figure 11.1 provides a very simplified overview of the minimum tax system. Start with your income for regular tax purposes, add tax preference items, and then subtract minimum tax itemized deductions.

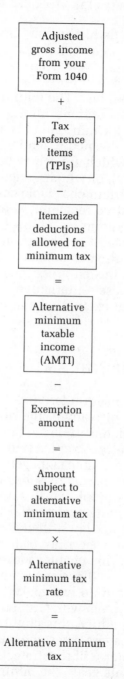

Figure 11.1 Alternative minimum tax—Simplified overview

Although itemized deductions are not called "tax preference items," Congress apparently believed that some of the deductions taxpayers were allowed were really special breaks—just like the special treatment afforded tax preference items like capital gains under the old law. The minimum tax takes the special breaks of itemized deductions into account by requiring that they be recalculated for minimum tax purposes using only the deductions Congress deemed essential. These are generally the types of deductions which are somewhat unavoidable in nature (medical and casualty), or which Congress did not want to limit for policy reasons (certain charitable contributions). Since itemized deductions must be recomputed for purposes of the minimum tax, the starting point for adding back the preference items is income (as calculated for the regular tax—i.e., on your Form 1040 tax return) before your itemized deductions. This amount is known as your "adjusted gross income" (AGI). The result is your minimum tax base—alternative minimum taxable income (AMTI). Subtract your exemption and multiply the result by the minimum tax rate.

TAX REFORM AND THE AMT

One of the basic premises underlying the Tax Reform Act of 1986 was the elimination of many of the preferential and special interest provisions which complicate the tax laws so that Congress could then dramatically lower tax rates. This would simplify the whole tax system and enable taxpayers to plan their investments and businesses for economic reasons rather than for tax reasons. The minimum tax is proof that this approach was not realized. If all the items receiving preferential tax treatment were really eliminated from the tax laws, then there would be no need for a minimum tax. The vast array of tax preference items which will be discussed in this chapter makes it apparent that the tax laws are still used to achieve social and political goals.

What tax reform did do was make the AMT a much tougher, more complicated system which will affect many taxpayers. The fairness and equity which this could achieve is to assure that most, if not all, taxpayers pay some minimum amount of tax. As the rest of this chapter will illustrate, Congress may come pretty close to achieving this goal. The minimum tax will unquestionably be much harder to avoid.

Basic Changes Tax Reform Made to the Minimum Tax

The key changes which tax reform made to the minimum tax are:

The minimum tax rate is now 21%; it had been 20%.

The exemptions available from the minimum tax are phased out when AMTI exceeds certain levels.

Foreign tax credits can only reduce up to 90% of your minimum tax liability.

A number of tax preference items have been changed and new preference items added to the list: accelerated depreciation on personal and real property; charitable contributions of appreciated property; certain tax-exempt interest; passive losses (with no phase in); the completed contract method of accounting must be used; the installment method of accounting is not permitted for some taxpayers; the tax preference for intangible drilling costs was made tougher, and so forth.

A new AMT credit was created which can be used to offset your regular tax liability in years when you are not subject to the minimum tax.

Perhaps the most important affect tax reform had on the minimum tax is the change in the relationship between the regular tax marginal tax rates as compared with the minimum tax rate. The change in this relationship is possibly the single factor most responsible for subjecting so many taxpayers to the minimum tax. Here's why.

The mechanics of the minimum tax are such that you only pay minimum tax when your minimum tax liability exceeds your regular tax liability. Under prior law this did not occur very often for many taxpayers. Many taxpayers avoided the minimum tax because their regular tax was calculated at a 50% rate. The minimum tax was then calculated at only a 20% rate—a 30 percentage point spread! Thus, even though their minimum taxable income base was much larger than their regular taxable income base (because of the tax preferences added back and the itemized deductions lost), the minimum tax often didn't exceed their regular tax.

Now look at what tax reform has done to this relationship. Your regular tax will be assessed at a maximum rate of 28%. Your minimum tax rate will be assessed at a rate of 21%. The spread in the tax rates under the two systems is now only seven percentage points!

Here's another way to look at the relationship. Under prior law the minimum tax rate was only 40% (20%/50%) of the maximum regular tax rate. After tax reform, the minimum tax rate is fully 75% of the maximum regular tax rate (21%/28%).

What this all means is that far smaller dollar amounts of tax preference items or itemized deduction adjustments are necessary to subject you to the minimum tax. For example, no deduction is allowed for state and local taxes in calculating the minimum tax. It is possible that even with no tax shelter investments the different treatment of state and local taxes could be sufficient to subject you to the minimum tax. This makes the minimum tax far more important than ever before. The minimum tax cost is far greater relative to the regular tax cost than ever before. Tax planning will be much harder—it will be much tougher to plan around the minimum tax since so much less is necessary to be ensnared by it.

With this overview of the minimum tax and the changes made by tax reform, a more detailed analysis can now be made. This analysis will expand on the prior discussions for certain aspects of the minimum tax. To maintain a perspective on how each area to be discussed fits into the minimum tax structure it may be helpful to refer back to Figure 11.1.

TAX PREFERENCE ITEMS (TPI)

This discussion of TPIs will note many tax preference items (and adjustments) which have no particular applicability to real estate investments. This is intentional. The impact of the AMT on your tax planning will be affected by all of your tax preference items. Therefore you must look at your entire tax picture, not just the real estate aspects.

1. *Pollution Control Facilities.* The excess of rapid 60-month amortization deduction of qualified pollution control facilities over the deduction which would otherwise have been allowable is a TPI. Note that this special provision has been repealed for purposes of the regular tax in 1986.

2. *Research and Experimental Expenditures.* Research expenditures qualify in certain instances to be deducted currently.

The excess of these current deductions over the deduction which would have been allowable had the expenditures been deducted ratable over a 10-year period is TPI. If the 10-year write-off period is chosen for purposes of the regular tax, then there won't be a TPI.

3. *Magazine and Newspaper Circulation Expenditures.* Expenditures to increase magazine and newspaper circulation and other preproduction expenditures can be deducted for the regular tax. The excess of this deduction over the deduction which would have been allowable had the expenditures been written off ratably over a three-year period is a TPI.

4. *Percentage Depletion.* The excess of percentage depletion over the adjusted basis in the property is a TPI, which is calculated separately for each property.

5. *Mining Costs.* Mining exploration and development costs which are deducted create a TPI to the extent that they exceed the amount which would have been deducted had the expenditures been deducted ratably over a 10-year period. The 10-year deduction can be used in order to eliminate this TPI.

6. *Depreciation.* Depreciation deductions can create a TPI to the extent that depreciation deductions claimed on property put into use ("placed in service") after 1986 exceed the depreciation deductions which would have been allowed had the new alternative depreciation system deductions been used. (See Chapter 10 for a complete discussion of the alternative depreciation system.) Thus for nonresidential real estate the excess of the deduction claimed using a 31.5-year period over the deduction which would have been allowed had a 40-year period been used is a TPI. For residential real estate the excess of depreciation claimed for purposes of the regular tax using a 27.5-year period over the deduction which would have been allowed had a 40-year period been used is a TPI.

For personal property, such as cars and furniture, the depreciation deduction is calculated using a 150% declining balance method over a period prescribed by law (the "ADR midpoint life"). This will be considerably lower in earlier years than the 200% declining balance method over what will generally be a five- or seven-year period for purposes of the regular tax. Explanations and examples of all these depreciation concepts are presented in Chapter 10.

Taxpayers can avoid the creation of TPIs for depreciation by electing to use the alternative depreciation system (i.e., the longer write-offs) for the regular tax. (See Chapter 10.)

The mechanics of making the depreciation adjustment for minimum tax purposes are important. Instead of just adding the excess depreciation back to the minimum tax base as a TPI (i.e., the excess of depreciation calculated for regular tax purposes minus depreciation calculated using the method required for the minimum tax), the depreciation calculated for purposes of the minimum tax using the alternative depreciation system is substituted (as an adjustment) for the regular tax depreciation. This is advantageous since in some years the minimum tax depreciation can exceed the tax for regular tax purposes. Thus, the net adjustment in those years would be a favorable one. Note the impact this will have on your investment (tax basis) in the property. Since depreciation deductions reduce your tax basis, you will have different tax bases for regular tax and minimum tax. This means that the gain or loss realized on selling an asset can differ for each. An example will illustrate.

Example. Assume you built and depreciated a $500,000 office building. Your deductions would be as follows:

REGULAR TAX DEPRECIATION

Investment (tax basis)	$500,000
Depreciable life	31.5 years
Annual depreciation	$ 15,873

MINIMUM TAX DEPRECIATION

Investment (tax basis)	$500,000
Depreciable life[a]	40 years
Annual depreciation	$ 12,500

[a] Under the alternative depreciation system required for the minimum tax, all real estate must be depreciated on the straight-line (ratable) method over a 40-year period (see Chapter 10). This alternative depreciation system may be elected for purposes of the regular tax as well, although for this illustration it is assumed that it was not.

Thus, for the first 31.5 years after the building is put into use, your minimum tax depreciation deductions will be $3,373 less than your deductions for regular tax purposes.

Let's say that after 10 years you sell the asset for $350,000. What is your gain (or loss) for the regular tax and for the minimum tax?

GAIN FOR REGULAR TAX

Sales price		$350,000
Less tax basis:		
Cost	$500,000	
Depreciation (10 × 15,873)	158,730	341,270
Gain		$ 8,730

GAIN FOR MINIMUM TAX

Sales price		$350,000
Less tax basis:		
Cost	$500,000	
Depreciation (10 × 12,500)	$125,000	375,000
Loss		$(25,000)

NOTE—The different depreciation deductions under each tax system result in different results on the sale of the asset. This is why separate books are required for each tax system—a tremendous record-keeping burden!

Planning Tip. One final point on depreciation. The amount of property deducted in the year it's acquired, using the special election to deduct up to $10,000 of personal property in a year, is not a tax preference item. Thus you can safely claim the benefits of this special tax treatment with no minimum tax risk.

7. *Depreciation on Pretax Reform Property.* For property depreciated under the rules applying before tax reform, the minimum tax rules existing prior to tax reform will apply for purposes of determining any depreciation tax preference with respect to such property. Thus for real estate put into use before tax reform, the excess of accelerated depreciation over straight-line depreciation (calculated over the ACRS period of 15, 18, or 19 years) is a TPI. For personal property (furniture, equipment, etc.) a TPI is only created by depreciation deductions on certain leased personal property.

8. *Completed Contract Method.* The percentage completion method of accounting for profits on certain long-term contracts must be used instead of the completed contract method of accounting. This applies to contracts entered into after March 1, 1986. See Chapter 3 for an explanation of these methods.

9. *Installment Method.* The installment method of accounting for profits as the payments are received is not allowed in

many instances for purposes of the minimum tax. Thus all gain on an asset sold on the installment method must be recognized in the year of sale. (See Chapter 5 for a complete discussion of this rule.)

10. *Tax-Exempt Interest.* Interest on certain private activity municipal bonds issued after August 7, 1986, which remain exempt from the regular tax, create a TPI for minimum tax purposes (see Chapter 2).

Planning Tip. Interest on most municipal bonds will remain tax-free. Be careful in buying bonds to ascertain whether the interest will be subject to the minimum tax. If you're not subject to the minimum tax you may want to look at the bonds which pay interest subject to the minimum tax—they may have a better yield.

11. *Charitable Contributions.* Contributions of appreciated capital gain property to a charity can create a TPI equal to the amount of unrealized appreciation which escapes taxation under the regular tax. This rule does not apply to gifts made before August 16, 1986.

12. *Intangible Drilling Costs.* Excess intangible drilling costs are generally the excess of the deduction for intangible drilling costs over the deduction which would have been allowed had such costs been written off ratably over a 10-year period, or deducted as cost depletion, whichever is more favorable. The amount of these excess intangible drilling costs which exceed 65% of the taxpayer's income from oil and gas properties is a TPI. Under prior law it had been 100% of income.

13. *Incentive Stock Options.* When shares of stock are issued in an incentive stock option plan, the excess of the fair value of the stock issued over the option price the recipient pays is a TPI. For minimum tax purposes executives receiving incentive stock options will now have to keep track of two investment (tax basis) figures. For regular tax purposes the gain on the eventual sale of the stock will be computed by subtracting the option price from the proceeds. For minimum tax purposes the tax basis will be increased by the TPI reported when the stock was issued. Thus the gain for purposes of the minimum tax will be lower. Just like depreciation, this TPI will require that additional records be maintained.

14. *Passive Losses.* Any losses incurred in rental real estate activities, in investments made as a limited partner, and in investments in which the taxpayer does not materially participate will be treated as a TPI. NOTE—There is no phase in for purposes of the minimum tax as there is for the regular tax (see Chapter 9).

Planning Tip. Investors must carefully consider the impact of this passive losses rule on the usefulness of their real estate and other tax shelter investments. The losses you may have thought you would be able to use may not be of any benefit because of the minimum tax. This also means that there may be a significant advantage to avoiding the minimum tax over the next few years to benefit from the passive losses the regular tax phase-in rules may permit you to take advantage of.

15. *Passive Farming Losses.* Losses from farming activities in which the taxpayer does not participate are treated as a TPI.

NOTE—A couple common TPIs of the past are gone. Since tax reform has eliminated the capital gains exclusion, this amount is no longer a TPI. Also, tax reform repealed the $100 dividends received exclusion so that this TPI is gone.

ITEMIZED DEDUCTIONS

As mentioned in the introduction to this chapter, only certain deductions qualify as itemized deductions for purposes of the minimum tax. Tax reform has made only a few technical changes to these. Itemized deductions for the minimum tax include medical expenses (in excess of 10% of AGI), casualty losses (less a $100 floor amount and then less 10% of AGI), qualified housing interest (which may be less than the interest you can deduct for your regular tax), and certain other interest expense. There are no other itemized deductions. You will therefore receive no benefit for payments of state and local taxes or any consumer interest expense! The personal exemption and the standard deduction are not allowed for the minimum tax (but see the discussion in the next section concerning the minimum tax exemption amount). Let's take a closer look at several of these itemized deductions.

The deduction for home mortgage interest has been adjusted so that it is similar to the home mortgage interest for regular tax purposes (see Chapter 7). Thus you can generally deduct interest paid on both a home mortgage and a mortgage on a designated second property. For regular tax purposes, the interest on your home mortgage will be deductible to the extent that the home mortgage doesn't exceed the purchase price of your home plus the cost of home improvements, medical expenses, and education expenses. The ability to deduct home mortgage interest for purposes of the minimum tax, however, appears to be more restricted. Only interest on a mortgage to construct or substantially rehabilitate your principal residence (or other qualified dwelling unit) can qualify. For purposes of the minimum tax, interest cannot be deducted on the portion of your home mortgage used to finance educational and medical expenses. Further, if you refinance your home mortgage for more than the original loan balance, the interest paid on the additional loan cannot be deducted.

Investment interest is also allowed to a certain extent for the minimum tax (see Chapter 2 for a description of the investment interest limitation). The computation for determining the allowable investment interest expense excludes any interest and income which is covered by the new passive loss rules (see Chapter 9). The calculation also excludes interest expense incurred in connection with an active trade or business. Thus the calculation will generally only include amounts with respect to certain oil and gas investments which have been specifically excluded from the passive loss rules (see Chapter 9), certain investments in low-income housing which have temporarily been excluded from the passive loss rules (see Chapter 6), and investments in portfolio assets (bonds, stocks, etc.).

Interest expense is allowed to the extent that it does not exceed net investment income. Net investment income is generally income from the investments listed in the preceding paragraph reduced by the expenses directly connected with those investments. Note that the expenses must be adjusted for any tax preference items or other minimum tax adjustments described in this chapter.

The Tax Reform Act of 1986 generally conformed the minimum tax investment interest limitation to that for the regular tax. Two of the differences warrant mention. Since income and deductions differ for purposes of the minimum tax, the amount of net investment income used in the minimum tax calculation can differ from the net investment income used for the regular tax. Also, the $10,000 additional interest allowance permitted under prior law is phased out over a four-year period for purposes of the regular tax. This allowance was never permitted for the minimum tax so it does not enter into the calculation.

EXEMPTION AMOUNT

For purposes of the minimum tax you subtract the minimum tax exemption amount from your minimum taxable income before calculating your minimum tax. The exemption amount is based on two things: (1) your tax filing status (e.g., if you're married filing a joint tax return you can get a $40,000 exemption); and (2) your level of AMT income. This will determine whether any of your exemption amount must be phased out. For example, if you're married filing a joint tax return and have minimum tax income of $310,000, the phase out of your exemption would have just been complete and you would not be entitled to any exemption. The exemption amounts and the AMTI levels at which the phase outs begin and end are illustrated in Table 11.1. The exemption phase outs occur ratably within the income ranges shown (i.e., at a rate of 25 cents for each dollar of income in the phase-out range).

Table 11.1   Minimum Tax Exemption Amount

Filing Status	Exemption	Phase-out Range
Married–joint	$40,000	$150,000–$310,000
Single	$30,000	$112,500–$232,500
Married–separate	$20,000	$ 75,000–$155,000

CALCULATING THE MINIMUM TAX DUE AFTER TAX CREDIT AND LOSS ADJUSTMENTS

Once all the steps described have been made, you will have the actual base on which to calculate the gross minimum tax. Multiply the resulting base by the new 21% minimum tax rate. The resulting gross minimum tax, to the extent it exceeds your regular tax liability, is the tax due.

This minimum tax cannot be offset by nonrefundable tax credits. Thus the investment tax credit (e.g., to the extent it is available for certain property subject to transition rules), the rehabilitation tax credit (see Chapter 3), and the low-income housing credit (see Chapter 6) cannot be used to offset your minimum tax liability. A number of additional complications affect the impact which the various tax credits can have on the final minimum tax you will owe. These are best left to a review with your accountant if they affect you.

Two final adjustments which may affect your minimum tax liability should be mentioned: foreign tax credits and net operating losses.

The foreign tax credit can be used to offset up to 90% of your minimum tax liability. Under prior law it could offset 100% of your minimum tax liability. Recomputations will be necessary to determine the foreign tax credit available for the minimum tax. The foreign tax paid or incurred on foreign source alternative minimum tax income will be used in the computation. "Foreign source alternative minimum taxable income" is foreign source income modified to reflect the required minimum tax preference items and other adjustments.

If you have a net operating loss, additional adjustments and computations may be required for purposes of the minimum tax. A net operating loss for an individual taxpayer, in very general terms, is a loss incurred in a trade or business which exceeds all other income for the year. In other words, you end up with negative taxable income as a result of losing money in your trade or business. This negative taxable income amount can, subject to a number of special rules, be carried over to other tax years to offset taxable income in those years. This carryover amount is called a "net operating loss." For the minimum tax, you will have to recalculate your net operating loss so that it reflects the various tax preference item limitations and other adjustments required by the minimum tax. The net operating loss can then be carried over to be used to offset minimum taxable income in other tax years. For the minimum tax these carryover amounts will differ from the carryover amounts used for regular tax purposes due to tax preference items and other adjustments. The net operating loss can only offset up to 90% of your minimum tax. Any unused amount is carried over and may be used in future years.

MINIMUM TAX CREDIT AVAILABLE TO OFFSET REGULAR TAX LIABILITY

One final step must be reviewed—the new minimum tax credit. A portion of the minimum tax you pay in excess of your regular tax liability will generate a tax credit you can use in later years to offset your regular tax when your regular tax exceeds your minimum tax. To understand the reasons for and the calculations of this new minimum tax credit, the two types of modifications you had to make to your regular tax to obtain your minimum tax base must be analyzed.

The first type of modification can be called an exclusion preference. This concerns items which do not enter into the regular tax calculation at any time. They are adjusted for only once in the minimum tax calculation. Examples include municipal bond interest on certain private activity bonds. Interest on these bonds cannot be excluded from the minimum tax, although it is never taxed for purposes of the regular tax. It is thus a permanent difference between the two tax systems (i.e., the regular and minimum taxes). A second example is the appreciated portion of donated capital gain property. It is taxed by the minimum tax system, although it is never taxed by the regular tax system. The minimum tax attributable to these types of modifications does not enter into the minimum tax credit.

The second type of modification is a timing adjustment, not a permanent difference. For example, if the installment method of accounting cannot be used for minimum tax purposes then the entire gain will be taxed in the year of sale. For purposes of the regular tax, however, the installment method may provide a deferral of some of the tax to a later year. Thus in later years, for the regular tax, installment proceeds will be subject to regular tax. The total amount taxed, by either the regular or minimum tax system, will eventually be the same. It is only the timing of the taxation that will differ.

What if you are subject to the minimum tax in the year you sell the asset? Then all of the gain would be taxed in that year. Assume that in the following year all the money due you is paid so that the entire gain is recognized for purposes of the regular tax in the second year. If you pay regular tax in the second year you could be taxed on the same amount you paid minimum tax on in the preceding year. The minimum tax credit is designed to mitigate this inherent unfairness. Thus the minimum tax attributable to timing-type preferences and adjustments (installment sales, depreciation, etc.) enters into the minimum tax credit.

Planning Tips. Planning for the minimum tax will be tougher than ever before. However, with the higher minimum tax rate, broader-based planning may be even more important than before.

A few general comments about minimum tax planning can be made. First, given the many new complications, comprehensive tax planning is essential. This will generally require that both the regular and minimum tax be reviewed together and that they both be reviewed for a number of years. Planning for a single tax year at a time could often lead to planning errors. Given the many complex interrelationships which must be considered, one of the best planning approaches will be to conduct various computer "what if?" projections. Project your regular tax and minimum tax for at least a three-year period under various possible scenarios. Then review the results with your advisors to choose an optimal strategy. Don't be led into making minimum tax decisions which are uneconomical or detrimental from a business standpoint unless the benefits are clearly worthwhile. Timing will be the key to all planning scenarios.

The tax planning ideas which can be used for the minimum tax can be organized in five categories. Remember no planning tip will always be of value. Each set of facts and circumstances requires careful analysis with your tax advisor. The many new complications and limitations tax reform created (passive loss limitations; investment, consumer, and home mortgage interest limitations, etc.) must be considered:

1. Tax Planning Which Benefits Both the Regular and Minimum Tax:

    a. Maximize the amount of depreciable property which can be treated as personal property rather than real property. Even though you will have a minimum tax adjustment it will still compare very favorably with the adjustment you otherwise would have had. (See Chapter 10.)

b. Make maximum use of the $35,000 deduction for removing architectural barriers to the elderly and the handicapped. It won't generate a tax preference. (See Chapter 10.)

c. Time elective medical expenses to maximize the expenses in any one year in order to attempt to exceed the percentage of adjusted gross income hurdle. (See Chapter 8.)

d. Maximize your use of home mortgage interest as compared with nondeductible consumer interest. (See Chapters 7 and 8.)

e. Structure and plan activities, to the extent possible, to avoid the passive activity taint which could subject the losses to strict limitations. (See Chapter 9.)

f. Carefully screen municipal bond investments in order not to inadvertently buy private activity bonds whose income is subject to the minimum tax. (See Chapter 2.)

g. Consider the merits of investing in insurance-type products which are treated favorably under both tax systems.

h. Take maximum advantage of pension and retirement plans.

2. Accelerate Income to a Minimum Tax Year:

a. In some instances it may prove beneficial to accelerate income into a year in which you are subject to the minimum tax. For example assume in year 1 you're subject to the minimum tax but in year 2 you won't be. It may be advantageous to accelerate certain income items into year 1 to be taxed at a maximum 21% minimum tax rate rather than to realize them in year at a maximum regular tax rate of 28%.

b. Time a bonus from your employer.

c. Recognize gain on an investment.

d. Pay a dividend from a close corporation.

e. Redeem government savings bonds.

f. If you have investment interest expense in excess of investment income, you may be able to earn investment income without incurring additional tax. Adjust your investments accordingly.

3. Time Unusable Itemized Deductions for a Nonminimum Tax Year:

a. If you're subject to the minimum tax you won't get any benefit from many itemized deductions. To the extent possible, try to accelerate or defer those deductions to an earlier or later year when you can get the benefit from them. This will be especially valuable over the next few years when passive losses, vestment interest, and consumer interest limitations will be partially available as deductions for the regular tax system, while they are entirely unavailable under the minimum tax system. Carefully review this type of planning in conjunction with the tax planning idea for "bunching" deductions. (See Chapter 8.)

b. Consider special elections to capitalize (i.e., add to your investment or tax basis rather than deduct) certain carrying costs for land.

c. Accelerate or defer medical expenses, consumer interest, and state and local taxes to nonminimum tax years. (See Chapter 8.)

d. Time above-the-line expenses (such as expenses of a business) for a nonminimum tax year when they will be more valuable.

e. Certain preference items can be deducted over elective longer periods. This can sometimes be used to save deductions for later years when the minimum tax won't limit them. It can also help you avoid the minimum tax by eliminating tax preference items (see 4 below). For example, circulation expenses, intangible drilling expenses, and so forth can be written off over longer periods (the "normative" election). For depreciation, the election to use the alternative depreciation system (see Chapter 10) can provide a similar result.

4. Time Controllable Preferences in Order to Avoid the Minimum Tax:

a. Many of the preference items can be timed to tax years when they won't trigger the minimum tax.

b. Time the exercise of incentive stock options (ISOs).

c. Elect out of the installment sale. This will eliminate the preference (adjustment) for minimum tax purposes and may thus enable you to avoid the minimum tax. This election could also be used to provide you with a loss for minimum tax purposes (because of different tax basis) which can be advantageously used. Defer an installment sale entirely if its inclusion would be the triggering item subjecting you to the minimum tax in a given year.

5. Other Minimum Tax Planning Ideas:

a. If certain assets can be depreciated using a method expressed in terms other than years (e.g., depreciate a machine over its estimated usable machine hours, instead of over the required five- or seven-year year depreciation period. For example, if the manufacturer says the machine will last for 500 hours of use and you use it 250 hours in the first year you would write off half its cost in the first year.) This type of depreciation will not create a minimum tax adjustment and in some cases it may prove more favorable than electing the alternative depreciation system.

    b. Plan to use any minimum tax credits as soon as possible.

    c. Plan to take maximum advantage of the phase-out periods of certain items (passive losses, consumer interest, etc.) while they are still available for the regular tax.

CHAPTER SUMMARY

The minimum tax is tougher then ever. Its expanded scope and increased cost make it imperative that it be incorporated into every tax planning analysis. The many new record-keeping requirements make it imperative that you review your current record-keeping practices with your accountant. Even if you're not subject to the minimum tax now, it may still be advisable to change or refine your record keeping.

12 MISCELLANEOUS TAX AND ADMINISTRATIVE CHANGES

The Tax Reform Act of 1986 made numerous changes which directly or indirectly affect real estate investors as well as the many real estate professionals with whom investors must deal. The most important of the changes have been reviewed in the preceeding chapters. This chapter summarizes a number of other changes which can be important in some situations. Since these changes are more administrative and technical in nature than those discussed in prior chapters, most planning concerning them will be left to your accountant or other tax advisors. Therefore the aim of this chapter is merely to alert you to these changes. If they might affect you, follow up with your tax advisor.

REGISTRATION OF TAX SHELTERS

Any person who organizes a tax shelter must register the tax shelter with the IRS. The registration must be filed not later than the day on which interests in the shelter are first offered for sale to investors. The person who is principally responsible for organizing the shelter is responsible for the filing. If this individual fails to register the shelter, then another person involved in the organization of the shelter will be responsible. Thus all those involved with a shelter should exercise care in assuring that the filing requirements are met.

What is a tax shelter for purposes of this requirement? An investment is treated as a tax shelter for registration requirements if it could reasonably be inferred that the investment's tax shelter ratio for any of the first five years of the investment is greater than 2:1. The tax shelter ratio is calculated as follows:

$$\frac{\text{Total deductions} + (350\% \times \text{tax credits})}{\text{Investment}}$$

If this ratio exceeds 2:1 then the test is met. In the past the calculation was made using only 200% of tax credits. The Tax Reform Act of 1986 increased this to the 350% reflected in the formula shown above.

In addition to the tax shelter ratio requirement, the investment must be: (1) required to be registered under a federal or state law regulating securities; (2) sold pursuant to an exemption for registration requiring the filing of a notice with a federal or state agency; or (3) exceed, in aggregate, $250,000 and be expected to be sold to five or more investors.

Although many real estate investments after tax reform will not be structured to provide large tax write-offs, they may still run afoul of these requirements. The safest approach is to have the accountant assisting in the organization of the investment make the necessary calculations.

If registration is required, then the seller must provide each purchaser with the tax shelter identification number issued by the IRS. The investor must then report this number on his tax return.

Many organizers of tax shelters are also required to maintain lists of investors containing certain required information.

Finally, there are a number of penalties which can be assessed for failing to meet these requirements and the Tax Reform Act of 1986 made many of them tougher than before. For example:

Failing to register a tax shelter can result in a penalty of up to 1% of the moneys invested in the deal, or $500, whichever is greater. CAUTION—This 1% penalty can be very substantial. Under prior law the 1% penalty had been limited in many situations to $10,000.

Failing to maintain an investor list can subject the shelter organizer or seller to a penalty of $50 per failure up to a maximum of $100,000 per year. The maximum penalty under prior law had been $50,000.

Failing to report the tax shelter identification number on your tax return can result in a $250 penalty. The penalty had been only $50.

REPORTING REAL ESTATE TRANSACTIONS

The Tax Reform Act of 1986 now requires that certain persons (it calls this person a "real estate broker"—but the definition is far broader than what you would suspect) file reports of real estate transactions. What real estate transactions must be reported? It appears that all sales and other transactions with the possible exception of refinancings will have to be reported. However, Congress noted that even refinancings may have to be reported in some situations. The Treasury Department will have to issue regulations further clarifying what constitutes a "real estate transaction" for these purposes. The definition is likely to be very broad.

Information as to the name and address of each party to the transaction, and probably the social security number or other identification number, will be required. Details as to the gross proceeds received by the seller or borrower and any other details the IRS decides necessary will have to be reported. The reporting will be done by completing a form similar to the Form 1099 used to report dividends, miscellaneous payments, interest, and so forth. Statements will also have to be given to each party to the transaction.

The final question is whose responsibility it will be to report this information. The new law sets up the following priorities: (1) the person responsible for closing the transaction (this could be the attorney or title company); (2) the mortgage lender; (3) the broker for the seller; (4) the broker for the buyer; (5) anyone else the IRS decides to designate in future regulations. Given this broad description, and the penalties which can be applied for failing to make the necessary reports, all those involved in a real estate transaction should take the precaution of verifying who will make the filings.

INTEREST CHARGED AND PAID ON TAX UNDERPAYMENTS AND OVERPAYMENTS

Before tax reform the rate of interest the IRS had to pay you on certain tax overpayments was the same rate you would have been assessed on a tax underpayment. The Tax Reform Act of 1986 changed this. Now the interest rate you will have to pay to the IRS will be based on a Treasury bill rate plus 3%. The rate the IRS will pay you, however, will be based on a Treasury bill rate plus only 2%. The rates will be revised on a quarterly basis.

PENALTIES INCREASED FOR FAILURE TO FILE REQUIRED INFORMATION RETURNS

If you fail to file a required information return or statement with the IRS, the penalties you face have just been increased. Failing to file a required information return can result in a penalty of $50 for each unfiled return, up to a maximum of $100,000. Transactions requiring reporting include exchanges of certain partnership interests and certain dispositions of donated property. The penalty for failure to report these is the greater of $100 for each failure or 5% of the amount which should have been reported.

PENALTIES FOR NEGLIGENCE AND FRAUD

The negligence penalty for failing to make a reasonable effort to comply with required tax laws, and for careless, reckless, or intentional disregard of the tax law requirements, can subject you to a penalty for negligence. The Tax Reform Act of 1986 also established that your failure to report an item on your tax return for which you received notice on an information return (such as a Form 1099-INT reporting interest paid to you) or on certain tax returns (such as a Form K-1 issued to you by a partnership in which you have invested) will automatically cause you to be subject to a penalty for failing to report the information shown on that return. To avoid this penalty you will have to make a strong argument that you were not negligent.

If you fraudulently fail to pay a tax which you owe, you will face an even tougher penalty. The new fraud penalty is 75% (it was 50%) of the tax underpayment due to fraud plus certain interest assessments.

ESTIMATED TAX PAYMENT REQUIREMENTS

If your tax liability for any tax year will exceed the amount of withholding tax paid on your behalf by $500 or more, you probably will have to make estimated tax payments. For most taxpayers these payments are due on the following dates:

April 15

June 15

September 15

January 15 (of the following year)

If you don't make the required estimated tax payments you can be assessed penalties. There are, however, two exceptions which can be used to avoid these penalties. These exceptions are:

1. The estimated tax payments which you made equal at least 90% of the tax liability shown on your tax return for the year. This percentage had been only 80%.

Example. You own and manage a real estate brokerage firm. You earn $100,000 in wages on which the firm withheld federal taxes of $20,000. You earned significant additional income on real estate investments you bought and sold. In 1989 your tax return (Form 1040) shows a tax liability of $45,000. You only made $16,400 in estimated tax payments. Thus your total payments-on-account of your 1989 tax liability are $36,400 ($20,000 withholding + $16,400 estimated tax payments). Since you have underpaid your tax liability you may be subject to a penalty. Does the exception help you avoid the penalty? You have paid in 80.89% of your actual tax liability [$36,400 ÷ $45,000]. Under old law this would have been sufficient. After tax reform, however, this will not be sufficient. You could be assessed a penalty unless you meet the next exception.

2. The estimated tax payments you made at least equal the tax liability shown on your tax return for the prior year.

Example. Let's assume the same facts as in the prior example and that your tax liability on your 1988 tax return was $35,000. Whether or not you met test one, you will be able to avoid the tax on underpaying your estimated tax since the payments you did make exceed the $35,000 you owed in the prior year.

What happens if you fail both exceptions? You will be assessed a nondeductible penalty. It is computed based on the amount of tax underpayment. This is the excess of the amount of tax you should have paid by an estimated tax due date (based on the exceptions) over your actual payments. For these purposes, withholding is treated as if it were paid in ratably throughout the year.

Planning Tip. Since the changes made by tax reform will make it harder to avoid an estimated tax underpayment penalty, carefully review your payment requirements with your accountant. When in doubt about the current year's tax liability, the safest course will be to assure that an amount at least equal to your prior year's tax liability has been paid in.

LARGER PENALTY IMPOSED ON SUBSTANTIAL UNDERSTATEMENTS OF TAX LIABILITY

A penalty is imposed if you substantially understate the tax due on your tax return. The Tax Reform Act of 1986 just doubled the penalty you could face. Here's how it works. A 20% (it had been 10%) penalty will be imposed on the amount of any substantial understatement of your tax liability. A "substantial understatement" is a tax liability which you report on your tax return which is 10% (or $5,000 if greater) less than the tax which should have been shown on your tax return.

The "substantial understatement" will be reduced to the extent that you had reason to believe that there was substantial authority for the positions taken on the tax return. "Substantial authority" means that the weight of the authorities (the Internal Revenue Code, temporary or final regulations, court cases, and certain other sources) supporting your position are substantial in relation to the authorities contrary to your position. This decision is to be made by considering all the facts and circumstances in the situation, including the pervasiveness, relevance, and source of the various authorities.

There is another out. If you adequately disclose the facts and treatment taken on your tax return you may be able to avoid the penalty. There are a number of detailed requirements which must be met for disclosure to be regarded as adequate for these purposes. This is really a decision which must be made with your accountant.

A tougher standard is applied to avoid the penalty for a substantial understatement of tax liability if a tax shelter is involved. In these situations you must have reasonably believed that the treatment of the questionable tax shelter items on your tax return was more likely than not an accurate statement and that there was substantial authority for the treatment used. Adequate disclosure must also be made.

Planning Tip. What does this all mean? Before taking a risky tax position you must carefully consider what penalties and interest charges (which probably won't be deductible) you could face. Your tax advisor should not only inform you of the tax planning ideas available, but of the support (or lack of support) which exists for them. You should then discuss whether the risks involved are reasonable for you. This must be a personal decision for you since each of your tax advisor's clients will have a different attitude toward risk and paying taxes.

For example, in discussing the applicability of the passive loss rules to real estate rental activities in Chapter 9, it was suggested that it may be possible that a few real estate activities may not be subject to these limitations because of the tremendous services the investors may render (certain shopping centers, as one example). There is very little support at the time this book goes to press for this position. This is in large part due to the fact that the laws are so new that the IRS has not had an opportunity to issue regulations and no court cases could have been filed.

If you consider taking the position that a particular real estate activity is so service-oriented that the passive loss rules should not apply, you should carefully consider the facts and circumstances in your specific case and review all the law presently available with your tax advisor. If the decision is then made to adopt that position, you should have your tax advisor carefully review the matter with the accountant preparing your tax return. It may also be advisable to have a memorandum written explaining the reasons for the decision, since it may be a number of years before the matter is raised by the IRS. Since memories fade with time, the memorandum may be essential to demonstrating the basis for adopting your position.

Finally, your accountant must review the disclosures which should be made on your tax return. If it is felt that the position you have taken is risky, you may want to disclose what was done in a detailed statement attached to the tax return. Whether such a statement is actually filed will have to be your final decision. Many taxpayers may feel that if a position is risky the less said the better. This strategy may work—but then again it may not. If it doesn't work the penalties discussed in this chapter (and this is but a small sampling of the many penalties and interest charges the Internal Revenue Code provides for) could make you regret trying to be secretive.

USE OF THE CASH METHOD OF ACCOUNTING RESTRICTED

To determine income subject to tax, some conventional set of rules must be followed. The various rules and conventions used to determine income are called an "accounting method." In very simple terms there are two methods of accounting which taxpayers can use to determine their income (or loss) for tax purposes.

The first and simplest method is the cash method of accounting. Under this method income is generally reported when cash is actually or constructively (i.e., reduced to your control) received. Expenses are generally reported when an item is paid for. There are numerous exceptions to these general rules. For example, if an expenditure is made for constructing a building or buying land these costs can't be deducted. They must be accumulated as part of your investment in the building or land (i.e., capitalized). Depreciation deductions may be allowed at a later time. (See Chapter 10 for a discussion of depreciation.) Tax shelters are subject to special restrictions.

The second major method of accounting is the accrual method. Under this method of determining income and deductions, income is generally recognized when it is earned, regardless of whether it has actually or constructively been received. For example, a lease requires a tenant to pay you $25,000 of rent in 1989. You will probably have to report that rental income even if the tenant doesn't pay you until January of 1990. Similarly, deductions on the accrual method are generally recognized when the liability is established (i.e., when they have been accrued or incurred), even if the actual payment occurs in a later year.

For a liability to be established it must meet the "all events test." This requires that all the events necessary to determine the liability have become fixed and certain and the amount of the liability can be determined. Economic performance must also have occurred—that is, the goods or services must have been rendered. For example, your attorney provides you advice in early December 1989 (the existence of the liability is determined and the services are rendered) and bills you before year end (the amount of the liability is determined). You should be able to deduct the legal fee even if you don't pay it until January 1990.

An exception is provided from this economic performance test. If the service or receipt of the goods is a recurring item and the services or goods are received within 8.5 months of year-end, economic performance will be considered to have occurred in the prior year, permitting a deduction in that year.

The Tax Reform Act of 1986 generally prohibits any tax shelter from using the cash method of accounting. Tax reform also prevents tax shelters from using the recurring item exception to the economic performance rule for accruing and deducting liabilities. Thus tax shelters must generally receive the goods or services they are paying for in the year they intend to claim a deduction for them. Finally, the cash method of accounting generally can't be used by any regular corporation (i.e., any corporation which is not an S corporation—see Chapter 1), any partnership with a regular corporation as a partner, and certain other taxpayers. Certain personal service corporations (law, engineering, health, accounting, architectural, consulting firms, etc.) are exempt from this latter requirement and may thus continue using the cash method of accounting.

CERTAIN CONVENTION EXPENSES
NO LONGER DEDUCTIBLE

Deductions are no longer allowed for expenses for attending a seminar or convention unless it is related to your trade or business. Since many real estate investors are merely investors, and are not sufficiently active for their real estate interests to constitute trades or businesses, this rule will eliminate the deductions for attending real estate investment, tax, and financial planning seminars.

SOLAR ENERGY TAX CREDIT EXTENDED

The tax credit for qualified expenditures on active solar systems which generate electricity, heat, cool air, or provide hot water for a building has been extended. For a solar energy system to be active it must use fans, pumps, and so forth to force the transfer of the solar energy which is harnessed. Mere passive solar panels which use conductive or radiant energy will not suffice.

The credit has been extended for three years—to 1988—at the following rates:

1986	15%
1987	12%
1988	10%

CHAPTER SUMMARY

This chapter has briefly reviewed a number of miscellaneous changes made by the Tax Reform Act of 1986. The important point is that the tax laws are complicated and cover many aspects of your real estate investment activities. Tax reform, in spite of claims of simplification, has only complicated the tax planning process further. If tax rates are raised soon, the importance for planning will increase, despite these complexities. With so many changes, and so many rules and planning ideas beyond the scope of this book, it is essential that you review any tax planning strategies with your tax advisor. Hopefully, this chapter—and this book—has given you questions and ideas, and an understanding of the more important rules, so that you can use your tax advisors effectively to achieve the best results. Good luck!

INDEX

[Note: Because all material in this book relates to the Tax Reform Act of 1986, that term is to be understood as applicable throughout this Index. It will not be used either as a main entry or as a subentry.]

Accelerated cost recovery system (ACRS), 230
Accounting:
 accrual method, 293–294
 cash method, 293, 294
 completed contract method, 28, 271, 275
 installment method, 28, 275, 281
 long-term construction contracts, 97–99
 methods of, 293
 taxable income; long-term contracts, 98–99
 see also Allocations
Acquisitions, *see* Brokerage costs; Financing investments; Investments; Leasing; Ownership; REITs; Sales agreement; Syndications
Active income, 217–218, 224
 see also Income; Materially participating; Passive loss rules; Portfolio income
Activity:
 definition, 203
 passive loss requirements, 217, 283
 planning tips, 224–225
Active real estate:
 definition, 218, 288
 minimum ownership requirement, 217
 see also REITs
Adjusted gross income, *see* Alternative minimum tax; Deductions; Income; Itemized deductions; Tax credits

Adjustments:
 minimum tax, 28–30
 see also Deductions; Tax credits
All events test, 294
Allocations:
 construction expenses: overhead, 86, 88
 cooperative housing, 177
 overstating interest portion, 66
 in partnerships, 11, 12
 purchase price, 250
Alternative minimum tax, 25, 54, 267–285
 adjustments, 28–30
 basic changes in law, 271–272
 calculating, 279–281
 credits, 30, 281–282
 definition, 267
 exemption, 30, 279
 foreign tax credit, 280
 installment sales, 149
 itemized deductions, 277–279
 net operating loss, 29, 280
 overview (figure), 269
 passive activity losses, 29, 226–227
 planning tips, 275–277, 282–285
 state and local taxes and, 272
 structure (figure), 26-27
 syndication and, 79
 tax-exempt bond interest, 64
 tax preference items and, 270, 272–277
 see also entities allocated: Interest; Rents; Time analysis; Vacation home; etc.

Amount realized, 122
Apartments:
    garden apartments, 92, 256
    like-kind exchange, 255
    rentals, 221
Applicable Installment Indebtedness
    (AII), 143–148
Applicable Installment Obligations (AIO),
    143–148
Application of proceeds, 61
Appraisal, 251–252
Architectural barriers;
    removing, 261–264, 283
    requirements for deduction, 263
Assets:
    definition, 120
    REIT status, 45
    REMICs, 38
    transferring to children, 190
At risk:
    investments in real estate, 56–60
    limitation on deductions, 55
    low income housing credits, 159
    participating in a number of
        projects, 59
    partnerships, 59
    S corporations, 59

Bad debts, 29
Bankruptcy, 64
Basis, see Tax basis
Bonds, see Municipal bonds; Tax–exempt
    bonds
"Boot," 254
Brokerage costs:
    deductibility, 111–112
Buildings:
    depreciation start date, 240
    useful life of, 229–230
Business meals deduction, 188

C corporations, 15, 17–30
    buying a business/allocating purchase
        price, 21–22
    compared with other structures, 18–20
    dividends-received deduction, 21
    lower tax rates, 21
    materially participating in, 211–212
    passive loss rules, 206
    planning tip, 223

Cancellation of debt, 64–66
Capital assets, 120–121
    definition, 120
    favorable rate eliminated, 134
Capital expenditures, 100–101
Capital gains and losses, 109–110, 170
    capital assets: old law, 122–125
    capital gains as goal, 134–135
    closing and other costs, 128
    "Code Section 1231 assets," 124–125
    considerations before selling, 128–
        129
    definition, 120, 121
    estate planning considerations,
        131–132
    exclusion eliminated, 277
    favorable tax benefits, 267–268
    holding period, 133–134
    investor vs. dealer status, 126–127
    long-term capital gains, 123–124
    old laws kept on the books, 120
    ordinary income, 125–126
    planning tips, 126–127, 130
    planning, with new rules, 119–135
    questions relevant to selling, 119–120
    rate of return, 132
    repeal of benefits, 119
    timing, 126
    vacation homes, 163
    see also Deductions; Installment sales;
        Selling real estate
Capitalization:
    construction expenses, 92–93,
        244–245
    equity kickers, 96
    example, 94–95
    loan prepayment prohibition, 95
    partners' and shareholders' loans, 96
    passive loss rules, 96–97
    refinancing, 95–96
    rentals, 252
Carry forwards (losses), 166, 200
"Carryover basis," 254
Cash flow:
    depreciation and, 231
    ground rentals, 259
    REITs, 52
Casualty losses, 189
Charitable contributions, 276
Clifford trusts, 191

Close corporations:
  losses in, 19
  see also Passive loss rules; S
    corporations
Collateral:
  installment notes as, 141–142
Collateralized mortgage obligations
  (CMOs), 38
Commercial real estate, 232
Completed contract method, *see*
  Accounting
Conduit entities:
  REMICs, 39
  see also Partnerships
Construction:
  contracts, long-term; accounting,
    97–99
  cost of, 154
  demand for, 81
  overbuilding, 81
Construction expenses:
  capitalization rules, 92–93, 244–245
  depreciation, 83
  direct material costs, 89
  indirect costs, 85
  interest expense; capitalization, 93–97
  labor costs, 83
  limits on, 82–93
  long-term projects; capitalization
    rules, 92
  overhead, 86, 88
  regression analysis, 90-92
  time analysis / daily log, 85–86
  wages: allocation percentage, 88
Construction period:
  accelerating the process, 243
  costs capitalized during, 82–84, 92–97
  deductible costs, 84–85
  delaying onset of, 92
  limiting duration rules, 97
Consumers:
  spending patterns, 109
Contracts:
  accounting methods, 275
  calculating income, 99
  contract price; formula, 98
  long-term; accounting, 97–99
Convention expenses, 295
Cooperative housing:
  allocation of interest and taxes, 177

Cooperative housing *(Cont.)*
  definition, 175
  tenant/shareholders, 176–177
Corporate alternative minimum tax,
  see Alternative minimum tax
Corporations:
  characteristics
    centralized management, 16
    continuity of life, 16
    free transferability of interests, 16
    limited liability, 16
  definition, 16
  desirability waning, 16
  master limited partnerships as, 14
  partnerships compared with, 20
  passive loss rules, 206
  profits taxed, 17
  property distributions, 22
  salaries, 18
  types (two), 15
  see also Cooperative housing
Credits, tax, *see* Tax credits
Critical Path Method (CPM), 243

Debt:
  average indebtedness, 148
  cancellation of, 64–66
  measure of borrowings, 143
  purchase money debt, 135
  recourse/nonrecourse, 57–59
Decision-making, 10
Deductions:
  architectural barrier removal, 261
  at-risk rules, 55, 56
  bunching, 284
  business meals, 109
  capital losses, 127
  consumer interest deductions, 54
  conventions and seminars, 295
  dividends-received deductions, 21
  excess losses carried forward, 166
  home equity loan, 190
  home mortgage interest, 168, 170–173
  home office expenses, 175
  installment sales, 141
  interest; limitations, 189
  interest on credit cards, 109
  investment interest limitation, 67–71
  minimum tax adjustments, 28
  mortgage interest on second homes, 54

Deductions *(Cont.)*
　passive loss limitations, 54
　standard deduction, 185
　state and local taxes, 109
　see also Depreciation; Itemized
　　deductions
Deemed payment, 147–148
Deferred losses, *see* Losses
Definitions:
　activities (passive/active), 13, 203
　alternative minimum tax, 268
　asset, 120
　capital assets, 121
　capital gains and losses, 120, 121
　cooperatives, 175
　corporations, 16
　depreciation, 229
　easements, 104
　elderly persons, 263
　general partner, 13
　handicapped persons, 263
　installment sale, 119
　like-kind exchange, 253
　limited partner, 13
　long-term construction contract, 97–
　　98
　material participation, 208
　net investment income, 70, 278
　net leases, 115, 116
　net operating loss, 280
　personal service corporation, 206
　preservation easement, 104
　rate of return, 132
　real estate activity, 218, 288
　REITs, 41
　residential property, 232
　residual interest, 39
　S corporations, 31
　substantial economic effect, 12
　tax shelter, 287
　tenant allowance, 114
Department stores, 266
Depreciation:
　accelerated, 73, 199
　adjustment, for minimum tax, 274
　calculating:
　　example, 237
　　new rules, 232–239
　　old rules, 231–232
　deductions, 141, 195, 293

Depreciation *(Cont.)*
　deductions for different tax
　　systems, 275
　deemed installment payments,
　　147–148
　definition, 229
　examples, 233
　fixtures and equipment, 236
　foreign real estate, 239
　important to investors, 230–231
　interest expense; capitalization, 93
　land improvements, 235, 239,
　　245–247
　leasehold improvements, 112, 113
　leases; planning, 117–118
　like-kind exchanges, 253–256
　maximize depreciable property,
　　282
　midmonth convention, 232
　minimum tax adjustments, 28
　multiunit projects, 241, 246–247
　new alternative system, 239ff
　passive loss limitations, 242
　personal property, 237–239
　placed in service, 233, 242–243
　planning tips, 240–245, 247–249,
　　250, 256, 264–266
　pretax reform property, 275
　rehabilitation credit, 105
　residential rental property, 161
　start date, 240–242
　tax-exempt bond financing, 63–64
　tax preference items, 239, 273, 284
　vacation homes, 162
　write-offs, 228–266
　see also Deductions
Development of real estate, 81–106
Distributions:
　REITs, 48
Diversification:
　REITs, 41, 45
Dividends:
　dividend-received deduction, 21
Double taxation:
　in corporations, 18, 19, 21, 22
　installment obligations, 148
　REITs, 42
　REMICs, 35
　S corporations, 31–32
Drilling costs, 276

Easement, 104
Economic performance, 294
Educational expenses, 171
Elderly, the, 261, 263
Entertainment expenses, 188
Equipment, depreciating, 236
Equity kickers, 96
Estate planning, 131–132
Estimated tax payments, 290–291
Excise tax:
    REITs, 49
Exclusions:
    dividend-received deduction, 21
    exclusion preference, 281

Family tax planning, 190–193
Farming losses, 277
Financial institutions:
    tax treatment of, 55–56
Financing investments, 53–80
    corporate taxation and, 55
    residential real estate, 161–162
    tax rates lower, 53
Finite-life REITs, 50
Fixtures, 236
Foreign investors, 40–41
Foreign real estate, 239
Foreign tax credit, 280
Fraud penalty, 290

General partner, see Partnerships
Gift and estate tax, 192
Goodwill, 253
"Greenmail," 22
Ground leases, 259–260

Handicapped persons, 261, 263
Historic buildings, see Rehabilitation
    credit
Home improvements, 172
Home mortgages, see Mortgages
Home office:
    new rules, 173–175
Homeownership:
    as investment, 168–177
    mortgages, see Mortgages
    sales affected by tax benefits, 170

Imputed interest, 139
Incentive stock options, 276–277

Income; Income tests:
    accounting methods, 293
    allocation, see Allocation
    bridges among three categories,
        213–218
    calculating; long-term contracts, 99
    investment income, 283
    low income housing, 155–156
    minimum tax year, 283
    net investment income, 70–71, 278
    partnership categories, 13
    passive, 73, 200, 260
    passive loss rules, 196–199, 207–212
        offsetting income, 198
        types (three) (figure), 197
    penalty for understatements, 99
    REITs, 43, 45–46
    taxable: reduce investment, 65–65
    types of, 19
    unrelated business income (UBI), 20
Income tax:
    calculation overview (figure), 182
    compression of rates, 184
    exemption amount, 279
    head of household status, 183
    income averaging, 184
    married filing separate tax returns, 183
    new structure, 181–185
    personal exemption, 185
    rates (table), 183
    single individuals, 184
    standard deduction, 185
Industrial development bonds (IDBs), 60
Industry:
    impact of tax changes, 108
Inflation hedges, 257
Information returns, 289
Installment method, see Accounting
Installment notes:
    pledging on and borrowing against,
        141–142
Installment sales:
    deemed payment on debt, 147–148
    definition, 119
    description, 135–136
    example, 136
    interest on unpaid balance, 137–141
    minimum interest rate, 137
    mortgage assumed, 137
    new rules, 119, 134, 135–150

Installment sales *(Cont.)*
  payment balance, 139
  payments received on old
    contracts, 134
  present value; calculation, 138–139
  profit percentage/recognized, 137
  proportionate disallowance rule,
    142–147, 149
  taxable portion, 136–137
  tax revisions, 170
Interest:
  allocation to tenant/shareholders, 177
  capitalization rules, 93–97
  deferred payment transactions, 65–66
  expense in excess of income, 283
  imputed interest, 139
  installment sales rules, 137–141
  limitation on deductibility, 67–71
  minimum tax, 278
  mortgage, 283
  overstating, 66
  personal interest expense, 69
  residual (REMICs), 39
  tax-exempt bonds, 64
  tax underpayments and over-
    payments, 289
  understating rate of, 66
Inventory assets, 147
Investment(s):
  chronological cycle, 3–4
  partnerships, the preferred vehicle, 12
  reduced benefits, 53–56
  residential real estate, 4–5
  structuring ownership, 9–52
  see also Financing investments;
    Interest; Partnerships; Rate
    of return
Itemized deductions, 187–190
  bunching, 186–187
  casualty losses, 189
  homeownership, 169
  interest deductions, 189
  medical expense, 187
  minimum tax, 270, 277–279
  state and local taxes, 192
  time unusable, 283–284

Labor:
  construction expense, 83
  low-income workers, 108
  time study, 87, 89

Land:
  ground leases, 259–260
  improvements; depreciation, 235–236,
    239, 245–246
Leasehold improvements:
  costs of capital repairs, 118
  tenant allowance, 114
  tenants and contractors, 244
  tenants: tax benefits, 113–115
  writing off, 112–118
Leasing:
  acquisition costs, 111–112
  brokerage costs, 111–112
  capital gains treatment, 109–110
  changes affecting, 107–110
  commencement clause, 118
  depreciation planning, 117–118
  ground leases, 256–260
  net lease: qualifying expenses, 116
  net leased property, 115–117
    planning tips, 117
    requirements, 222
    options, 112
    passive loss rules, 115, 222
    "placed in service," 117
    rental property value and, 107
    tax planning, 110
Leverage:
  in syndications, 74
Liability:
  all events test, 294
  limited, in corporations, 17
  limited partnerships, 13, 209–210
Like-kind exchanges:
  definition, 253, 254
  depreciation deductions, 253–256
  passive losses, 256
  time period for transaction, 254
Limitations:
  at-risk rules, 55, 56
  capital losses: the $3,000 limit,
    126, 127
  interest deductions, 189
  investment interest, 54, 67–71
  low income housing, 156–157,
    159–160
  minimum tax, 29
  net operating losses, 23
  private activity bonds, 63
  see also Accounting; Passive loss rules
Limited partner, *see* Partnerships

Liquidations:
  general utilities doctrine, 22
  in REMICs, 40
Liquidity:
  partnerships, 13
  REITs, 42, 43
Loans:
  home equity loans, 190
  nonrecourse, 57–58
  reschedule loans due, 65
  see also Capitalization; Debt;
    Mortgages
Long term contracts, see Contracts
Look back rule, 99
Losses:
  carry forwards, 200
  in closely held corporations, 19
  corporate structure and, 18
  deferred, 201–205
  excess, carry forward, 166
  net operating losses, 23
  offsetting income, 215–216
  suspended, 199–200
  see also Capital gains; Limitations; Net
    operating losses; Passive loss rules;
    Tax losses
Low income housing:
  additions to building, 159
  at-risk rule, 159
  calculating the credit, 158–159
  credit formula (figure), 157
  financing, 159–160
  income tests, 155–156
  limitations on state-by-state basis,
    156–157
  limitations on use of, 159–160
  passive loss rules, 160–161
  qualifying basis, 159
  rate for new credit, 155
  recapture of, 156
  rental projects, 161–162
  requirements for qualifying, 155–156
  tax credit for, 154–160, 197

Magazine expenditures, 273
Maintenance and repair;
  capital expenditures, 100–101
  deductible repairs, 100
  depreciation, 100
  ongoing and regular program of, 101
  planning, 99–102

Maintenance and repair (Cont.)
  rotational basis, 101
  tax planning, 102
Management:
  centralized, 16
  services, 47
Master limited partnerships, 13–14
Materially participating, 207–212
Mechanical equipment, 243
Medical expense deduction, 187, 283
Mergers, 24
Midmonth convention, 232
Milestone dates, 244
Minimum tax, see Alternative
    minimum tax
Mining costs, 273
Mortgage-backed securities, see REMICs
Mortgages:
  credit certificates, 63
  deductions, for second homes, 54
  home mortgages; deductions, 170–173,
    277, 283
  loans made after 16 Aug. 1986, 172
  pools, 35–36
  qualified, 38
Multiunit/use projects, 241, 246
Municipal bonds:
  screening, 283
  tax-free interest, 276
Mutual funds:
  REITs compared with, 41

National Register of Historic Places, 102
Negligence penalty, 289
Net investment income, 278
  defined, 70
  limitation, 71
Net leases, see Leasing
Net operating losses;
  changes in ownership, 23
  minimum tax calculation, 29, 280
Newspaper expenditures, 273
Nonrecourse debt:
  at-risk rules, 57
  related lenders, 59
  requirements for qualifying, 57–58

Office buildings, 266
Old buildings, see Rehabilitation credit
Operating losses, see Net operating losses
Overhead, see Construction expenses

Overpayments, 289
Ownership:
    change tests, 24
    changes in; losses carried over, 23–24
    decision making process, 10
    factors in deciding type of, 9–10
    REITs, 47
    structuring, 9–52

Partnerships:
    at-risk rules, 59
    capitalization rules, 96
    corporations compared with, 11, 20
    flexibility in, 11, 12
    general, 16
        active income, 13
    income allocation, 11–12
    limited, 16, 20, 204, 209
        liability, 13
    liquidity, 13
    management, 16
    master limited, 13–14
        as "corporation," 14
        formation, 14
        planning tips, 14–15
    partnerships and, 72
    preferred investment vehicle, 12
    S corporations and, 32–33
    special allocations, 12
    tax treatment, 11–15
    tax year, 11
Passive income, see Income
Passive loss rules, 19
    "actively participate," 216–217
    allocating purchase price, 250
    alternative minimum tax, 276–277
    capitalization rules, 96
    categories (three) of activities, 13
    corporations subject to, 206
    deductions limited, 54, 242
    effective dates, 226–227
    examples, 200–201, 223
    ground leases, 260–261
    homeownership, 169
    income types (figure), 197
    installment sales, 141, 149
    investment interest and, 66–69, 278
    limitations, 196–227
    low income housing, 160–161
    master limited partnerships, 14

Passive loss rules (Cont.)
    "materially participate," 207–208,
        210–212
    net leases, 115
    partnerships, 12–13
    persons subject to rules, 205–207
    planning tip, 277
    portfolio income, 212
    rehabilitation credit, 105
    REITs, 42–43, 46, 47, 49
    rental real estate, 292
    suspended losses, 204, 256
    syndications, 74
    tax shelters, 72–73
    unused, 13, 15
    vacation homes, 164, 166
Penalties:
    estimated tax, 290
    information requirements, 287–288
    "look-back" rule, 99
    for negligence and fraud, 289
    REITs, 49
    understatements of liability, 291–293
Percentage depletion, 273
Personal exemption, 185
Personal property:
    depreciation rules, 231, 236, 264
    special write-off of, 237–239
Personal services, see Services
PERT (Program Evaluation and Review
        Technique), 243
Placed in service, 242–243
Pollution control facilities, 272
Portfolio income, 43
    passive activity and, 196, 212–215
Preferential tax items, see Tax preference
        items
Present value calculation, 139
Preservation easement, 104
Private activity bonds, 60–62
    requirements for tax exemption, 61–62
    state volume limitations, 63
Profit:
    installment method of reporting, 54
Property:
    movable, 265
    value, 251–253
Property distributions, 22
Property taxes;
    allocation to tenant/shareholders, 177

Property values, 150
Proportionate disallowance rule,
    142–147, 149
Purchase price:
    residual method, 21–22

Qualified mortgage bonds, 62–63

Rate of return:
    calculation, 133
    defined, 132
    example, 132–133
    length of time of ownership, 133–134
Real estate:
    investment, *see* Investment(s)
    professionals in, 2
Real estate investment trusts, *see* REITs
Real estate mortgage investment con-
    duits, *see* REMICs
Real estate rental activity, *see* Rents
Real property, 231
"Recapture," 232
Record keeping:
    REITs, 49
    see also Accounting
Recourse debt, *see* Debt
Refinancing:
    capitalization of interest, 95–96
Regression analysis, 90–92
Rehabilitation credit:
    additions to the building, 103
    depreciation, 105
    old and historic buildings, 102–106
    passive loss limitations, 105
    preservation easement, 104
    qualification for, 103, 106
    tests for qualification, 104
    time period, 104
REITs (real estate investment trusts), 15,
    36, 41–52
    asset requirements, 45
    cash flow, 52
    comparison with other vehicles, 42–43
    definition, 41
    distribution requirements, 48–49
    diversification, 41, 45
    excise tax on excess, 49
    financing investments, 55
    finite-life REITs, 50
    income requirements, 45–46

REITs *(Cont.)*
    income treatment, 43
    installment sales, 149
    as investment: factors in choosing a
        REIT, 51–52
    key advantage, 42
    liquidity, 42, 43
    management services, 47
    mutual funds compared with, 41
    organizational requirements, 44
    ownership interests, 44, 47, 51
    passive income, 46
    passive investments, 49
    passive losses, 42–43
    penalty taxes, 49
    performance, 43
    planning tip, 46–49
    prohibited services, 47
    qualifying requirements, 43–46
    real estate sales, 50
    record keeping, 49
    rental activities, 46, 48
    subsidiaries, 48
    taxation, 49–50
    tax losses, 42
    tax requirements, 42
    tax year, 44
    transferable shares, 44
    types of, 50–51
Related parties, 59
REMICs (real estate mortgage investment
        conduits), 15, 34–41
    asset requirements, 38
    collateralized mortgage obligations
        and, 38
    creation of, 35, 36
    excess servicing, 39
    financing investments, 55
    foreign investors, 40–41
    growth of the industry, 34, 36
    key benefits of, 37
    liquidation, 40
    multiple-class arrangements, 35
    ownership interests, types of, 38–39
    penalties, 40
    REITs and, 36, 41
    requirements to be taxed as, 37–38
    residual interest, 39, 41
    taxation of the intermediary, 35
    taxation as a conduit, 39–40

REMICs *(Cont.)*
  transferring assets to, 39
Renovation, *see* Rehabilitation credit
Rent controls, 153
Rents:
  businesses treated as real estate
      activities, 218–226
  capitalization, 252
  passive activities, 208
  percentage rentals, 108
  period (length) of rental, 221
  placed in service, 233
  property values, 107
  rates, 107–108, 153
  REITs, 46, 48
  scope of rental activity, 222–224
Repair and maintenance, *see* Maintenance
    and repair
Reporting requirements, 288
Research expenditures, 272–273
Residential real estate:
  depreciation, 161
  investing in, 4–5, 153–167
  see also Low income housing; Rents;
      Vacation homes
Restaurants, 266
Return on investment:
  ground rentals, 259

S corporations, 15, 16, 18, 23,
    30–34
  at-risk rules, 59
  capitalization rules, 96
  comparisons with other structures,
      31–32
  definition, 31
  limited liability, 31
  partnerships and, 32–33
  planning tip, 34
  requirements for status as, 33–34
  stock requirements, 33
  tax attributes, 31, 206
Salaries, 18
Sales agreement, 250–251
Sales of real estate:
  installment method of reporting
      gains, 54
  REITs; penalty tax, 50
Sales taxes, 109
Secretary of the Interior, 102, 104

Securities:
  multiple-class, 35
Selling real estate:
  amount realized, 122
  capital gains rules, *see* Capital gains
      and losses
  estate planning, 131–132
  examples, 128–129, 130, 132
  expenses of sale, 129
  installment sale, *see* Installment sales
  market prices after tax reform, 128
  planning tips, 126–127, 130, 133
  present value calculations, 139
  revolving credit plan, 149
  tax basis, 122, 132
  tax considerations in decision, 129
  transfer costs, 128
  warehouses, 124
Seminars, 295
Service businesses, 108–109
  materially participating, 208
Services (in rental real estate), 219
Shares:
  free transferability of, 17
  REITs, 44, 51
Shareholders, 16
Shopping center industry, 219–220
Small businesses, 188
Small-issue bonds, 61–62
Solar energy tax credit, 295
State and local taxes, 272
Stock redemption payments, 22
Stocks:
  incentive stock options, 276
  in S corporations, 33
Subchapter S corporations, *see* S
    corporations
Supermarkets, 266
Syndications, 55, 72–80
  fee structures, 75
  hypothetical investment (table),
      76–77
  leverage, 74
  minimum tax and, 79
  objectives, 72
  partnerships and, 72
  passive income or loss, 204–205
  passive loss limitations, 73, 74
  planning tip, 78–80
  zero coupon bonds, 74–75, 79

Takeover attempts, 22
Tax assessor's values, 252–253
Tax basis:
    sale of real estate, 122
    "stepped-up basis," 131–132
Tax benefits:
    value of, 248–249
Tax credits:
    foreign tax, 280
    low income housing, 154–160
    minimum tax, 30, 279–281
    offsetting income, 217–218
    in passive activities, 202
    solar energy expenditures, 295
Tax-deferred exchange, 254
Tax-exempt bonds:
    financing, 55, 60–64
    qualified mortgage bonds, 62–63
    residential real estate, 161–162
    "tainted," 61
Tax losses:
    at-risk rules, 56
    business continuity test, 24–25
    inability to use, 18–19
    ownership change tests, 24
Tax planning, 5, 181–193, 282–285
    complicated since tax reform, 2
    computing value of, 249–250
    objective of this book, 2
    syndications and, 72
Tax preference item (TPI), 28, 239, 268,
    270, 272–277
Tax rates:
    C corporations, 21
    corporations, 19
    lower (assumption), 53, 109
    maximum marginal rate (1981), 196
    tax planning, 110
    see also Income tax
Tax shelters:
    accounting method, 294
    depreciation and, 230

Tax shelters (Cont.)
    home ownership, 169
    passive loss rules, 72, 196
    registration of, 286–288
    special restrictions, 293
    tax planning, 195, 200
    understatement of liability, 292
    vacation homes, 162
Tax year, 11, 44
Time analysis (form), 87
Time study, 89
Transfer costs, 128–129
Trusts:
    ownership interest, 36

Underpayments/understatements,
    289–293
Useful life, 229–230

Vacation homes:
    capital gains, 163
    depreciation, 162
    example, 164, 165–166
    excess losses, 166
    interest deductions, 163
    as investment, 162
    passive loss rules, 164
    personal use: number of days, 164,
        165, 172
    planning tips, 165, 166
    tax benefits, 167
    tax losses from rentals, 162
    tax rates, 163
    tax shelter, 162
    tax treatment of, 164
    value related to tax policy, 163

Warehouse, 124, 254
Write-offs, see Depreciation

Zero coupon bonds, 74–75, 79